natural English

upper-intermediate teacher's book
Ruth Gairns & Stuart Redman

OXFORD
UNIVERSITY PRESS

contents

introduction

how we wrote this course

Before we established the language syllabus for the **natural English** course, we wanted to be sure that what we set out to teach upper-intermediate learners corresponded to what they actually needed to learn at that stage in their language development. So, instead of starting with a prescribed syllabus, we began by planning a series of communicative activities with certain criteria:

- they should be achievable, engaging, and purposeful
- they should be language rich in that they would push learners into extensive and varied language use, and could not be accomplished with a very limited range of expression
- they should range across different time frames (past, present, and future)
- they should have different topics and themes
- they should include different activity types, e.g. role play; discussion; giving, justifying, and reacting to opinions; planning and negotiating; exchanging information; presenting ideas; sharing experiences; telling stories, etc.
- finally, they should each be different in tone: fun, business-like, factual, nostalgic, etc.

We then wrote the activities. Initially, we produced more than we needed, and after trialling, we eliminated those which did not work as well as we had hoped, or that overlapped with others which were richer in language or more successful. Those that remained became the extended speaking activities and role plays which you will find in the **student's book** in a much refined and reworked form, thanks to the learner data and feedback received from teachers during piloting of the material. Here are two examples:

you're going to:	you're going to:
collect ideas listen to some people talking about reading in their lives	**collect ideas** choose the members of your band, decide on their musical style and image, and how you will promote them
share experiences talk to a partner about either sport or reading at different stages in your life	**present your ideas** describe your band to the rest of the class
write a summary write a short summary about your partner	**write a profile** create a website profile of one of the band members
but first ... look back at the **extended speaking** boxes in this unit. You can use this language in the activity.	**but first ...** look back at the **extended speaking** boxes in this unit. You can use this language in the activity.

from **student's book unit one** *p.18* and **unit three** *p.42*

trialling and recording the activities

We asked teachers to use the material with their upper-intermediate classes and record small groups doing the activities. We also piloted them ourselves with small groups. In all, we recorded over two hundred learners who came from more than twenty countries in Europe, South America, and South East Asia. We also did a limited amount of piloting of native speakers doing the activities. However, following on from our experience at the intermediate level, we also did more extensive and systematic piloting of the material with higher level learners. In other words, we recorded upper-intermediate learners doing the activities, and compared this with the performance of advanced learners doing the same activities. We felt that they provided a more realistic and attainable model than native speakers, whose language was often too colloquial and idiomatic, and often included too many irrelevant cultural references (see **what is natural English?** below).

analysing the learner data

Finally, we transcribed the recordings. This data enabled us to look at the differences between upper-intermediate and advanced level learners. We examined how each group performed, what the language differences were, and what achievable goals we could set for upper-intermediate learners in terms of language and performance strategies. This data influenced our selection of language in preparation for the role plays and extended speaking activities, although we also decided to include other language suitable for the level to ensure that the syllabus was as comprehensive as possible. At that point, we were able to start writing the **student's book**.

To summarize, the development of the course involved the following stages:

1. devise the extended speaking activities / role plays for trialling
2. trial and record upper-intermediate and advanced level learners
3. transcribe and analyse the data
4. select appropriate language for the syllabus
5. write the learning materials in each unit leading up to the extended speaking and role plays (and refine them).

what is natural English?

As we have already said, native speaker talk did not provide us with a model of English that was necessarily the most appropriate for upper-intermediate learners. In a nutshell, the gap between the two was just too great, and the native speaker model represented a target that was still largely unattainable for upper-intermediate learners of English. One of the features of native speaker talk, especially with native speaker to native speaker, is its highly idiomatic nature. Native speakers can use *at the end of my tether* or talk about *getting their head round a problem*, and when they do, it sounds perfectly natural. Transferring that language and trying to integrate it within an upper-intermediate learner's current interlanguage often has the opposite effect; it sounds very unnatural.

There are, however, degrees of idiomaticity. At the extreme end are the more picturesque but often opaque expressions such as:

He's got a finger in every pie.
She's full of beans.
When all's said and done.
They're thick as thieves. etc.

But at the other end are much lower levels of idiomaticity in expressions such as:

I haven't a clue.
It's getting on my nerves.
We've got nothing in common.
It cost a fortune. etc.

This second group contains phrases that are very natural for native speakers, and, in most cases, much more frequent than the more opaque idiomatic expressions above. For upper-intermediate learners of English though, they have a further benefit: being less idiomatic and more neutral in style, they are more accessible and easier to use alongside the rest of their current interlanguage.

This lead us to a general principle for language selection: choose language proficient speakers and native speakers of English use naturally, which upper-intermediate learners could incorporate into their evolving language and also use naturally. Hence, natural English.

the natural English syllabus

How does anyone decide exactly what language will fulfil these criteria? It is, of course, highly subjective. As yet, there isn't a readily available core lexicon of phrases and collocations to teach upper-intermediate learners on the basis of frequency, let alone taking into account the question of which phrases might be most 'suitable' for learners at this level. Our strategy has been to use our own classroom knowledge and experience to interpret our data of upper-intermediate and advanced level language use, in conjunction with information from the *Longman Grammar of Spoken and Written English*, a range of ELT dictionaries and data from the British National Corpus. In this way, we arrived at an appropriate language syllabus for upper-intermediate learners.

what else did we learn from the data?

These are some of the general findings to emerge from our data, which influenced the way we then produced the material.

developing conversation

Although upper-intermediate learners were better at sustaining monologue than intermediate learners, they were not very good at responding naturally to conversation or sustaining and developing it. Our approach was to provide natural English examples and controlled and freer practice that would help them sustain conversation. For example:

– challenging opinions
  e.g. *Why do you say that? / I can't see the point of that.*
– asking follow-up questions
  e.g. *What sort of thing? / What does that involve?*

– relating what you hear to your own experience
  e.g. *That happened to me too. / It wasn't like that for me at all.*
– moving the topic on
  e.g. *Shall we go on to the next point?*

linking

As mentioned above, upper-intermediate learners were capable of longer utterances than intermediate learners, but they were often not very good at linking their ideas together. We focused on these in both written and spoken texts, often by introducing sets of linkers which could serve as a framework to structure their discourse. For example:

linking events in a 'bad news' story
Initially, … As time went by …
The situation deteriorated …
Things went from bad to worse …
Eventually, …

linking reasons together
There are several reasons why …
First of all, …
Secondly, …
… and another thing is …

adding ideas (informal)
What's more, …
… also …
… as well.

becoming more 'language rich'

The use of linkers (like the ones above) can help learners both to extend their discourse and use more complex and varied forms. Throughout the data, we noted that many upper-intermediate learners tended to 'play safe' with language and rely on fairly simple structures and lexis, which prevented them from expressing more complex ideas and using greater subtlety. We endeavoured to put them in situations where more complex language was required in order to achieve the tasks we set them. Of course, this meant providing them with necessary language through input in grammar, vocabulary, and **natural English** phrases. For instance:

– expressing willingness
  I'd be willing to do that.
  I'd be a bit reluctant to do that.
  I wouldn't mind doing that.

– saying what you like
  X appeals to me.
  Y doesn't appeal to me at all.

– using attitude adverbs
  Understandably, …
  Obviously, …
  Presumably …

accuracy

Students at this level were clearly familiar with a wide range of grammar but they were very inconsistent in their accuracy. For instance, a learner could use the structure *should have done* correctly in one utterance, but within the same conversation, go on to use it inaccurately two or three times. At the same time, a different learner in the group might use it inaccurately throughout. We felt that learners now had a degree of fluency and knowledge of the language which should enable them to focus on getting things right.

With lexis, learners were similarly inconsistent, and could produce the correct word form one moment, then get it wrong the next. We therefore focus on the grammar of lexis in the **wordbooster** sections, for example, phrasal verbs, prefixes and suffixes, uncountable and plural nouns. (By lexis we mean both individual words and phrases.) Inevitably at this level, learners need to expand their vocabularies, both productively and receptively. A final area that we needed to work on was collocation, which was a common source of error for all the upper-intermediate learners in our data.

how to use the key features of natural English

- life with Agrippine / do you get it?
- natural English boxes
- wordbooster
- language reference / cover & check
- the listening booklet
- test yourself!
- workbook
- puzzle book
- teacher's book

life with Agrippine / do you get it?

Alternate units in the course (1, 3, 5, etc.) begin with a section including a Bretécher cartoon called **life with Agrippine**, while the other units (2, 4, 6, etc.) begin with a recorded, illustrated joke section called **do you get it?** Each of these sections begins with personalized speaking practice, followed by the cartoon or joke, with **natural English** features derived from the reading or listening input. The jokes also include a vocabulary development activity.

why cartoons and jokes?

They provide a light-hearted and engaging lead-in to the theme of the unit through listening or reading for pleasure. The Bretécher cartoons raise recognizable and universal issues to do with contemporary life, and although aimed at adults, they are also appealing to younger adults. The jokes have been chosen to be linguistically and culturally accessible – and, we hope, amusing for a wide audience.

how to ... use the cartoons

With the **Bretécher cartoons**, there will be a temptation for learners to read ahead to the next cartoon strip if they like them. If they do so, at least it will mean that learners are very motivated.

- You could do the first speaking activity in the cartoon section with books closed, either by telling learners orally what to do or by writing the questions / prompts on the board. This will prevent learners from reading the cartoon before you want them to. The speaking activity can be done in pairs, groups, or as a whole class.
- You can then tell learners to look at the pre-set questions and read the cartoon. In the early units, point out the glossary so that learners can read quickly and understand the humour. Avoid getting involved in a detailed study or word-for-word translation at this stage: as a text, it has been written to be read for pleasure.

- Decide whether you want to use the recording. It will help your learners get a feel for natural sounding English, although some teachers may prefer not to use it, as the cartoon was originally written as a text to be read, not listened to.

Once you have dealt with the **natural English** focus, you could consider other activities:

- Some of the cartoons lend themselves well to reading aloud and acting out in pairs or small groups (e.g. units seven, nine, and eleven.) This could either be done in a very controlled way, or learners could read the conversations a couple of times, then shut their books and improvise them.
- Some cartoons might stimulate discussion, depending on the teaching context; e.g. unit five: cheating / homework / education; unit seven: where does parental responsibility stop?
- You may find other well-known cartoon strips in the local culture which you could take into class and learners could translate, or you could blank out the mother tongue dialogue and write an English version yourself, or ask your learners to write the dialogue.

how to ... use the jokes

You can use the lead-in speaking activity as with the Bretécher cartoons.

- The pictures are there essentially to help learners understand the joke by setting the scene. You can pre-teach key vocabulary, or give learners time to work out the story and use the glossary themselves. If anyone recognizes the joke, and knows the punchline, do your best to prevent them from revealing it – otherwise it will spoil the listening activity.
- Always read the joke yourself before the lesson in case there is anything culturally problematic. You can then decide, in advance, how to deal with it.
- The response bubbles (*That's a good one.* / *I don't get it.* / *That's pathetic!*, etc.) are important, and it should be no stigma if a learner doesn't get the joke; it often happens to native speakers too. You can use the second listening and the **listening booklet** to clear up any misunderstandings. By the end of the book, learners will have acquired quite a lot of ways of reacting to jokes. Even groans indicate involvement and recognition, and that is a common response to jokes. Don't be put off by them!

After dealing with the **natural English** box and vocabulary activity, there are other possibilities:

- You can suggest that they learn the joke for homework. Jokes, like songs, are often very memorable, and they are excellent for building confidence.
- Learners could translate a joke from their mother tongue into English to tell the class.

natural English boxes

Most of the **natural English** boxes consist of natural English phrases. They normally occur five or six times in each unit, with one or two boxes in each main section (excluding **wordbooster**) leading up to the **extended speaking** activity.

what do the natural English boxes contain?

These boxes focus on important aspects of everyday language, some of which fall outside the traditional grammatical / lexical syllabus. They include:

– familiar functional exponents: e.g. making and responding to requests, asking for and making recommendations
– communication strategies: e.g. clarifying your position (*That's not what I meant*); introducing and focusing information (*The trouble is, the thing is ...*)
– common features of spoken English: e.g. *so anyway, ... and things like that*
– lexical chunks: e.g. *that was brave / silly of you; all over the place / country / world*

The language here is presented in chunks, with each box containing a limited number of phrases to avoid memory overload. The phrases are practised on the spot, and then learners have the opportunity to use them later in freer activities, (e.g. in **it's your turn!**) and the **extended speaking** activity at the end of each unit.

how to ... use the natural English boxes

These boxes have been positioned at a point within each section where they are going to be of immediate value. Some of the phrases are recorded to provide a pronunciation model. There is always an instruction in each **natural English** box for controlled practice of the phrases, and in many cases it is followed by a personalized practice activity. In the classroom, you could vary the presentation of the language in the following ways:

– If the target phrases have been recorded, you could ask learners to listen to them first. They could do this with books shut and treat it as a dictation, then compare their answers with the **student's book**; or they could listen and follow in the **student's book** at the same time, and then repeat from the recording or the model that you give them yourself.
– You can read the phrases aloud for learners to repeat; alternatively, you can ask individual learners to read them out as a way of presenting them.
– You can ask learners to read the box silently, then answer any queries they have, before you get them to say the phrases.
– You could write the phrases on the board or OHP for everyone to focus on. Then ask learners about any problems they have with meaning and form of the examples before practice.
– You could sometimes elicit the phrases before learners read them. For instance, ask them how they could ask for repetition, or what they would say when meeting and greeting people in interview situations. Write their suggestions on the board, and then let learners compare with the **natural English** box. In some cases learners will know some important phrases, but they may not be very accurate or know the most natural way to express these concepts.
– Once learners have practised the phrases, you could ask them to shut their **student's book** and write down the phrases they remember.
– If you have a weaker class, you might decide to focus on one or two of the phrases for productive practice; for a stronger group, you may want to add one or two phrases of your own.

– For revision, you could tell learners they are going to be tested on the **natural English** boxes of the last two units you have done; they should revise them for homework. The next day, you can test them in a number of ways:
  – give them an error-spotting test
  – fill gaps in phrases or give stimuli which learners respond to
  – ask them to write four-line dialogues in pairs.
– The **workbook** provides you with a number of consolidation and further practice exercises of **natural English** (and, of course, other language presented in the **student's book** – see below for more details).
– Because the phrases are clearly very useful, you may want to put some of them on display in your classroom. You could also get learners to start a **natural English** and vocabulary notebook and record the phrases under headings as they learn them. You should decide together whether natural (rather than literal) translations would be a useful option for self-study.

wordbooster

Wordbooster is a section in each unit devoted to vocabulary development. It is divided into two parts, each one focusing on a different lexical area: one is often topic-based, the other may be based on the grammar of vocabulary, e.g. compound and plural nouns or phrasal verbs.

why wordbooster?

Throughout the other sections in each unit, you will find vocabulary input which is practised within the section, and is often needed for the **extended speaking** activity. Some of the vocabulary in **wordbooster** is also useful for the **extended speaking** activity, but the main role of **wordbooster** is to provide essential vocabulary expansion for learners at this level that goes beyond the immediate requirements of the unit. In this way, learners cover a comprehensive vocabulary syllabus.

The **wordbooster** section is designed to have a different feel from the other more interactive sections in the course, and it provides a change of pace and activity type. In this teacher's book, the teaching notes for all the **wordboosters** are in a separate section, from *p.132* to *p.145*.

how to ... use wordbooster

Each **wordbooster** will take approximately 25 to 30 minutes to complete, and it can be used flexibly.

– In some units, you can do the **wordbooster** activities earlier or later than they appear in the unit. This will be highlighted in the teacher's notes.
– You don't need to do the whole **wordbooster** in one session. As it is divided into two sections, you can do one part in one lesson, and the other part in a later lesson. In other words, you can use this section to fit in with your own teaching timetable. For instance, if you have 15 minutes at the end of a lesson, you can do one of these sections.
– You can do some of it in class, and some of it can be done for homework.
– You can bring in a competitive or fun element by turning some of the exercises into team games or *against the clock* activities (e.g. unit two, **health and medicine**). This approach is not suitable in all learning contexts, however. If you are new to your teaching environment, consult your colleagues for advice.

– Encourage learners to record the language learnt in these sections in their **natural English** and vocabulary notebooks.

test yourself!

Test yourself! is an end-of-unit test or revision activity enabling learners to assess their progress, and consider how they performed in the **extended speaking** activity. It is a short, easily administered test covering lexis, **natural English** phrases, and grammar from the unit in a standardized format:

– producing items within categories
– transforming sentences
– correcting errors.

how to ... use test yourself!

You can use it either before the **extended speaking** activity, for revision purposes, or afterwards, as an end-of-unit test. You may want to give learners time to prepare for it, e.g. read through the unit for homework, or make it a more casual and informal revision activity. Make it clear to learners that their answers in the test should only include new language from the unit.

The test can be used in different ways:

– A formal test. Ask learners to complete it individually, and then collect in their answers to mark.
– An informal test. Ask learners to complete it individually, then go through the answers with the whole class.
– A more interactive test. Ask learners to complete it in pairs. Go through the answers with the class, or ask a pair to mark the answers of another pair.
– You could get learners to complete the test individually or in pairs, then they can check their answers by looking back through the unit. Asking learners to search for answers in this way may not give <u>you</u> as much feedback on their progress, but it may be more memorable for them as learners.
– You could give the test for homework. Learners can then use the unit material as they wish.

Refer learners back to the checklist of the language input at the beginning of the unit. They can then tick which areas they feel more confident in. This is an important way for you to discover which areas they feel they need to revise. You may still have **workbook** and **cover & check** exercises which you can use for this revision.

why ask learners to mark their performance?

Asking learners to give themselves a mark for their performance in the speaking activity may seem an unusual thing to do. Clearly the precise mark is irrelevant, but we have found it a useful way to encourage learners to reflect more generally on their ability to communicate, and their contribution to the activity, without getting too involved in minor errors, grammar mistakes, etc. It also gives you a chance to have a one-to-one chat with learners, and provide them with some positive feedback and encouragement. It may take several units before learners are able to do this effectively, so your support will be essential in the early stages.

listening booklet

The **listening booklet** is a separate booklet in the back cover pocket of the **student's book**. It provides:

– complete tapescripts for all of the **student's book** listening material
– tapescript based exercises
– optional listening and pronunciation activities
– the phonemic chart on the back cover, with example words for each sound.

The activities and exercises focus on:

– features of natural English
– pronunciation in context, including focuses on individual sounds, wordstress, sentence stress, and intonation
– development of listening sub-skills.

why a separate booklet?

Until recently, tapescripts have often been buried in the back of coursebooks and largely under-exploited. In **natural English**, listening is a very important part of the syllabus, with the majority of recorded material being improvised, unscripted, and delivered at natural speed. It is, therefore, an invaluable source of natural spoken English, so we have set out to exploit the material as much as possible, both for acquiring new language and developing listening sub-skills. Following the tapescript after one or two attempts at listening is a valuable way for learners to decode the parts they haven't understood; it is not only useful, but also a popular activity.

Learners should find the separate booklet very convenient, and it also allows them to make greater use of the listening material.

how to ... use the listening booklet

Use the **listening booklet** whenever you want to refer learners to the tapescript.

Within the main listening section of each unit in the **student's book**, there's a page reference to the listening booklet for the related tapescript(s) and accompanying exercise(s).

You may decide to do the **listening booklet** exercises in class. Alternatively, the learners can do them at home, using the **student's audio CD** and answer key.

You might also wish to devise your own activities around the listening material, along similar lines to those already provided in the **listening booklet**.

language reference and cover & check exercises

The **language reference** section contains more detailed explanations of the key grammar and lexical grammar in the units, plus a large bank of exercises (**cover & check**) for further practice and consolidation. **Cover & check** exercises have been included for two main reasons:

– they make the language reference much more engaging and interactive
– they provide practice and consolidation which teachers and learners can use flexibly: within the lesson when the grammar is being taught, in a later lesson for revision purposes, or for self-study.

Most of the exercises are objective with a right-or-wrong answer which makes them easy for you to administer.

how to ... use language reference and cover & check exercises

- Use them when the need arises. If you always tell learners to read the **language reference** and do all the **cover & check** exercises within the lesson, you may have problems with pace and variety. Rather, use them at your discretion. If, for instance, you find that the learners need a little more practice than is provided in a grammar section, select the appropriate exercise (e.g. unit one: -*ing* form and infinitive: do exercise 1.3 in **cover & check**). Areas of grammar are not equally easy or difficult for all nationalities. **Cover & check** exercises provide additional practice on all areas; you can select the ones which are most relevant to your learners.
- The **cover & check** exercises are ideal for self-study. Learners can read the explanations on the left, then cover them while they do the exercises on the right. Finally, they can look again at the explanations if necessary. You can give them the answers to the **cover & check** exercises, which are at the back of this teacher's book, *p.181* to *p.183*.
- If learners write the answers in pencil or in a notebook, they will be able to re-use the exercises for revision. Some learners also benefit from writing their own language examples under the ones given in the **language reference**. They can also annotate, translate, etc.

workbook

The **workbook** recycles and consolidates vocabulary, grammar, and **natural English** from the **student's book**. It also provides language extension sections called **expand your grammar** and **expand your vocabulary** for stronger or more confident learners. These present and practise new material that learners have not met in the **student's book**. Another important feature of the **workbook** is the **say it!** sections, which encourage learners to rehearse language through prompted oral responses. There are two other regular features: **think back!** (revision prompts) and **write it!** (prompts for writing tasks). You can use the **workbook** for extra practice in class or set exercises for learners to do out of class time. The **with key** version allows learners to use the **workbook** autonomously.

puzzle book

what's in the puzzle book?

The 32-page **puzzle book** features a wide range of word games, word lists, puzzles, jokes, cartoons, and anecdotes, and comes complete with an answer key. It includes the following topic-based pages:

crime (*pp.4* and *5*)
health (*pp.8* and *9*)
shapes and dimensions (*pp.12* and *13*)
the media (*pp.16* and *17*)
sport (*pp.20* and *21*)
feelings (*pp.24* and *25*)

how to ... use the puzzle book

The **puzzle book** is designed to expand learners' vocabulary, and to encourage reading for pleasure and learner independence. It's not directly linked to units in the **student's book** – rather, it is intended as a fun and motivating optional extra. You may wish to refer learners to particular pages for homework (the topic pages listed above, for example) or you might want all your learners to have the **puzzle book**, so that it can be used in class for warmers and fillers. Otherwise, the 'dip-in' nature of the **puzzle book** means you can just encourage learners to use it as and when they like.

teacher's book

This **teacher's book** is the product of our own teaching and teacher training experience combined with extensive research carried out by Oxford University Press into how teacher's books are used.

lesson plans

The teaching notes are presented as flexible lesson plans, which are easy to dip into and use at a glance. We talk you through each lesson, offering classroom management tips (**troubleshooting**), anticipating problems (**language point**), and suggesting alternative ways of using the material (**ideas plus**). In addition, each lesson plan provides you with the exercise keys, a summary of the lesson contents, and the estimated length of the lesson.

At the beginning of each teacher's book unit, there's a photocopiable list of **natural English** phrases and vocabulary items from the **student's book**. This is a useful reference for you, and a clear, concise record for the learners, which they can annotate with explanations, translation, pronunciation, etc. and use for their own revision.

teacher development chapters

You'll find the teacher development chapters after the lesson plans, starting on *p.148*. These practical chapters encourage reflection on teaching principles and techniques. At upper-intermediate level the areas covered are:

- how to ... do informal testing   *p.148*
- how to ... motivate higher level learners   *p.154*
- how to ... develop lexis at higher levels   *p.160*
- how to ... teach reading   *p.167*
- how to ... use dictionaries with learners   *p.174*

The chapters are regularly cross-referenced from the lesson plans but you can read them at any time and in any order.

Each chapter contains the following features:

- **think!** tasks for the reader with accompanying answer keys (see *p.148*)
- **try it out** boxes offering practical classroom ideas related to the topic of the chapter (see *p.149*)
- **natural English student's book extracts** to illustrate specific points (see *p.151*)
- **follow-up** sections at the end of each chapter providing a short bibliography for further reading on the topic (see *p.153*).

This **teacher's book** also contains a photocopiable key to the **student's book** language reference section (*p.181* to *p.183*).

welcome

use natural English phrases to say what they notice about people they meet
study and use phrases appropriate to greeting people in different contexts
discuss how they would react in situations about meeting people with a focus on *would, should, could*
listen to someone greeting a stranger
describe and say how they feel in different situations

lead-in

- This section could be used with learners who already know each other, or with a newly-formed class. Although the topic is meeting people for the first time, the situations learners discuss are suitable for use at any stage in the course. If the learners have never met each other before, spend time at the beginning so they can learn each others' names and get a little background information. This will give you the chance to find out about the learners yourself in an informal setting. See **ideas plus** on the right.

- Notice the **Think!** instruction in **exercise 1**, which appears throughout the **student's book**. This allows learners time to prepare what they are going to say and rehearse mentally, perhaps even look something up in a dictionary. Our research showed that this helped learners speak with more confidence and for longer. Discourage learners from writing out what they are going to say.

- Before learners discuss their answers, go over the phrases in the **natural English** box. *Notice* /ˈnəʊtɪs/ = to see (or hear) something which is important or memorable for you. If necessary, remind them of the meaning of *tend to* (= generally happens). Read the first phrase aloud, completing it in your own way, and ask learners to repeat it. Then practise in pairs. They can then go on to **exercise 2**.

Want to know more? Go to introduction: **natural English** boxes *p.5*

- You could give learners the opportunity to brainstorm what they know before looking at the phrases in **exercise 3**. Some quick oral feedback will lead into the exercise, where some of their suggestions will probably come up. Learners could complete the table with a partner. Check the answers with the class, and deal with the meaning of any new phrases, e.g. *What've you been up to?* is a very informal phrase meaning *What have you been doing?; How are things?* and *How's it going?* are informal ways of saying *How are you?* Model the phrases yourself using appropriate intonation and enthusiasm.

- In **exercise 4**, learners can give any appropriate answer and most of these are obvious. Here are some natural responses you might like to feed in:

  How are things? / How's it going?   *Oh, pretty good, actually.*
  It's nice to see you.   *Yes, you too. / Yes, it's been ages.*
  What've you been up to?   *Oh, nothing much. / Just working as usual.*

- You may wish to brainstorm with the class possible ways of continuing initial conversations with strangers before they mingle and do **exercise 5**, e.g. how long they have been in the school, why they need to study English, etc. Encourage learners to use the language studied, and monitor the mingling activity, noting good use of language and one or two points to give feedback on at the end.

grammar *would, should, could*

- Ask learners to read the situations in **exercise 1**, and then briefly discuss in pairs which situation they would find more difficult. Don't get them to discuss the answers to the questions at this stage. They should find the texts quite easy to understand, although you may need to explain *do*s and *don't*s in situation 2 d, i.e. things you should or shouldn't do.

- **Exercise 2** can be done alone, then learners can compare their answers before class feedback.

- You have a choice in **exercise 3**: let learners themselves decide which situation they want to discuss, or divide the class in half and each half discusses a different situation. In **exercise 4**, monitor to see how well they are doing, and to check that learners are involved and speaking. You could suggest a time limit of about five minutes, but be flexible: if it is going very well, let the discussion run its course.

- For **exercise 5**, you can do this as a pair activity or as an open class discussion.

listen to this

- Tell learners that they are going to listen to a German student in situation 1. Give them time to read questions 1 to 4, then play the recording. Monitor to see how accurate their answers are, and if they have not grasped it, replay the recording. At the end, your learners may wish to listen and follow the tapescript in the **listening booklet**, *p.2*.

- **Exercise 2** is intended as an opportunity to react briefly to the content of the recording, and could be done in open class.

exercise 3

meeting people for the first time

Hi!

Sorry, I didn't catch your name.

Is this the first course you've done here?

I'm Joao.

Nice / Pleased to meet you.

Do you live locally?

greeting people you already know

Hi!

How are things?

It's nice to see you.

What've you been up to?

How's it going?

You're looking well.

ideas plus 'getting to know you' activities

There are many activities you can use on the first day with a new class who do not know each other.

Want to know more fun and interesting ice-breaking activities? Go to **Classroom Dynamics** by Jill Hadfield (OUP) and **Keep Talking** by Friederike Klippel (CUP).

Here are two further simple ideas, done in pairs to encourage confidence:

• Learners work in pairs. Put some suitable speaking topics on the board – their home life, family, job, hobbies, an achievement, an unusual experience, etc. They should each choose three different topics. They then tell their partner what the topics are, e.g. their job. The partner then asks questions to find out what the job is, e.g. *Do you work in an office? Did you have to train for a long time?*, etc. They work through student A's first topic, then swap and do student B's, and so on. At the end, they tell the class one or two facts about their partner.

• In pairs, learners write five questions to ask the teacher about him / herself, e.g. *How long have you been working here? What's the most important decision you've ever had to make?* Go round and monitor. If a question has already been written down by one pair, tell any other pair who writes it to cross it out and think of another question. Bring the class together and let them ask their questions, answering them as truthfully as possible. If you don't want to answer, say, *I'd rather not say*. Learners can adapt the questions to ask each other in pairs.

exercise 2

1 We use *would* because we are talking about an imaginary situation.

2 *How should you greet him?* means *What is **the right way** to greet him?*
   How would you greet him? means *Imagine that situation. What are you personally going to say?*

3 *What could you do?* means *What possibilities are open to you in that situation?*
   What would you do? means *Imagine that situation. What are you personally going to do?*

troubleshooting it's your turn!

If this is a new class, this speaking activity will be an ideal opportunity to see how well learners cope with speaking in English, and whether some of them lapse into their mother tongue, are shy, or feel they have nothing to say. Use the time to monitor and notice which learners are confident and tend to dominate speaking activities, and which learners will need more encouragement. As you accumulate more information about the speaking abilities of different learners, you can think about how to group learners. You could try putting less confident learners together, or place them with someone who is happy to encourage them and is sympathetic. Naturally you will need to encourage quiet learners yourself, reassure them that the goal is communication and not to worry about mistakes, and praise their efforts where possible. At the beginning, it is probably better not to give too much negative feedback, but some constructive suggestions or different ways of expressing an idea in English will be welcomed.

exercise 1

1 friendly

2 tries (by offering him a coffee)

3 Dan

4 his lecture

one

wordlist

natural English

showing impatience
Oh, honestly!
For goodness' sake!
Oh, really!
You're hopeless!
Not again!

talking about activities
I play a lot of (tennis).
I don't get much exercise.
I do a bit of (judo).
I don't do any sport at all.

describing difficulty
I found it hard / easy to ...
I found ... quite tricky / challenging.
I was hopeless /good at ...

describing your language ability
I'm fluent in ...
I speak ... reasonably well.
I can get by in ...
I speak ..., but it's a bit rusty.
I know a few words of ...
I wish I could speak ...

asking follow-up questions
How do you mean (exactly)?
What does that involve?
How come?
What for?
What's it like?
What sort of thing?

sharing experiences
That happened to me too.
That was / wasn't true for me.
I remember (doing) that (too).
It wasn't like that (for me) at all.

vocabulary

learning
keep sth up
get used to sth
persevere with sth
get discouraged
get better at sth
pick sth up
have a go at sth
give sth a try

wordbooster

sporting collocations
go rollerblading / for a run
go in for a competition
take part in a race / the Olympics
join a club / a team
lose a match / the final
win a match / a prize
practise your tennis serve / your technique
do aerobics / weightlifting

glossaries

posh ⊚
kid ⊚
brat ⊚
go berserk ⊚
tip (n)
go to pieces
asset
index finger
outstretched

mind and body

life with **Agrippine**   25 – 30 mins

read for pleasure
nE showing impatience

Want to know more? Go to introduction: **life with Agrippine** / **do you get it?** *p.5.*

- This section starts with personalization to motivate and relax the learners. You could change the questions to make them more relevant to your group, e.g. if your learners are parents themselves, ask them about their experience of using babysitters. Let anyone with an amusing or interesting anecdote tell the class.

- Before you tell learners to read the cartoon, show them the **glossary**. These are provided to make it easier for learners to read quickly and therefore enjoy the humour of the cartoon. You'll see phonemic script here (and throughout the **student's book**). You could check learners' pronunciation after the listening activity.

Want to know more? Go to intermediate **teacher's book, how to ...** teach phonemic script *p.158.*

- If learners listen to the conversation, they will be able to focus on the stress and intonation in the phrases in the **natural English** box. You could use the recording a second time to focus on pronunciation of the phrases, or provide your own model for learners to repeat.

cartoon time
possible answers: lazy, selfish, irresponsible, unhelpful, obsessed with money, rude
Oh, honestly! For goodness sake!

language point informal language
Here and throughout the **student's book**, you will find informal language highlighted with a ⊚ symbol, which you will need to point out to your learners. Note that informal language and slang are not the same thing. Informal language is used in <u>normal conversation</u>, but may not be suitable in certain formal contexts. Slang is <u>very</u> informal language, which is often restricted to certain groups of people and may be offensive to some others. Learners at this level should be very aware of stylistic differences; once their English is of a reasonably accurate and fluent standard, errors of style may stand out.

reading would you pass the fitness test?

75 – 90 mins

talk about their family's physical activities using **natural English** phrases

read texts on physical tests

tell a partner how to do the tests and react to them using **natural English** phrases

focus on the use of *-ing* form and infinitive

lead-in

- **Exercise 1** sets up the need for the phrases in the **natural English** box. Ask learners to repeat the phrases, and then think about how to use one or two of them to talk about their family. At the end of **exercise 2**, ask a few learners to tell the class about their family.

read on

- Before you do **exercise 1**, look at **ideas plus** on the right.
- Divide the class to make sure that half read one text and half read the other. You will find that glossaries for texts are provided throughout, and often learners have to complete the glossary, match words and definitions, etc. The aim of this is to help learners with new vocabulary items, but also to practise contextual guesswork. Go over the **glossary** answers when they have read the texts.
- Before moving on to **exercise 2** give learners an opportunity to rehearse giving instructions. Working with someone who has read the same text will allow them to practise giving clear, oral instructions. Also if there are any parts they don't understand, they can work co-operatively, or ask for your help as a last resort. They will also have fun trying out the tests.
- In **exercise 2**, when they work with a new partner who has read a different text, they should be able to give the instructions more confidently and without looking at the book.

Want to know more? Go to **how to ...** teach reading *p.167.*

- Before learners discuss the tests in **exercise 3**, go over the phrases in the **natural English** box using the recording. Learners should understand the phrases, but they may not produce them naturally using these lexical chunks.
- At the end, give learners a couple of minutes to read the other text; in the next section they will be looking at the grammar in the first text.

grammar *-ing* form and infinitive

- In **exercise 1**, do the first example together, then let learners work alone or in pairs.
- After **exercise 2**, you can go to **language reference** *p.151* to show learners where the grammar summary is. You will find extra **cover & check** exercises there which can be used either during the lesson, if you think learners need extra controlled practice at that point, or for homework, or for revision later. Notice, however, that in **exercises 3** and **4**, learners are given a more personalized activity to practise the structures.

Want to know more? Go to key features: **language reference** *p.7.*

- Ask learners to look through the list of verbs in **exercise 5**, and to tell you if there are any they don't understand. You may need to explain *used to* versus *get used to*. *Used to* = something that happened often or continuously in the past; *get used to* = become accustomed to. *Be willing to do sth* = be prepared or happy to do sth.
- When you have checked the answers to **exercise 5**, you will see a **test your partner** exercise. These are used throughout the **student's book** to let learners practise intensively together. One learner shuts their book and is tested by their partner, then they swap. Once learners have done this exercise type a couple of times, they can set it up themselves quickly and easily.
- **Exercise 6** focuses on three verbs (*remember*, *try*, and *regret*) where the meaning changes depending on whether the verb is followed by *-ing* form or infinitive.
- **Exercise 7** is a game which practises the verb patterns focused on in **exercise 5**. In the game, the sentences are not planned: one person says a word, the next person has to continue with a logical word, and so on. Play it as a class with a couple of sentences to demonstrate what to do, then let learners work in small groups to invent more sentences. If you like, give them a time limit of five minutes to produce as many sentences as possible.
- Draw your learners' attention to the **extended speaking** box at the end of this section. Explain that this includes key language from the reading section that they will be able to use again in the **extended speaking** activity at the end of the unit.

 wordbooster *go to p.132* This **wordbooster** can be used at any point in **unit one**.

sh7325na

exercise 1 glossary

text 1: tips, index finger
text 2: tips, asset

nE

hard, tricky, very, hopeless

ideas plus total physical response (TPR)

If you think your class would enjoy it, try this TPR activity which is very suitable for following instructions and a fun introduction to the text. Get the class to stand and move chairs / tables out of the way. Give them instructions which they must carry out to demonstrate they have understood what you say. Here are some suggestions:

Lift your right leg ... then put it down again slowly. Now lift your left leg ... and raise your right arm.
Put your leg down slowly, but keep your arm raised. Stretch that arm as high as possible. Finally, keep that arm up and swing your left leg backwards and forwards without falling over.

Once you have done it, see if learners can remember the instructions; you can prompt them by doing the actions. They can give each other the instructions in pairs, or give them a handout for this purpose. Alternatively, learners can think up their own list of instructions to try out on another pair.

exercise 1

a try (doing), involves (using)
b for developing, after letting, by trying, as a result of playing
c Shutting your eyes ..., Practising also makes ...

exercise 2

a is more natural than b in both cases

exercise 5

verb + -*ing* form: keep, give up, get used to, practise, finish, mind, look forward to, take up
verb + infinitive: be willing to, used to, be prepared to, tend
verb + -*ing* form or infinitive: try, remember, regret, start

exercise 6

1	reading / looking at	4	using
2	to take	5	learning
3	to get / to buy	6	to tell / to inform

language point -*ing* form and infinitive

Focusing on -*ing* form and infinitive is useful at this level, as learners often still have the following problems:

- They don't know which verbs are followed by an -*ing* form and which by an infinitive.
- They seem reluctant to use the -*ing* form as the subject of a sentence. This doesn't happen in many other languages. Learners use the infinitive instead which doesn't sound natural.
- Learners have particular problems with preposition +*ing* when the preposition is *to*. They treat *to* as part of the infinitive, e.g. not ~~get used to do~~ but *get used to + doing*.
- They don't realize that both forms are sometimes possible, e.g. *start to do / doing*, but that sometimes the meaning changes, e.g.
  remember to do (= not forget to do something)
  remember doing (= recall something happening before now / in the past)

This is a clear case for good record keeping by learners; suggest devoting space in a notebook to this feature, and noting down when new vocabulary is followed by -*ing*, infinitive, etc.

listening learning

70 – 90 mins

Want to know more? Go to **Practical English Usage** by Michael Swan, *pp.278–285.*

talk about their language ability using **natural English** phrases

focus on present and past wishes and regrets

listen to people talking about subjects they have learned

talk about their own learning experiences using new vocabulary

lead-in

- You could begin **exercise 1** by looking at the **natural English** box. Go through the phrases and explain any new items, e.g. *get by* = manage / survive, *rusty* = not used for a long time, *wish + could* = I want to be able to do this now, but I can't. This last example is a quick preview of what is coming up in **grammar**. Here, it can be learned as a lexical item; don't get involved in the grammar at this stage. Then, **in exercise 2**, learners can think about the questions and discuss them in groups using the **natural English** phrases.

grammar wishes and regrets

- For **exercise 1**, do the first couple of sentences at least as a class. With the first example, compare with the sentence in the **natural English** box (*I wish I could speak Italian*). Does this mean now or in the past? It clearly means now, although learners may be put off by the past tense form (see **language point** on the right). Contrast this with sentence 2, *I wish I hadn't done Greek at school,* which is talking about past time using the past perfect. You could ask, *Did the person do Greek at school?* (yes). *Do they regret it now? / Are they sorry about it now?* (yes). Either do more of the sentences together, or let learners work in pairs and check their answers.

- **Exercise 2** will help to clarify the concepts. **Exercise 3** is a personalization activity to consolidate the concepts. If you want to give learners further consolidation before this activity, go to the **cover & check** exercises in **language reference** on *p.152.*

- **Exercise 4** is an opportunity for learners to generate their own examples. Give them time to think of a few questions before they work together, and do a model with one learner before they work in pairs.

listen to this

- Each unit has a listening section which includes the main listening activity. This consists of:

  tune in The aim is to overcome the limitations of recorded material by easing learners into the recording with a fairly guided task. The **tune in** extract is very short (in most cases, it is just the first part of a longer passage). This enables learners to get used to the voices and the context.

  listen carefully Here, the learners listen more intensively to the whole passage with a more demanding task, such as completing tables, completing a summary, etc.

  listening challenge This is an opportunity for learners to test their understanding of a new listening passage which is parallel to the first listening on a similar topic or of a similar genre.

  listening booklet Here, learners get an opportunity to analyse and learn from parts of the tapescript which contain a rich source of natural English. There are also exercises on pronunciation and / or vocabulary.

- After **exercise 2**, where learners hear a very brief extract, **exercise 3** gives them the opportunity to predict what might be said, which helps learners to tune in to the topic, and gives them a reason for listening.

- Let learners read the table in **exercise 4** first, and then play the recording. Replay the tape if learners need to hear it again. Go to the **listening booklet** *p.2* to *p.5,* where learners can listen and follow the tapescript and / or do further exercises on the tapescript. See **troubleshooting** on the right.

Want to know more? Go to introduction: **listening booklet** *p.7.*

Go to intermediate **teacher's book, how to …** teach listening *p.150.*

vocabulary learning

- You could start by checking that learners understand and can pronounce the word in the title; *persevere* = continue trying to do something even when there are difficulties. Do the first example in **exercise 1** together, then let learners work alone or in pairs to fill the gaps, using dictionaries if they have them. Tell them not to answer the questions at this stage so that you can concentrate first on the new items, and move on to discussion later.

- For **exercise 2**, look at **ideas plus** on the right. You could do this with the class as a training exercise.

- During **exercise 3**, monitor and note any problems with the vocabulary, but listen to the content which will tell you something about your students' attitude to learning.

exercise 1
sentences 1, 3, 5, and 8 refer to the present / future
sentences 2, 4, 6, and 7 refer to past events or situations

exercise 2

1 I wish I knew how to

2 I wish I was / were

3 I regret not ... -ing / I wish I'd done

4 I wish I hadn't done

---

language point wishes and regrets

1 Learners' main difficulty with these constructions is the use of the past tense after *wish* to talk about the present or future, and the use of the past perfect to talk about the past. There is a parallel, however, with the past forms in *if* sentences, and learners will already have come across the past simple used in the second conditional, e.g. *If Helen had more money, she'd go out more.*
You can use the board to highlight the forms and reinforce the concept, like this:

I wish I <u>was</u> better at maths <u>NOW</u> (past simple)

I wish I <u>hadn't done</u> Greek at school <u>IN THE PAST</u> (past perfect)

2 Using paraphrase is a useful way to help learners with the concepts, as in **exercise 2**: *I **can't** do it, but I'd like to.   I wish I **could.***

Want to know more? Go to **Practical English Usage** by Michael Swan *p.628.*

---

exercise 1 possible answers
learning to drive; learning a language / sign language; learning to dance, e.g. the tango; learning to cook; learning yoga / breathing exercises

exercise 2
Trude chose Russian and Julia chose yoga.

exercise 4

1 Julia	3 Trude	5 Julia
2 Trude	4 Julia	6 Trude

exercise 5
Eric learnt to do the Lindyhop, a kind of rock and roll dance. He really enjoyed it.

---

troubleshooting time management

As this is a long section, with quite a lot of new language input, you may decide to divide it over two lessons. If so, there is a natural break after the listening before starting on the vocabulary. You may even decide to leave the **listening challenge** until the next lesson and use it as a way into the vocabulary and speaking activity. If the listening activity in T1.3 proved to be more time-consuming than you had anticipated, this might be another reason for deferring the listening challenge. Throughout the **student's book**, you will notice that sections are subdivided into two, three, or four parts, each with a heading, and these allow you convenient breaks if you are unable to complete a section in one lesson.

---

exercise 1

1 keep	4 pick
2 used; persevere	5 have
3 get; making; better	6 give

---

ideas plus keeping a record

When learners make a note of new lexical items, they should:

1 try to include words that <u>commonly combine</u> with it, e.g. *persevere* is usually followed by *in* or *with;* this will be important for active use.

2 put items into <u>a simple context</u>, e.g. *You should persevere with your studies.*

3 note <u>phonemic script</u> and <u>word stress</u> of items which are difficult to pronounce.

4 think about how to record the <u>meaning</u> of the item: a translation / a paraphrase / a dictionary definition / a line drawing.

Want to know more? Go to **how to ...** develop lexis at higher levels (Self-study) *p.165.*

how to ... have a great conversation

---

speak for three minutes on different topics

read and **discuss** a text about successful conversation

develop a conversation using **natural English** phrases

listen to people talking about their childhood

talk about their own schooldays using **natural English** phrases

---

keep going

- Some learners might be quite surprised at being asked to keep a topic going for three minutes in **exercise 1**, but the topics are very simple and it will improve their confidence when they find they can do it. You could time them, and give them a warning when there is only one minute left. If a pair is running out of things to say, they can move on to another topic. It would be sensible to give learners a minute to choose their topic and think before they start. See **ideas plus** on the right.

- In **exercise 2**, don't expect learners to agree with everything; we wouldn't! There may be cultural differences and differences of degree, i.e. they may agree with some points to a certain extent. This activity can be done in pairs or groups. Ask each pair or group to summarize their ideas for the class.

---

develop the conversation

- Focus on the follow-up questions in the **natural English** box, then do the activity as a class. In **exercise 1**, do the first one together, then let learners work in pairs. Make it clear these are separate conversations. Accept any logical answers, then move on to **exercise 2**. Practise these short dialogues in open class so that you can correct learners' pronunciation and intonation.

- If you have done the **ideas plus** activity on the right, it will serve as a useful model for **exercise 3**. Give learners a moment to choose their topics and think of things to say. Monitor the pairwork and at the end give positive feedback on examples of good follow-up questions and balanced conversation.

---

talk about your childhood

- This recording acts as a model for the speaking activity in **it's your turn!** It also introduces some of the phrases in the **natural English** box, which will be very useful later to facilitate the conversation in the **extended speaking** activity.

---

it's your turn!

- Give learners time to choose a topic and think what to say. During the activity, monitor and note any language points for feedback at the end. Listen to their stories and pick out an interesting one that a learner could tell the class at the end.

ideas plus jigsaw activity

You could write out the text in **exercise 2** on a piece of paper, cut it into six pieces, and give each learner one point (if you have twelve learners, make two copies of the text, etc.). Each student has to learn their point and is told that there are five other points to discover. Before they mingle, they should check any unknown words with a dictionary or you. They then circulate until they have understood all six points. Learners don't have to be word perfect; they just have to remember the main idea.

They then go back to their place and read the full text to see if they have understood the points correctly. Then go on to the discussion in **exercise 2**.

nE

1 f 2 a 3 e (d is also possible)
4 d 5 b 6 c

exercise 1

1 What for?
2 What's it like?
3 What sort of thing?
4 What does that involve?
5 How come?
6 What do you mean exactly?

ideas plus interrupted monologue

As a lead in to **exercise 1**, you can do this activity with your class. Tell them you are going to talk about your last holiday, but that they must try and interrupt you and ask you about the things you tell them. It might go like this:

T I had a really wonderful holiday last summer. I went to the north coast of Spain to stay in an old farm.

S1 Oh really? Where exactly was it?

T It was in Gijon, which is on the coast.

S2 And are the beaches nice there?

T Yes, they're lovely, sandy beaches. Anyway, I went with my brother and his wife …

The activity will continue the theme of *good conversation* with active listening, and lead into the language point.

exercise 1

1 they talk about visiting their grandparents and getting dressed up
2 their experience was similar

exercise 2

1 they talk about holidays
2 their experience was different

exercise 3

all the phrases are used

language point lexical chunks

The phrases in this **natural English** box are a good example of lexical chunks which learners will almost certainly understand, but be unlikely to construct themselves in this natural way. They are more likely to say, for example, *for me it was not the same / it was different,* etc. It may be worth pointing out to your learners that these are very natural ways to express the ideas, and that if they can practise and assimilate phrases like these, they will make their English sound more natural overall.

Want to know more? Go to **how to …** develop lexis at higher levels *p.161*.

extended speaking are you a runner or a reader? 50 – 70 mins

listen to people talking about reading in their lives

prepare to talk about reading or sport in their lives

speak to a partner about their topic

write a summary of reading or sport in your partner's life

- It is important that learners understand at the beginning of this activity what they are going to do in the lesson. You can ask them to read the menu in the left-hand column, or put it on the board, or tell them in your own words what is going to happen.

- You should also give them time to look back at the **extended speaking** boxes which occur at the end of each section in every unit. This will enable them to see how language learnt can be used in the activity, and will refresh their memories. As this is the first **extended speaking** activity, it is important that they see how each section works towards the final activity.

collect ideas

- For **exercise 1**, get learners to mingle and find someone who likes the same topic. They shouldn't start to discuss it yet. If you have an odd number of learners in each category, let them work in a group of three. Get learners to sit with their new partner. See **troubleshooting** on the right.

- The listening activity in **exercises 2** and **3** serves as a model for the learners. The task in **exercise 3** is included here to make learners aware of the importance of listening, reacting, and contributing to conversation. Although Michael talks more initially, Trude is more dominant later in the conversation. If you point out the conversational implications and learners adopt these, it should improve the quality of their conversations.

- For **exercise 4**, focus learners on the notes about reading and sport and point out that they should cover as many points as possible from A, and choose two relevant topics from B (or their own ideas). This will give pairs a clear conversational structure to get them started, but produce some unpredictability later on. If they have any language queries, let them ask you at this point.

exercise 2
reading in my childhood, what I had to read at college / university, particular likes and dislikes

exercise 3
1 true   2 true   3 false   4 true   5 true

share experiences

- Don't be worried if learners take a minute or two to get into the conversation; this might well happen in their own language. Once the conversation takes off, monitor and note down points for feedback at the end, including positive comments as well as some language correction. If one pair finishes early, you could ask them to talk about one more point from B, or even tell them to split up and listen to another pair (but not interrupt). At a suitable point, when most of the class seems to be finishing, go on to **exercise 6**. Explain the activity, then give them a few minutes to write.

- You can point out the uses of *both / neither* in the **language reminder** before they feed back to the class.

Want to know more? Go to intermediate **teacher's book, how to ...** do free speaking *p.162*.

write a summary

- **Exercise 8** could be done as homework, and you could also collect in the work and mark it. Alternatively, each pair could make a poster of their similarities and differences, to be displayed on the walls. If you do this, omit **exercise 7**, otherwise it will be repetitive.

feedback checklist

During the **extended speaking** activity, note down examples of …

- **good language use**

- **effective communication strategies**
  (turn-taking, interrupting, inviting others to speak, etc.)

- **learner errors**
  (vocabulary, grammar, pronunciation, etc.)

- **particular communication problems**

Make sure you allow time for feedback at the end of the lesson. You can use the notes you make above to praise effective language use and communication or, if necessary, to do some remedial work.

---

troubleshooting engaging conversation

For this **extended speaking** activity, learners don't need to be very serious readers or avid sports fans. Much of the conversation which follows will be factual and personalized and involves information about what learners read or sports they did at school and in their free time. You could point this out to anyone who isn't interested in either topic, although we didn't come across any learners like this in our research.

When we devised this activity, we asked pairs to work together who chose different topics, i.e. a reader and a runner together. This did not prove to be wholly satisfactory, because learners were not always interested in the other topic, and the result was an interview rather than a genuinely interactive conversation. When we changed to the present form where learners chose the same topic, the conversations were longer, more engaging, and more animated with more sharing of experiences.

test yourself!

Encourage learners to use **test yourself!** to reflect on their progress as well as doing the test activities. Give them a few minutes to mark the line before they do the **test yourself!** activities and to go back to the unit contents and tick the language they can now use confidently. This should motivate learners and will help them to be analytical about their own learning.

Want to know more? Go to the **introduction** *p.7* for ways of using **test yourself!**

1 **go / do** rollerblading; **join** a club; **do** aerobics; **practise** your tennis serve; **win / lose** the final
2 be good **at** sth; flick **through** a book; take part **in** a race; persevere **with** sth; have a go **at** sth
3 get used to; look forward to; keep

1 I wish I hadn't left the company.
2 I decided to give it a try.
3 I got better at it.
4 I get discouraged easily.

1 I wish I could speak French.
2 I can't remember meeting him before.
3 Reading is the best way to relax.
4 I'm fluent in Dutch, and I can get by in German.

two

wordlist

natural English

That was ... of you!
That was very (brave / nice / clever) of you!
That wasn't very (kind) of you!
That was a bit (silly / careless) of you!

saying how things sound
That sounds right / fine.
That doesn't sound polite / very appropriate.
That isn't natural.
That's wrong / odd / rude.
That sounds wrong. It should be ...

though and although
I enjoyed it, though not everyone did.
I enjoyed it. Not everyone did, though.
Although we need to ..., the results are ...

asking for and making recommendations
Can you recommend any places to see?
Is there anything else you can recommend?
It's worth going to ...
... is well worth a visit.
You should go and see ...
I'd (really) recommend ...

vocabulary

physical actions
bend down
lose your balance
reach up
lean against sth
grab hold of sth
get down on your knees

tourists' phrases
youth hostel
bed and breakfast accommodation
tourist attractions
historic monuments
opening times
admission charges
places of interest
bus / train timetable
holiday resorts
guided walks
sightseeing tours
day trips

on board a plane
How much longer do we have to wait?
I'm afraid (the light) isn't working.
When do we land at ... Airport / in ...?

Please ensure your seatbelt is fastened.
Extinguish all cigarettes.
We're cruising at an altitude of ...
Do you need to fill in a landing card?
Please remain seated until the plane has come to a standstill.
cabin crew
turbulence
an aisle / window seat
scheduled / charter flight
terminal building
jet lag
steward / stewardess
runway
overhead locker

wordbooster

health and medicine
earache
a sore throat
a cough
a pain in my (elbow)
a nose bleed
sunburn
a bandage
tablets
a plaster
tissues
eyedrops
ointment

tourist information
What's the best way of getting to ...?
Do I have to book in advance?
Is there any chance of getting tickets for ...?
How much does it cost to get in?
Can we get something to eat round here?
What's the best place to get (souvenirs)?

glossaries

parrot
(pretty) fed up ⑥
grab hold of
burly
broccoli
cauliflower
tap
loo ⑥
flick through sth
syringe

in unit two ...

do you get it?
joke flying high
natural English *That was ... of you!*
vocabulary physical actions

listening airport experiences
natural English saying how things sound
listening airport stories
grammar *should have* + past participle

wordbooster
health and medicine
tourist information

reading lost for words
reading Words fail me
natural English *though* and *although*
grammar possibility and probability

how to ... get the information you want
vocabulary tourists' phrases
natural English saying how sure you are
listening conversation in a tourist information office
natural English asking for and making recommendations

extended speaking produce a page from a phrasebook
correct and **discuss** a sample page from a phrasebook
produce a phrasebook page of useful phrases for the chemist's
role play at the chemist's using the language from their phrasebook
write a postcard about a holiday health problem

test yourself!
revision of the unit

do you get it ?   25 – 30 mins

listen for pleasure
nE *That was ... of you!*
vocabulary physical actions

Want to know more? Go to introduction: **life with Agrippine / do you get it?** *p.5.*

- This section starts with personalization to motivate and relax the learners. If the first activity is not relevant to your class, go straight into the picture activity. If some learners in your class have never flown, put them with someone who has, or do this warmer as a class discussion.
- When they look at the pictures, show them the **glossary**. These words may help them when piecing the story together. This activity is best done in pairs. If anyone knows the joke and what happens in the final frame, ask them not to tell the class, or they will spoil the joke. Elicit their suggestions for the end of the joke, but don't confirm or reject any at this stage.
- As this is the first time they hear a joke in the **student's book**, point out the phrases in the speech bubbles. These will give them ideas for responding to the joke, which they should do as soon as they've heard it.
- Learners can look at the phrases in the **natural English** box, then follow the tapescript and repeat the phrases. Learners are often not familiar with this construction (*That was ... of you*) and tend to say *You're kind / nice*, etc.
- The vocabulary slot, **physical actions**, contains some useful lexical phrases. Demonstrate the meaning of any that learners don't understand, or ask a learner to demonstrate.

physical actions possible answers
bend down to pick something up / put your shoes on
lose your balance if the plane dropped suddenly in an air pocket
reach up to get something from the overhead locker
lean against something if you were trying to sleep
grab hold of somebody if you were going to fall / if the flight were bumpy
get down on your knees to pray if you were frightened / to look for something under your seat

ideas plus have a go!
Some learners really enjoy telling jokes, and because of their narrative structure, they are easy to memorize and retell. You could ask learners to think of a joke for homework, or find one in a book / on the Internet, which they are able to tell in English and other learners will be able to understand. They should practise telling it on their own. In the next lesson, they tell their jokes in small groups. If learners really respond to jokes, you could get them to produce a little booklet of jokes written in English. For an interesting website, go to laughlab.co.uk, where an international experiment is running on different nationalities' sense of humour.

listening airport experiences

60 – 80 mins

discuss accuracy and politeness using **natural English** phrases

talk about how they would behave in certain situations

listen to people describing airport experiences

focus on *should(n't) have* + past participle with controlled and freer practice

lead-in

- If your learners are studying in an English-speaking country, they can compare their experience of home and abroad. You could ask learners whether there are particular professions in their country where people tend to be rude or difficult.

- Go through the **natural English** box first. Ask learners to repeat some of the phrases, particularly *That doesn't sound very appropriate* /ə'prəʊprɪət/, and explain any new items, e.g. *odd* = strange.

- You could write the example in **exercise 3** on the board. Tell them the context is of a passenger talking to an airline check-in stewardess, and ask them to respond using one of the **natural English** phrases (make sure they know what the correct response should be). Do another example from the activity if necessary before learners work in pairs. In feedback, learners can practise the corrected forms, with appropriate intonation, in a question and answer format.

- Give learners time to read and think about the situations in **exercise 4**. If you like, they can add their own situation. If the discussion generates quite a lot of ideas, let it run. You could also consider getting learners to role play one or two situations. Monitor the discussion and collect examples for feedback at the end.

listen to this

- Once learners have done **tune in** in **exercise 1**, let them try to guess what happens. This will be motivating when they come to hear whether their guess was correct. See **ideas plus** on the right.

- All three listening extracts are referred to again in the grammar practice activity, **exercise 3** on *p.24*, so you will need to do all of them. The first two extracts are not particularly difficult for the level. If you are running out of time, omit the **listening booklet** activity. Don't replay the **listening challenge** if learners have understood it the first time.

grammar *should have* + past participle

- The explanations in **exercise 1** are a way of checking concept. You could also check the first sentence by asking concept questions: *Did he check? Was that a bad idea?* Be sure to give plenty of controlled practice of the pronunciation in **exercise 2**.

- For **exercise 3**, you will need to give learners time to recall the stories and the parrot joke. Be prepared to remind them where the tapescripts are in the **listening booklet** (*p.6*), so that they can refer to these if they can't remember. Ask the pairs to read their examples to the class at the end, especially if any sentences are different.

Want to know more? Go to **how to ...** do informal testing (concept questions) *p.150.*

it's your turn!

- If you are running out of time at the end of your lesson, you could ask learners to think up and plan their anecdote as a homework activity. You could then use it as a warmer in the next lesson. During the mingling activity, monitor and make a note of interesting examples of language use, and provide class feedback at the end. If anyone has a particularly nice story, get them to tell the class.

Want to know more? Go to intermediate **teacher's book, how to ...** monitor and give feedback *p.156.*

exercise 3

2 wrong; it should be *Why do I have to pay for excess baggage?*
3 correct
4 wrong; it should be *What time does the plane land?*
5 sounds odd; you don't use *sir* or *madam* (see **language point** on the right)
6 correct
7 doesn't sound polite; it should be *I'm afraid this suitcase is in the way. Could you possibly move it?*
8 wrong; it should be *I'm afraid your flight is delayed.*
9 doesn't sound correct or natural; it should be *Could I see your ticket?* or *I need to see your ticket.*
10 correct

language point style

1 In the **natural English** box, the phrase, *That sounds wrong* is more direct than, *That doesn't sound right.* In discussing the sentences in **exercise 3**, learners can use either form, but if they are commenting on each others' use of language, it would be more tactful if they used the more indirect form, *That doesn't sound right / appropriate*, etc.

2 In British English, it is only appropriate to use *sir* or *madam* if you are in the position of serving a member of the public, e.g. a bank employee serving a client; a shop assistant serving a customer. Even here, it would only tend to happen in quite formal settings. They may be used in a smart restaurant, but are unlikely to be heard in a sandwich bar. Learners often use *sir / madam* inappropriately because of translation.

---

exercise 1

1 check-in
2 a hamster
3 a Greek man has arrived at check-in with a hamster in a cardboard box; he wants to take it on the plane

exercise 5

1 false (she discovered the problem at check-in)
2 true
3 false (it was the week before)
4 true
5 false (they arranged another flight for her)

exercise 6

He was in Israel / the Middle East. The customs official asked him to take a photo to prove his camera was real and not a weapon. He didn't realize why he was being asked to do this, and pointed the camera at the official.

ideas plus prediction

In **how to ...** teach reading, on *p.167*, we talk about the use of prediction; this also applies to **tune in** activities for listening. You may want to teach the following phrases, which are very useful for talking about predictions:

It's hard to say, but I think ... / It could be all sorts of things / One possibility is that ... / He'll probably... / He might ...

Learners will be focusing on ways of expressing possibility and probability in the reading section.

---

exercise 1

1 didn't do   2 did

exercise 3

1 Lynne should have checked her ticket in advance.
2 Ralph shouldn't have pointed the camera at the customs official.
3 The customs official should have explained why he wanted Ralph to take a photo. Or he should've told him to point the camera at the ceiling.
4 The parrot shouldn't have been rude.
5 The passenger shouldn't have shouted at the stewardess.
6 The stewardess should've remembered to bring the passenger's drink.
7 The steward shouldn't have thrown the man out of the plane (without a parachute!).

language point *should / shouldn't have* + past participle

Learners at this level already know *should* + infinitive and they have just seen another use of it in the **natural English** box on *p.22 (That's wrong; it should be ...)*. If they aren't familiar with the past form, the concept itself is not difficult, i.e. you did something and it was the wrong thing to do, or you didn't do something and that was also wrong. You will need to point out the pronunciation of the weak form and the contractions *should've* /ˈʃʊdəv/ and *shouldn't've* /ˈʃʊdəntəv/, and get learners to practise in **exercise 2.**

You could also revise the form *I wish I'd / I hadn't ...* which learners focused on in unit one on *p.13*. You could ask learners in which sentences in **exercise 3** the speakers might use *I wish I'd / I hadn't ...*

Want to know more? Go to **Practical English Usage** by Michael Swan *pp.516–517.*

reading lost for words

60 – 75 mins

practise communicating without words

read and **discuss** a text about communicating without words

focus on *though* and *although*

study the grammar of possibility and probability and **use** the language to talk about Dieter Graf's book, and in a personalized activity

lead-in

- The warmer in **exercise 1** is a fun way into the lesson and introduces the topic. You could start by demonstrating a particular request through mime or gesture, e.g. *What time does the film start?* or, *Can I borrow your mobile phone?* Then get learners to look at the possible ways of communicating and try the sentences in pairs.

- After feedback, go on to **exercise 2**. Give learners time to decide how they are going to communicate their ideas before they act them out in front of the class.

read on

- In **exercise 1**, draw the learners' attention to the pictures in the **glossary**, which illustrate items (in **bold**) in the text that they may not know.

- Give learners time to prepare the questions or re-read the text to find the answers in **exercise 2**. When they have finished, ask each pair to sit facing each other as in an interview, and to act the roles. At the end, have one pair act their interview out while the others listen to see if they are correct.

- Talk through the **natural English** box before asking learners to find the examples of *though* and *although* in the text and do the exercise. Bear in mind that there is a fuller treatment of adverbs of concession in unit eight **grammar** *p.99*.

- You may wish to do **exercise 4** before the **natural English** box to allow learners time to react to the text while the ideas are still fresh in their minds.

Want to know more? Go to **how to ...** teach reading *p.167*.

grammar possibility and probability

- For **exercise 1** do one example with the class before they work on the task alone or with a partner. When you check the answers, be sure to check the pronunciation before doing **test your partner**. Look at **language point** on the right.

- **Exercise 2** relates the language in the exercise back to the text. You also have a useful set of vocabulary in this exercise: they are all superordinates, i.e. general words which cover many examples, e.g. *jewellery* includes *ring, necklace, brooch*, etc. Incidentally, Dieter Graf's book has 64 pages and 1,200 photos altogether, a fact you might want to pass on to your learners.

it's your turn!

- The section concludes with a freer, personalized activity to practise the grammar. If you feel from your knowledge of the group that there are more relevant topics to discuss, you could add them. Give an example yourself to start with, put learners into small groups, then monitor the activity and do feedback on content and language at the end.

 **wordbooster** *go to p.132*   This **wordbooster** can be used at any point in **unit two**.

exercise 2

1 Where are you from? Munich.
2 What do you do for a living? I'm an architect.
3 Have you done a lot of travelling? Yes, I've travelled all over the world.
4 Why did you decide to produce this book? Because I found myself unable to say things in lots of situations around the world.
5 Why is the book unusual? Because it's only pictures.
6 What kind of people use it? A wide range of people / tourists (such as Swiss UN workers and the Dutch Olympic team).
7 Did you have any problems producing it? Yes, sometimes it was dangerous.
8 Has it been successful? Yes, it has sold over half a million copies.

exercise 3

What if there is nothing to point at, though ...
It can be dangerous, though ...
... although several women were worried about ...

possible answers

1 We went to Spain for a week.
2 The trip was very successful.
3 Sometimes it's stressful, though.
4 It doesn't include everything you need, though.

ideas plus acting out text

Comprehension of written texts is commonly tested through true / false, multiple choice, and general comprehension questions, etc. However, it can be motivating for learners to take the information in the text and act it out, usually in a dialogue. This wouldn't work with all texts, but some lend themselves to this treatment well, especially if they are about people's experiences, e.g. *Single white female* in unit eight and *Excuse me, is it day or night?* in unit five. The learner who is the interviewer in each case could be asked to plan five or six suitable questions that will elicit most of the information in the text. In the case of *Single white female*, there are two characters, Michelle and Sophie, which could produce two interviews and allow learners to be both interviewer and interviewee.

exercise 1

It'll definitely happen.
It's bound to happen.
It's likely to happen.
It might happen.
It's unlikely to happen.
I doubt if it'll happen.
It's highly unlikely to happen.
It definitely won't happen.

language point possibility and probability

The language items in this section are all very high frequency: *doubt, might, definitely,* and *likely* are within the first thousand words of spoken and written English, for instance, and yet some of them are rarely used productively by learners at this level. Another way to introduce or revise this language is to put the phrases on separate cards (see answer key), make several copies, and give them to your learners to rank in order from *sure to happen* to *sure not to happen.*

As well as focusing on the meaning of these phrases, you will need to highlight the forms, i.e. which ones are followed by *to,* and the word order, e.g. we say *it'll **definitely** happen* but *it **definitely won't** happen.*

Want to know more? Go to **language reference** and **cover & check** exercises *p.154.*

how to ... get the information you want

learn vocabulary and read about tourist information offices

discuss what happens in them using **natural English** phrases

listen to a conversation in a tourist office

role play a similar situation using **natural English** phrases asking for and making recommendations

vocabulary tourists' phrases

- The phrases in **exercise 1** are all compound nouns, e.g. *youth hostel*, or common collocations, e.g. *historic monuments*. This means words that <u>might</u> combine together, e.g. *cheap hostel*, *dirty hostel*, are <u>not</u> what you are looking for. Learners need to provide combinations that are both frequent and predictable. You can remind learners that they studied common sporting collocations in **wordbooster** in unit one on *p.12*.

- Let learners work in pairs, then check their ideas in the text in **exercise 2**. You will need to have a round-up activity at the end where they can ask you if the words they wrote are correct. The text includes *holiday resorts*, for example, but *ski resorts*, *mountain resorts*, or *seaside resorts* are also fine. Learners can check these in dictionaries.

- Look at the phrases in the **natural English** box and play the recording as suggested. After practising the questions and answers, they can use these phrases in the discussion in **exercise 3**. Look at **language point** on the right.

Want to know more? Go to **how to ...** develop lexis at higher levels *p.160*.

make enquiries

- **Exercise 1** is a simple prediction activity to help learners tune in to the context and familiarize themselves with the map. You could do this as a class activity.

- In **exercise 2**, learners are tuning in to the tone of the conversation as well as the setting.

- Monitor the learners while they are listening to see how well they are coping with the comprehension task. Replay the recording if you feel it is necessary.

make recommendations

- Replay the recording, pausing at appropriate points where learners hear the phrases in the **natural English** box. There is also a short controlled practice stage where you can focus on pronunciation, e.g. *worth* /wɜːθ/.

it's your turn!

- This **it's your turn!** brings together much of the language learners have worked on in the lesson and in the second part of **wordbooster**. In **exercise 1** learners prepare information as tourist information advisors. They should both make notes about the attractions they have devised in pairs, so that they can talk about them in exercise 3 with a new partner.

- With the same partner, learners prepare the role of tourists in **exercise 2**. Explain that they will be working with a new partner for the role play.

- Organize learners into new pairs for the role play in **exercise 3**. They have prepared both roles so they can take turns to be the tourist information advisor and the tourist. Monitor and check that they are doing the role play effectively. Make notes for feedback at the end.

exercise 1

1	youth hostel	7	places of interest
2	bed and breakfast accommodation	8	bus / train timetable
3	tourist attractions	9	holiday resorts
4	historic monuments	10	sightseeing tours
5	opening times	11	guided walks
6	admission charges	12	day trips / river trips

nE

Is the museum open on Sundays?
Yes, I'm pretty sure it is.
Do students get a reduction?
I'm not too sure about that.
Do they provide sightseeing tours?
I don't really know, to be honest.
Do you know what time the river trips are?
I haven't a clue.

language point nE box modifying and extending

The phrases here help learners to modify and extend what they want to say in a way that makes them sound more natural. You may wish to further extend their knowledge of phrases in this context and include: *I'm absolutely certain (tourist information offices tell you about …)*; *I'm 100% certain*.

exercise 2

They both sound friendly and interested.

exercise 3

The woman is very interested in the river trips; she's interested in the castle; she's not interested in the Modern Art and Photography Museum; we don't really know if she's interested in the Theatre Museum or the bird park.

nE

Can you recommend any places to see? (the same)
Anything else you can recommend? (different)
It's worth going to … (the same)
… is well worth a visit (the same)
You should go and see … (the same)
I would recommend … (different)

ideas plus recommending places

You can practise the language in the **natural English** box in a personalized activity.

1 With multilingual classes who are not studying in their own country, ask learners to think of four or five places in their local area to recommend to people visiting for the first time.

2 With classes who are studying in their own country, ask learners to choose a different region or country which they have visited and think of several places in that area to recommend to people who have not been there.

Organize the class into groups of learners who have chosen different places to talk about. They should ask each other questions to find out as much information as they can. Monitor and take notes for feedback at the end, focusing particularly on the **natural English** questions. If you have time, ask groups for the most interesting recommendations.

ideas plus writing project

Learners might enjoy producing a collage, posters, or even a booklet describing tourist attractions in and around their town / city or the place where they are studying. They could get information from tourist information offices or from the Internet, and possibly contribute photographs. They could also have restaurant, bar, or club reviews to which other learners add comments. Learners studying in an English-speaking country could produce a booklet for new learners arriving in their school, which would have a genuine purpose.

extended speaking produce a page from a phrasebook 60 – 80 mins

collect ideas

- If possible, take in some phrasebooks for different countries to show learners, and ask them if they ever use them. What do they think of them? Then refer them to the phrasebook page, *On board a plane*, which will be a model for the page that they produce themselves. Point out that there are three sections, and there is a distinction between what they might say (productive language) and what they might hear (receptive language). This is a useful distinction for learners, and will help them to structure their page.

- Before they begin to correct the errors, remind them of the **natural English** box on *p.22*: *saying how things sound*. They can work alone and then compare with a partner, or work together throughout. Then go over the answers to **exercise 1**. Be prepared to explain new items in the phrasebook, e.g. *come to a standstill* = when a vehicle, plane, etc. stops moving, and *turbulence* = strong air currents causing a plane to move suddenly. Then go on to **exercise 2**.

produce a phrasebook page

- This is a writing activity, but in fact, because learners are writing co-operatively, there is a great deal of oral interaction: making suggestions, accepting and rejecting them, negotiating the phrases, correcting each other, etc.

- The **checklist** is very important here if learners are to get the most out of the activity. Crucially, they shouldn't include words and phrases which are elementary or likely to be of little value. Trying to think through problems for their own level is what will make this a challenging activity. They should be able to teach each other some new language by the end of the exercise; they will certainly need to call on you for help and use dictionaries.

- Your role in **exercise 3** will be to stimulate ideas where necessary, guide the learners if they run out of ideas, and help them to polish their phrases into accurate and natural language (see **troubleshooting** on the right). If you find a group has run out of ideas, suggest one or two ailments to get them thinking, e.g. medical problems you might have on holiday. You can also refer them back to **wordbooster** on *p.25*. Try to monitor so that everyone has a correct version by the end. We have provided a sample answer sheet here but this is only for your guidance, and learners' own versions are more important.

- Give them a time limit to start with, for instance fifteen minutes, but then adapt this as necessary.

- When the groups are all more or less ready, reorganize them as suggested in **exercise 4**. This should be a further opportunity for them to learn from each other and add to their lists.

role play

- If you are running out of time, you could stop the lesson at this point, and do the listening and role play as revision in the next lesson. The aim of this role play is to encourage learners to use the language they have produced. This listening activity in **exercise 5** is a simple model for the role play, so you don't need to spend a lot of time on comprehension.

- While learners are doing the role play, monitor and provide feedback at the end. This role play can be repeated several times.

write a postcard

- You can ask learners to write their postcards at home and show them to their partner the next day. Collect them in and correct them.

exercise 1 collect ideas
section 1
1 How much longer **do** we have to wait?
2 I'm afraid ~~but~~ my light isn't / my earphones aren't working.
3 Could I have another blanket? (not *Give me* ...)

section 2
4 Please ensure that your seatbelt is fasten**ed** and extinguish all cigarettes.
5 Can I get you anything ~~for~~ to drink?
6 Do you need to fill **in** a landing card?

exercise 2
You can use the first three phrases.
Can I put my bag under the seat? may be possible on certain trains.
The other questions are very unlikely (although you could ask someone for another blanket / a newspaper on a sleeper).

exercise 5 role play
1 He has insect bites.
2 She recommends an anti-itching cream and an insect repellent spray.

write a postcard possible answer

AT THE CHEMIST'S
phrases you may need
Can you recommend something for ... (constipation / diarrhoea)?
Have you got anything ... (cheaper / stronger)?
Does it contain ... (penicillin / aspirin, etc.)?
How often / when do I have to take it?
Do I need a prescription for (antibiotics / this drug)?
Does it have any side effects?
Is it safe to take ... (when you are driving / with alcohol)?

phrases you may hear
Are you allergic to ... (penicillin)?
Are you taking any other medicine?
Is it painful / sore? / Does it itch?
You take (two tablets) twice a day with / after meals.
Do you prefer (tablets / cream / drops)?
You should see a doctor if it gets any worse.

useful vocabulary

cotton wool	tablets / pills / ointment / drops	feel dizzy
plasters	tube / bottle / packet	to faint / pass out
bandages	painkillers	feel sick
a sling	dosage / dose	bleed

troubleshooting produce a phrasebook page
helping learners with language

In this and similar activities, don't be tempted to just supply learners with the language they require. When they produce phrases and want you to check them, look for ways of making them more natural in English, e.g. if learners write *How often must I take this medicine?* you could suggest they use *have to* and then check they reformulate the question correctly. There will also be specific vocabulary they will want to ask you for. If possible, you should provide dictionaries, but if they explain the meaning of a word in English, then give it to them. You may decide to tell the class you won't give answers in translation; upper-intermediate learners have enough English to explain what they mean.

ideas plus phrasebook pages

If learners have enjoyed this activity, you could repeat it for a different topic, or try it at a different level with another class. For example, you could revise the tourist information office language using this type of activity, or focus on classroom language, or airport / clothes shop language, etc. Learners can keep these phrasebook pages in their vocabulary notebooks, or they can produce posters for the classroom.

test yourself!

Want to know more? Go to the **introduction** *p.7* for ways of using **test yourself!**

1 earache, a sore throat, a cough, a rash, a pain, sunburn; plasters, a bandage, tablets / pills, eye drops, ointment
2 Can you recommend any places to see? Anything else you'd recommend? (see also the questions in **wordbooster**, e.g. How much does it cost to get in to ...?)

1 I haven't a clue.
2 The castle's (well) worth a visit / worth seeing.
3 That was very brave of you.
4 That doesn't sound very polite.

1 It was bound to happen.
2 You shouldn't have gone there.
3 He's highly unlikely to come.
4 Sightseeing's fun. It's expensive, though.

three

wordlist

natural English

fancy (v)
Do you fancy (a drink)?
Do you fancy + -*ing*?
I don't fancy ... (much).

describing group size
There are five of us in my family.
There are five of us in all / altogether,
including (my grandparents).

agreeing with and challenging opinions
That makes sense.
That seems sensible.
I think you're right.
Why do you say that?
I can't see the point of that.
I don't see why.

talking about your background
Originally, I'm from ...
I was (born and) brought up in ...
I come from a (sporty / musical) family.
My proudest moment was ... + -*ing*.
I've always dreamt of + -*ing*.

reaching a decision / moving on
So that's decided / we agree on that, then.
Shall we go on to the next point?
Let's go on to the next one.

vocabulary

good and bad relationships
consult sb
quarrel with sb
compete with sb
relate to sb
get on with sb
hug sb
stick up for sb
clash with sb

wordbooster

personality phrases
articulate
a good laugh
eccentric
a pain in the neck ⊚
out of control
a big ego ⊚
want to get on in life
supportive

glossary
wanna ⊚
telly ⊚
There's ... on.
stuff ⊚
the pictures
broke (adj) ⊚
pathetic ⊚
put sb on
too much on ⊚
wouldn't be seen dead ⊚
kid ⊚
let your hair down ⊚
go on about
ruin
booze ⊚

in unit three ...

life with Agrippine
cartoon free time
natural English *fancy* (v)

reading family ties
natural English describing group size
vocabulary good and bad relationships
reading Disco with Dad ... Why not?
grammar *each other / one another, -self / -selves*

listening creating a community
grammar obligation, necessity, and prohibition
natural English agreeing with and challenging
   opinions
listening interview with a TV producer

wordbooster
personality phrases
paraphrasing

how to ... write a website profile
listening profile of an Edenite
natural English talking about your background
grammar sequencing information in a text

extended speaking create a band
choose the members of a band
discuss their musical style and image, and how
   to promote them
present ideas to the rest of the class
create a website profile of one of the band
   members
natural English reaching a decision / moving on

test yourself!
revision of the unit

life with Agrippine   25 – 30 mins

read for pleasure
nE *fancy* (v)

- The procedure for using this section is standard. As you have already used the first Agrippine cartoon, you will be familiar with this format. Most learners will have plenty to say in the warmer.

- When learners have read and discussed the cartoon and listened to the recording, you could take a few minutes to go over the **glossary**, as there are some useful phrases. See **language point** below. Focus on the stress in the phrases with *on* (*There's only kids' stuff on*; *There's nothing on*; *I've got too much on*).

- When you look at the **natural English** box, you could point out that there is another meaning of *fancy* in informal English; *to fancy someone* means to find someone sexually attractive. When they practise the phrases, make sure that they contract *do you fancy* /djuːˈfænsi/.

Want to know more? Go to introduction: **life with Agrippine / do you get it?** *p.5.*

nE
Do you wanna watch the telly? Do you fancy watching the telly?
How about the pictures? Do you fancy going to the cinema?
What about going down to Megastore? Do you fancy going down to Megastore?

---

language point *on*

In the cartoon, there are three examples of *on* being used with a similar general meaning of something happening, now or in the future.
There's only kids' stuff on (TV). = being broadcast
There's nothing on (at the cinema). = showing
I've got too much on. = I'm too busy

---

reading family ties

talk about their families using **natural English** phrases
focus on and **discuss** relationships vocabulary
read and **discuss** a text about parents and teenagers
focus on reflexive and reciprocal verbs

lead-in

- For **exercise 1**, do a quick version of the diagram on the board for your own family (but don't write the words *nuclear* or *extended*), and include a few members of your extended family. Take a minute or two to describe your family, using the **natural English** phrases and answering the questions in **exercise 2**. Elicit, or if necessary teach, the words *extended* and *nuclear family* from the diagram. Write them on the board. This phase will have acted as a demonstration for what learners now have to do. Go over the **natural English** box before they talk in pairs.

- Most learners are very happy to talk about their families, but make it clear that no one should feel obliged to say anything about their families that they do not wish to.

vocabulary good and bad relationships

- For **exercise 1**, learners should only use dictionaries as a last resort. Once they have done the matching exercise, they can compare with a partner. When you go over the answers, clear up any confusion with meaning, and focus on the pronunciation. See **ideas plus** on the right. Highlight the form of the vocabulary items on the board, focusing on the prepositions which collocate with these verbs and phrasal verbs, e.g. *compete <u>with</u>* sb, *stick up <u>for</u>* sb, etc. and encourage learners to copy them into their notebooks.

- Bear in mind that later in the lesson there is a grammar focus on *each other, one another, -self / -selves*, so don't get involved in explaining it here. Learners will probably understand it receptively, in any case.

- Before going on to **exercise 2**, you could get learners to do a **test your partner** activity with this vocabulary. Give them a minute or two to study the verbs, then take turns to test each other.

- When they are comparing their ideas in **exercise 3**, monitor and collect examples of correct or incorrect language for feedback at the end. This activity could be done in small groups if you prefer.

read on

- The discussion in the previous section is a good introduction to the text, so you can go straight into the reading activity. Point to the headline, *Disco with Dad … Why not?* and ask learners what they think the article will be about.

- Let learners compare their answers in **exercise 2** before feedback. This should lead easily into **exercises 3** and **4**. At the end, ask one person in each group to briefly summarize their groups' opinion.

different opinions

- These recordings in **exercise 1** are *vox pops* (= very short interviews with members of the public, broadcast on TV, radio, or in the press). People are simply asked to respond to the idea in the text, and give their opinions. Don't spend too long on this activity; it is just an opportunity for exposure to natural English.

grammar *each other / one another, -self / -selves*

- In **exercise 1**, learners look back at the article to identify the items in context. This will focus them on the aim of **exercise 2**, which is to distinguish the meanings. Do the first example in exercise 2 together, then let learners work in pairs on the others. See **language point** on the right.

- If you are teaching a multilingual class, you will need to rely on the learners' understanding of their own language for **exercise 3**. If you are not a proficient speaker of the learners' language in a monolingual context, ask your colleagues for advice.

- Do one or two examples together for **exercise 4**, so that learners see that they must use a pronoun and their own ideas.

exercise 1

1 g   2 c   3 f   4 h   5 a   6 d   7 e   8 b

---

ideas plus pronunciation

At this level, instead of providing a pronunciation model yourself for vocabulary, you could ask your learners to provide the model (in this case, for the verbs in **bold** in **exercise 1**). If a learner gets the pronunciation right, get the other learners to copy that model. If nobody gets it right, ask them to find the correct pronunciation from the phonemic transcription in a dictionary. Over a period of time, this is one way of teaching or reinforcing phonemic symbols. Words they might find difficult in this exercise are *consult* /kən'sʌlt/, *quarrel* /'kwɒrəl/, *compete* /kəm'piːt/, and *hug* /hʌg/.

Want to know more? Go to intermediate **teacher's book, how to ...** teach phonemic script *p.168*.

---

exercise 1

kid   let your hair down   go on about   ruin

exercise 2

a Dan thinks it's a good idea. At first he didn't, but it gave him something in common with his father, so they could relate to each other.
b The author has mixed feelings. From a parent's point of view it can be enjoyable and a good thing, but she found it embarrassing if somebody saw her dancing with her parents when she was a teenager.
c Kelly thinks most teenagers would prefer to go out without their parents.

---

exercise 1

3 and 5 are the teenagers. They both talk about their parents.

exercise 2

a 2   b 3   c 4   d 5   e 1

---

exercise 2

1 In **1a** each child looks after himself or herself; in **1b** each child looks after the other children.
2 The sentences have the same meaning.
3 **3a** means, *Did you do your homework alone?*
   3b means, *Did you do your homework together?*
4 *Get dressed* means put on one's clothes – this is a normal situation. We only use the reflexive verb here (dress oneself) to suggest that it is an exceptional or difficult thing to do, e.g. a young child or someone who is ill.
5 If people talk to themselves they are having a conversation alone; people talking to each other means people talking to other people.

---

language point *each other / ourselves*, etc.

There are two main points of difficulty here.

1 The first relates to *myself / herself*, etc. In some languages, reflexive pronouns are used extensively in contexts where it would be wrong in English, e.g. (French) *Je me suis habillé*. *I dressed myself*. English speakers would normally say *I got dressed*. Certain verbs are reflexive in other languages but not in English, e.g. *hurry, meet, relax*. Some verbs are reflexive in English, but in other languages an object pronoun is used, e.g. *I hurt myself*, not *I hurt me*.

2 Some languages do not distinguish between *ourselves* and *each other*, using a reflexive form for both.

It can help to demonstrate the concepts physically, by acting out sentences with learners, e.g. *They are talking to themselves* as opposed to *each other* can be illustrated by two learners in front of the class.

listening creating a community

60 – 80 mins

lead-in

- The lesson is closely based on a real TV adventure survival show that took place in an Australian rainforest during 2002; and the website profiles in the next lesson carry on the theme of this section. This may add extra interest to the lesson. If there are similar survival shows in the country where you are teaching (e.g. *Big Brother, Survivor*, etc.), you could ask the group what they think about them.

- Get the learners to look at the advert and the picture. Do they know, or can they guess, the meaning of *remote* (= far from towns and built-up areas)? Do they notice anything unusual about the first sentence in the advert? How would they expect this sentence to be written? See **language point** on the right.

- Allow learners a couple of minutes to think about **exercise 1**. You could point out that a *contribution* could include a skill such as *cooking* or *carpentry*, or a particular quality they think they possess such as *strength* or a *good sense of humour*. There is plenty of opportunity to discuss conditions in the rainforest during the lesson, so keep **exercise 2** quite brief.

---

grammar obligation, necessity, and prohibition

- The **laws of Eden** develop the theme of the lesson and place the target grammar in context. Learners should already be familiar with most of the items in **bold**, but they still present problems at this level, and learners often need to refine their understanding of the differences. See **language point** on the right. In addition, *ought to* may be completely new, and many learners are unclear about the meaning of *have got to*.

- Give learners plenty of time to read the laws and think about the differences. Put them in pairs to discuss **exercise 2**. While they are doing this, walk round the class to find out which pairs of words / phrases are causing the most difficulty; this is where your focus will be in feedback. If there are still problems, you may wish to use the **cover & check** exercises in **language reference** on *p.156* and *p.157* at this point. If you want to provide some extra speaking, you could ask learners to discuss whether they think the laws are sensible and fair.

- **Exercise 3** can be done in pairs or small groups, and is an opportunity for learners to test their understanding of the target language but also contribute ideas of their own. Point out *have access to* (= be available for use), as this could be a very useful item for learners here, e.g. *They have to have access to medical supplies.*

---

listen to this

- You could demonstrate **exercise 1** with your own ideas using some of the language from the previous grammar section, e.g. *I think we **ought to** (have the same number of men and women); I think we **should** (only have people over twenty / thirty).* You could also point out that if you feel very strongly about something, you could use verbs of obligation, e.g. *We've **got to** have equal numbers of men and women.* Then let learners complete the notes individually. If they choose to write full sentences including different modal verbs, that's fine, but notes will do.

- Elicit one or two examples to make sure they have got some ideas, then talk through the **natural English** box showing ways of agreeing with and challenging opinions. Highlight the stress on the underlined words, and practise the pronunciation of the phrases, before pairs discuss **exercise 2**. Monitor to see how they are using the phrases and the verbs from the previous grammar section.

- **Exercise 3** helps to establish the context and gives learners a chance to get used to the voices. In **exercise 4** learners may wish to take notes. You could pause the recording at several points where the TV producer has finished answering a question, or play the recording twice if necessary. Give learners a minute to finish writing at the end of the conversation and let them compare their answers with a partner before feedback.

- **Exercise 5** contains information about the selection process. If you didn't do this earlier, you could go back to exercise 1 and elicit the class's ideas for the selection before they listen, so that it is fresh in their minds. If you put these ideas on the board, learners can listen to see which are mentioned.

language point ellipsis

We can sometimes leave out words in a sentence to avoid repetition, or when the meaning is clear without them. This is called <u>ellipsis</u> and is particularly common in spoken English. Examples include:

1 omission of full infinitive at the end, e.g. A: *Are you going to the match?* B: *I'd like to (go)*.

2 omission of auxiliary at the beginning, e.g. *Ready? (Are you ready?)*

3 omission of a relative pronoun + *be*, e.g. *Who was the man (who was) driving the car?*

At the beginning of the advert there is an example of omitting the auxiliary verb plus subject at the beginning of a sentence: *(Are you) looking for ...?* Elicit this sentence beginning from the learners and explain that it is an example of ellipsis. See if the learners can explain why it is being used here. (In this case, it offers a shorter, snappier form of prose than the full sentence, and it is also more dramatic, which is what the advert wants to be.)

Want to know more? Go to **Practical English Usage** by Michael Swan *pp.181–186*.

exercise 2

1 *have got to* and *have to* have the same meaning here, i.e. it is necessary / compulsory; *have got to* is used mainly in spoken English (see **language reference** *p.156*)

2 *be allowed to* and *be permitted to* have the same meaning but *be permitted to* is more formal and less common; *mustn't* means it is dangerous, wrong, or prohibited; *shouldn't* means it is not a good idea, so the meaning is different here

3 *mustn't* and *aren't permitted to* have a similar meaning here

4 *should* and *ought to* mean the same in this context

5 *are allowed to* means they can / are permitted to, and this has a very different meaning from *ought to*, which implies a degree of obligation; *mustn't* means it is dangerous, wrong, or prohibited, whereas *don't have to* means it's not necessary, so the meaning is completely different

6 as in example 5, the meaning is different

7 *can't* and *aren't allowed to* have a similar meaning here

language point obligation, necessity, and prohibition

Learners at this level still confuse certain items (*mustn't* and *don't have to* being the most common example), but the biggest difficulty perhaps is that some of the items overlap in meaning in some contexts but not others.

- *Should* can almost command the same degree of obligation as *have (got) to / must* in some contexts, but is much weaker in others.

- *Must* and *have to* are interchangeable in certain contexts, but in others, native speakers express a clear preference for one over the other (see **language reference** *p.156* for details).

- *Have got to* is interchangeable with *have to* in many contexts but *have got to* is largely restricted to spoken English.

- *Ought to* and *should* are very similar when talking about duty, or offering advice or an opinion, but *ought to* is less frequent and rarely used in negative and interrogative sentences, where *should* is preferred, e.g. *You shouldn't go to work with that cold. Should we tell him now?*

exercise 3
The interviewer is talking to Candy Duncan, the producer of the Eden survival show.

exercise 4

1 six men and six women
2 eighteen to twenty-five
3 people under eighteen would need their parents' consent; they designed the programme for that age range
4 no; they would be given basic survival training and basic skills; they were more interested in selecting interesting people
5 they needed to be moderately fit (not super-fit) and would be given a medical check up

exercise 5
each person prepared a one-minute talk, selling themselves
variety of group activities to assess how they mixed, natural leaders, etc. e.g. play team games, make a simple rope bridge to get across a river
used psychologists in selection, plus individual interviews too

how to ... write a website profile

60 – 70 mins

choose personal information

- In **exercise 1**, learners discuss how they would like themselves to appear (in words with a photo) on a website. A real photo is not necessary, but if you want to make it more realistic, you could ask learners (in the <u>previous</u> lesson) to find a photo of themselves to bring to class the next day. Explain that it will be for a personal profile. You could demonstrate the activity by bringing in your own photo and telling the class what sorts of things you would write about yourself. Monitor the group work, then go on to the listening.

express information in writing

- Link the website profile to the previous lesson about the Edenites, by asking learners to look at the photo on *p.38* in pairs and comment on it. After giving learners time to read, you could pause the recording in **exercise 1** at certain points to allow time to write, and replay the recording on request. Point out the word *motto*, as learners will have to think up a motto for themselves later on.
- When you move on to the **natural English** box, ask learners to find two of the phrases in Katie's profile (*Originally I'm from …*; *My proudest moment was …*). Focus on the pronunciation of the items given in phonemic script.
- Let learners put the profile in order in **exercise 2**, then compare with a partner. This is an exercise in coherence, and you can highlight a few points here across the line breaks: the collocation *public relations (PR)*, *shortly before* (which is dealt with in the next grammar point), *dream of + -ing*, and the verb + noun collocation *have fun*. If you have access to a photocopier, you could make several copies of this profile, then cut them into separate lines for learners to unjumble in pairs.
- **Exercise 3** contextualizes the other phrases that learners saw in the **natural English** box.
- **Exercise 4** gives learners a chance to focus very intensively on one of the texts, and puts a little gentle pressure on them to memorize. Many learners enjoy this kind of challenge, and it can be a good way to reinforce collocations, grammar, and lexis.

grammar sequencing information in a text

- For **exercise 1**, you could do this either in pairs or as a class activity. If the latter, draw a table on the board with three columns: time before, time after, and same time. Elicit where the phrases in **bold** fit, and add them to the board. As learners answer questions b, c, and d, you can add the information they give you to the table (-*ing*, + noun, or + clause). Point out to learners that *prior to* is formal. (You will find more practice exercises in the **language reference** on *p.157* and *p.158*.)
- For **exercise 2**, elicit one or two ideas for the first gap, then let learners work alone or in pairs. Monitor so that you can identify and deal with any problems individual learners have with these constructions.

plan your website profile

- This section encourages learners to look at the way information is ordered in a text. Both Katie and Jonny's profiles are fine, though different. Learners could follow either pattern for their own profile.
- **Exercise 2** can be done in different ways. Some learners (or some classes) may prefer to have some silent time to think and plan, and use the opportunity to consult you individually for advice. Others may prefer to make it more interactive. If so, you could set up paired interviews, e.g. student A asks student B which of the topics in the spray diagram they would like to include, and what they want to say. A conversation at this point may also be helpful for learners who don't feel confident about what to write; peer encouragement may help them to find suitable things to say. Whichever way you decide to do it, refer learners to the diagram with prompts to help them. A time limit of about ten minutes would be suitable for this activity.
- When learners know what they are going to write, you could ask them to write it at home, and then collect it in the following lesson and correct it.

ideas plus write your own profile

Instead of using the second profile (Jonny Wood), you could write about yourself. Learners will probably find this interesting. Keep it to under 100 words, and include something about your past, present, and future. Be sure to include a couple of the linking phrases from the **natural English** box. Then, cut it up into about ten separate lines, and give copies to pairs to unjumble. You could include one or two facts that are not strictly true, and ask learners to decide which they are.

exercise 1

1 it wasn't for me
2 on a cruise ship
3 I'm a keen
4 winning a silver medal
5 run it as a tourist business
6 a train, bus, or man
7 another will come along

exercise 2

1 d 2 h 3 g 4 b 5 i 6 a 7 f 8 j 9 c 10 e

exercise 3

I was born and brought up in …
I come from a (musical) family
I've always dreamt of + -ing

ideas plus using short texts

Short texts, especially those with a narrative structure, can be exploited in different ways. Here are some ideas.

- **dictation** or **dictogloss**, i.e. learners listen to a short text, note down the key words and reconstruct the text with a partner.

Want to know more? Go to intermediate **teacher's book, how to …** introduce new language (try it out) p.146.

- **pronunciation** You can highlight and practise a range of features: marking pauses in the text so that it can be read coherently, with appropriate intonation, linking, contractions, and weak forms, etc. Learners can also listen to the recording and shadow read, i.e. listen and read aloud with the recording.
- **fill the gap** After studying a text, student A reads the text to student B (whose book is shut), stopping at appropriate points for B to say the next word. This is very useful for collocation and syntax, e.g. A: *Originally, I …* B: *… I'm from Glasgow.* A: *Correct. But I was brought …* B: *… brought up in Manchester.* A *I've always had itchy …* B *… itchy toes.* A: *No! Itchy feet.* etc.

exercise 1

a *time before* = prior to, shortly before, long before; *time after* = soon after and since; *same time* = while
b they can all be followed by *-ing*
c they can all be followed by a noun except *while*
d all except *prior to*

exercise 2 possible answers

1 Julie took her final exams shortly before her baby was born.
2 David was interested in archaeology long before he started studying it seriously.
3 Soon after leaving home, Lucy got a job in a health club.
4 Since being made redundant, Claire's been unemployed.
5 While he was unemployed, Don learnt to drive a heavy goods vehicle.
6 Prior to attending university, Geri spent two years in South East Asia.

exercise 1

1 Katie's profile includes the following information in this order:
a where she was born and brought up
b her career in chronological order
c her most recent job
d her achievements
e how she would spend the prize money
f her motto

2 Jonny's profile includes the following information in this order:
a where he was born and brought up
b his family background
c his career in chronological order
d his most recent job
e his feelings about Eden
f his attitude to the prize money
g his motto

ideas plus profiles

For this writing task, you could tell learners to write their profiles anonymously, i.e. they write their text without referring to themselves by name. The profiles can be displayed around the class for the learners to guess who wrote each one. If learners bring in photos, these can then be matched to the texts. This would provide an interesting and motivating reading task. You could also produce a class booklet (including photos) or even a page on the school or college website.

extended speaking create a band

choose the members of a band

discuss their musical style and image, and how to promote them

present ideas to the rest of the class

create a website profile of one of the band members

collect ideas

- Learners have already looked at different kinds of groups in this unit: party groups, the Edenites, and now a pop group. You could point out this link to them. Since we devised this **extended speaking** activity, there have been several television programmes with a similar aim: to create a pop band, a pop star, and a family for a TV soap opera. It is possible that such programmes have appeared in the learners' own country. If so, you could refer to them.

- For **exercise 1**, make sure learners know what an *audition* is (= a 'live' test prior to taking part in a performance, or joining a group). They don't need to look at the pictures and profiles yet.

- Go over the notes in **exercise 2** together. Then give the learners several minutes to look at the profiles and think about their answers.

- **Exercise 3** allows learners to share ideas before the full discussion in exercise 4.

- Look at the agenda in **exercise 4** together, and deal with any problems with vocabulary or the task itself. At this stage, they will be discussing some points from exercise 3 in groups, and moving on to further considerations such as the group's appearance and image. Allow a little time for learners to think about this alone. The phrases in the **natural English** box help learners to direct the meeting. Go over them before they start the discussion.

- You could suggest a time limit of ten to fifteen minutes to your class, but be flexible. Don't allow the discussion to wane, but equally, don't cut them off if they are really involved in it. During the discussion, monitor the group work and make notes for feedback at the end of the lesson. You may wish to use the **feedback checklist** opposite.

present your ideas

- Direct learners to the **checklist** before they start to prepare and rehearse. Be available to offer advice and encouragement. For some learners, this will be a useful activity for other areas of their life, e.g. work or study.

- If your class is large (more than twelve learners) it will probably take too long to do each presentation one after the other. Instead, divide the class into two large groups, e.g. if you have eighteen learners, form two groups of nine, with three mini-groups in each one. They can then do their presentations to their half of the class at the same time. If this creates a noise problem, try to find an area nearby where half the class could go. You would need to move between the two groups to monitor. Alternatively, have some presentations in one lesson, and some in another.

- Encourage learners to listen to each others' presentations and discuss them after each one. If you like, tell the listeners to think of questions to ask each speaker at the end. This will be motivating for both listeners and speakers.

- Provide feedback on the group work and the presentations themselves. Be sure to praise these wherever possible.

write a profile

- Once learners have written their profiles, they can show them to others in their group.

feedback checklist

During the **extended speaking** activity, note down examples of …

- **good language use**

- **effective communication strategies**
  (turn-taking, interrupting, inviting others to speak, etc.)

- **learner errors**
  (vocabulary, grammar, pronunciation, etc.)

- **particular communication problems**

Make sure you allow time for feedback at the end of the lesson. You can use the notes you make above to <u>praise</u> effective language use and communication or, if necessary, to do some remedial work.

---

ideas plus recording presentations

Using video or audio, you could record learners giving their presentations to the class and use the recordings diagnostically and to provide feedback at the end. Some learners will be very keen on this, and others might find it a bit nerve-wracking. Just choose groups who are confident and happy to do it. If your class find this useful, you could do it on a regular basis. It will also be interesting for them to review the recording at the end of the course to see their progress. Some learners might like to write a transcript of their presentation from the recording, and then polish it, i.e. write out a full corrected version. You would have to lend them the recording to do this in their own time.

test yourself!

Want to know more? Go to the **introduction** *p.7* for ways of using **test yourself!**

test yourself!

1 These verbs can be reflexive: *hurt, enjoy, entertain, look after*
2 *articulate* = express yourself very well; *eccentric* = have strange ideas; *wild* = out of control; *ambitious* = wanting to get on in life; *supportive* = always there to help; *annoying* = a pain in the neck
3 compete with, relate to, quarrel with, stick up for, hug, get on with

1 Do you fancy going out?
2 We've got to provide accommodation.
3 That makes sense.
4 Prior to coming here he was a teacher.

1 There are five of us in our family.
2 You don't have to wear a tie if you don't want to.
3 Since retiring, she's been ill.
4 They ought to get a car.

four

wordlist

natural English

connecting ideas
I was surprised that ..., but what was
  even more amazing was that ...

frequency phrases
whenever I can
about twice a week
roughly once a fortnight
every month or so
now and again
once in a while
hardly ever
it varies

'sitting on the fence'
It's a difficult issue.
Well, it depends, doesn't it?
It's hard to say.
I can see both sides.

Internet language
. dot
@ at
/ forward slash
co
upper case / capital letters
lower case
all one word

making and responding to requests
I was wondering if you could ...
Do you think you could (possibly) ...
Is there any chance you could ...
Sure.
I'll see what I can do.
I'm afraid I can't.

vocabulary

adjectives describing reactions
surprising
irritating
strange
odd
weird
peculiar
annoying
amazing
astonishing
infuriating

synonyms
film / movie
fans / (movie) buffs

mistakes / errors / howlers
compile / assemble
ruin / spoil

the language of editing
It's in the wrong tense.
It should be double 's'.
There's a question mark missing.
This isn't spelt correctly.
It should be in italics.
It doesn't need a hyphen.
This should be a comma, not a full stop.
There should be an apostrophe.
You have to close the brackets.

wordbooster

words of similar meaning
check / examine
restrict / limit
ban / prohibit
boost / increase
allow / permit
censor / remove
decline / deteriorate
reduce / cut
lack / not have enough
expand / grow
regulate / control
raise / improve
boost sales / morale
increase prices / sales
raise efficiency / taxes
improve your English / efficiency
the weather / your health can deteriorate
your health /population figures can decline
the economy / metal can expand
the economy / trees can grow

making the most of your dictionary
occasion
opportunity
chance
possibility

glossary

weird ⊚
(be) taken aback
blink
briefs
kilt

in unit four ...

do you get it?   25 – 30 mins

listen for pleasure
nE connecting ideas
vocabulary adjectives describing reactions

- The irritating habits mentioned are certainly relevant to cinema goers in Britain, but in the country where you are teaching, there may be other more common sources of irritation. If so, feel free to adapt the exercise. Either way, most learners should have something to say about the topic. You could also ask them if they are guilty of any of the habits mentioned. If they are, how do they feel about it?

- If anyone looking at the pictures realizes they know the joke, ask them not to tell others and spoil it for them. Learners can discuss what's happening and what's going to happen next in pairs or as an open class. Point out the **glossary**, and refer them to the phrases in the speech bubbles. These build on the previous joke section by adding one or two new ways of responding to a joke. Check they understand *pathetic* (= awful or terrible in this context), then play the joke and let them respond.

Want to know more? Go to introduction **life with Agrippine** / **do you get it?** *p.5.*

- Put learners in pairs for **adjectives describing reactions**. They will be familiar with some of the words, so they should be able to identify three different groups quite easily in **exercise 1**. They can use dictionaries if they have them, and do **exercise 2** at the same time, marking the stress on the words.

- Go over the answers and practise the pronunciation. Learners at this level need to start developing a grasp of the differences between partial synonyms. However, you may not feel it is necessary to get too involved in all of these at this stage.

- The adjectives here are *-ing* forms, but in the practice activity for the **natural English** box that follows, learners will have to manipulate both *-ing* and *-ed* forms. Learners at this level should know the difference, but they still make mistakes and confuse the two forms, so ask someone in the group to explain the difference, i.e. *-ed* forms are used to say how people feel and *-ing* forms describe the people or things that cause the feelings, e.g. *I was very interested in the book. It's a very interesting book.* That reminder may be all they need to monitor their use of the forms in the next exercise.

- The **natural English** box shows one way in which ideas can be connected, and it results in two long example sentences. Learners will need to practise saying these sentences. To get the rhythm correct, they need to put extra stress on *more* and *gorilla costume* in the first sentence, and *last one* in the second.

- You could ask learners to use their own ideas to make similar sentences using the language in **adjectives describing reactions**, then they can tell a partner their completed sentences. Listen to some examples at the end to make sure they are correct and sound natural.

nE
but, what's even more weird is that ...
adjectives describing reactions
strange, odd, weird, peculiar
surprising, amazing, astonishing
irritating, annoying, infuriating

reading don't believe everything you see in films   60 – 70 mins

talk about cinema-going habits using **natural English** phrases

listen to people talk about cinema-going habits

read about mistakes in films

study how synonyms are used in text

focus on the grammar of nouns in groups

lead-in

- You could start this section by putting learners in small groups to give one-minute talks, e.g. What was the last film they saw? Who did they go with? What was the film about? What did they think of it? Give them a minute to prepare mentally, then start the groups off. Listeners can comment on the films too at the end. Monitor and give feedback on language at the end.

- Once learners have read the questions in **exercise 1,** go over the language in the **natural English** box, checking understanding. For more information, look at **language point** on the right. Check learners' pronunciation of the phrases, especially *roughly* /ˈrʌfli/ and *it varies* /ˈveəriːz/.

- Go on to the practice activity in **exercise 2**. If you prefer, do this as a mingling activity to give learners a greater opportunity to hear the phrases.

- **Exercises 3** and **4** give learners a set of *vox pops* to listen to, which provide some very natural exposure to English. They will also hear a couple of the phrases from the **natural English** box. It is not necessary to exploit the listening any further, but you could ask learners to listen again with the tapescript in the **listening booklet** on *p.14* to see if they can identify any other frequency phrases, e.g. *once or twice a month, it depends how much time I've got; Sometimes I go every night for a phase; I may not go for a month or so.* You could ask learners to go and find out from their families how often they go to the cinema, and come back with the information in the next lesson. This would be a neat way to revise the phrases.

read on

- **Exercise 1** leads into the topic of the text, so discuss the first possible answer together, then ask learners to think up their own ideas with a partner. They could produce their own examples for other learners to complete.

- Give learners time to read the questions in **exercise 2**, then go straight into the text. You could suggest that they underline the possible answers in the article.

- You could ask learners if they know any other examples of mistakes in movies or TV programmes, and go on to the short discussion in **exercise 3**.

vocabulary synonyms

- Look at the example together and ask learners how *fall asleep* and *nod off* are related and why they are used. (The answer is to avoid repetition).

- Give learners a few minutes to find the answers to **exercise 4**. This kind of text search for partial synonyms is a useful exercise, and at the same time is a useful way to expand learners' vocabulary. You could keep an eye open for examples of this in other texts that you use. (See **language point**.)

grammar nouns in groups

- Go over the grammar explanation and move on to **exercise 1**. Alternatively, look at **ideas plus**.

- **Exercise 2** provides learners with noun phrases which will be useful in the **extended speaking** activity at the end of the unit. When they have worked out the phrases, make sure they keep a record of them in their notebooks. You could turn this into a game by making sets of cards in two different colours for learners to match in pairs.

- In many countries there are TV programmes which show things going wrong while films / TV programmes are being made, i.e. *outtakes*. If you can find a video of these, a short selection of outtakes might be a fun and motivating listening activity at some point, perhaps at the end of this section.

Want to know more? Go to **how to ...** motivate higher level learners *p.156.*

exercise 4

	How often do they go?	What's unusual about their cinema habits?
1 Juliet	whenever she can	likes to go alone
2 Julia	quite a lot	goes every night for a period, then not at all
3 Michael	hardly ever	only sees children's films
4 Eric	whenever he can	watches everything, including the credits; tries to get into all the films in a multiplex

language point frequency phrases

Some of these phrases are likely to be new for learners at this level, or will certainly not be part of their productive repertoire.

- *roughly* = approximately; (number / amount) + *or so* = approximately; these are both examples of vague language, as are the phrases *now and again / once in a while* = occasionally

Want to know more about vague language? Go to intermediate **teacher's book, language point**, *p.35.*

- *hardly ever* = almost never. Learners confuse this because they think that *hardly* is the adverbial form of *hard*.
- *it varies* = it changes according to the situation. This is a useful phrase.

exercise 1 possible answers
1 in the next shot, the car is black.
2 you see that an actor's wearing a watch / trainers.
3 in the next shot you see him moving / blinking.

exercise 2
1 He thought it would be interesting.
2a *An elderly man who gets his arm chopped off, reappears ... with it back again. A character picks up the Beatles album* **Let It Be**, *which was not released until a month after the launch.*
2b *Gibson ... jumps over a roof, revealing a pair of modern black briefs under his kilt. Wallace's executioner has shoes with red rubber soles.*
2c *One of Wallace's men speaks his only line in a southern Californian accent. Richard Gere calls Julia Roberts 'Julia'.*

language point synonymy

There are words which are synonymous in one context, but not in others. Here are some examples of semantic overlap in **exercise 4**.

- **film / movie**: *movie* is originally American English, but is now widely used in British English
- **fans / buffs**: a *fan* is someone who enjoys a particular activity, e.g. *football fan, Beatles fan*; a *buff* is someone who is very knowledgeable about a subject e.g. *film buff, wine buff, computer buff*
- **mistakes / errors / howlers**: *mistake* is the most commonly used; an *error* tends to be more serious than a mistake, perhaps causing problems; a *howler* is a silly mistake which makes people laugh
- **compile / assemble**: *compile* is to bring things together specifically in a book or list; *assemble* is to bring things (or people) together in a group
- **ruin / spoil**: *ruin* means to damage something so badly that it loses all value; *spoil* means to make something less successful or satisfactory

exercise 4
film / movie   fans / film buffs   mistakes / howlers / errors
compiled / assembled ruin / spoil

exercise 1
1 a film maker   4 people's enjoyment
2 Cary Grant's suit   5 the end of the film
3 a list of mistakes 6 the Atlantic Ocean

exercise 2
wildlife documentary; weather forecast; the quality of TV programmes; the danger of mobile phones; chat show; use of the Internet; the government's responsibility / decision; the parents' responsibility / decision

ideas plus dictogloss

You could teach this language point through a dictogloss. Here is an example text using all the forms; you could adapt it to your teaching context.
The latest horror film to come from Colombian director, Pablo Escolar, is sure to be a massive box office hit. The film is about a young female Dracula, and the child's part is played by an eight-year-old girl. The title of the film is **Dracula's Child** *and film fans will not be disappointed.*
Read the text once quickly, then again, allowing learners to note key words. As they reconstruct it from memory, they may make mistakes with the noun phrases. You can then teach these remedially.

Want to know more? Go to intermediate **teacher's book, how to ...** introduce new language (try it out: dictogloss) *p.146.*

listening — the mobile phone police

70 – 90 mins

discuss mobile phones using **natural English** phrases

listen to one half of a mobile phone conversation

discuss the Internet

focus on *will* and the future continuous with guided and freer practice activities

lead-in

- Most learners will have something to say about this topic, but keep **exercise 1** quite short as there are further opportunities to discuss the pros and cons of mobile phones in the lesson.

- Go through the phrases in the **natural English** box, practise the pronunciation, and provide some quick practice round the class by giving stimuli that will allow learners to offer one of the **natural English** phrases in response, for example,

  Do you think it's right to stop cars going into busy city centres? / keep animals in cages in zoos? / let people choose which country they want to live in?

  You will obviously have to exercise your own judgement in selecting topics that are relevant to the culture you teach in but not too sensitive.

- Go through the questions in **exercise 2**, and explain any new items, e.g. *ban* (= forbid, prohibit), *hands-free set* (= a phone which does not need to be held), and *stationary* (= not moving). Give learners time to think about their answers then let them move on to **exercise 3**. It is important to stress that this is a discussion with an opportunity to use the **natural English** phrases if appropriate, not a controlled exercise in which they are under an obligation to use the language.

listen to this

- The use of mobile phones on public transport has already been discussed in exercises 2 and 3, so you can move into the listening without much introduction. In Britain, they have now introduced carriages on some trains where you are not allowed to use mobile phones. Is it the same in the country where you teach?

- Play the first part of the listening passage, **exercise 1**, and elicit answers. Play it again only if necessary.

- Get the learners to read through the questions in **exercise 2** before playing the whole conversation. At the end, they can compare their answers with a partner while you monitor. If you feel the majority of the class have got the gist, elicit answers from individual learners. If not, play it again.

- **Exercise 3** moves away from the content of the dialogue to focus on its character. Have they grasped the fact that the conversation is largely meandering and probably unnecessary? Recognizing the tone and attitude of the speakers here is an important part of understanding the passage.

- The **listening challenge** in **exercise 4** is a similar context, i.e. a phone conversation involving one speaker on a train, only this time the information content is important. Play the recording (twice if absolutely necessary), elicit the key information, then let learners listen again with the tapescript in the **listening booklet** on *p.16*. You could follow up using the suggestion in **ideas plus** on the right.

grammar future simple and continuous

- Not everyone will use the Internet, but there should be enough learners who do use it and have things to say about it in **exercise 1**. You could pair these learners up with others who have little or no experience.

- Ask learners to read *Weird websites,* the short text about the website in **exercise 2**, then check their understanding before they move on to the website itself. Ask them what *Your Cyberfuture* is, and how it works. Then tell them to read the website page and write down the answers they would give to each of the questions. They can discuss their answers in pairs or small groups.

- **Exercise 3** focuses on the grammar in the website text. Learners may not be able to answer these questions, but it will be interesting for you to monitor their discussions to see exactly how much or how little they do know. At this level, some learners also begin to have a strong sense that something is wrong or right by the way it sounds, even though they may not be able to explain why.

- Discuss the answers in open class and provide more examples to help them see the differences. Look at **language point** on the right and get learners to do the **cover & check** exercises in **language reference** on *p.159* now or for homework. If you do them now, you may wish to leave **exercise 4** until later.

it's your turn!

- This section concludes with a personalized activity in which learners use the grammar, but this time in their own invented questions about the future. They do this in pairs in **exercise 1**, and they could also produce cards with *yes* and *no* written on them, so that in **exercise 2** they can hold up their answers when they are asked a question. You could also do this in open class at the end.

exercise 1

He's talking to his wife (or partner), and he's just calling to pass the time.

exercise 2

1 The woman has had an ordinary day.
2 He isn't very interested.
3 His secretary is leaving her job.
4 She isn't very interested.
5 She's cooking the dinner.
6 She wants him to buy some cream on his way home, because they're having strawberries for dessert.

exercise 4

The woman is on a train. She's calling because she's been delayed, and she arranges to meet the man in a restaurant near his office.

---

ideas plus role play

By this stage the learners will be very familiar with the content of the conversation in the **listening challenge**, and as it is a common and largely predictable dialogue, it would be a suitable one for them to role play in pairs. Assign roles and give each learner a couple of minutes to look through the transcript on *p.16* and remember the key facts (it doesn't actually matter if they change some of the details as long as it is coherent). When they role play the phone conversation, seat the learners back to back, so they don't have any face-to-face contact; this makes it more realistic. If learners complain they can't hear one another because of the noise from other pairs, so much the better. This is also a fact of life in many real phone conversations, and learners will just have to tell each other to repeat things or speak up. Point this out before they begin.

Monitor the conversations and make a note of the way they use, or don't use *will* and the future continuous. The next part of the lesson looks at this language point and it will be useful for you to have some idea of how they might handle it.

---

exercise 3

1 No. In 1, *catch on* is not something that continues for a period of time, and the same is true for *crash* in 3. In 2, *own* is a state verb, so we cannot use a continuous form.
2 Sentence 4 refers to something in progress, so you can't use *will* + verb. In 5, both forms are possible, but the meaning would be different. *Will I have dinner at 8.00?* means *Will I start dinner at 8.00? Will I be having dinner at 8.00?* means *Will the dinner be in progress at 8.00?*

   In 6 and 7, *will* + verb is also possible.

exercise 4

1	will be working; will be free	4	will be revising
2	will be using	5	will be seeing; will tell
3	will have	6	will win

---

language point *will* and the future continuous

One difficulty with the future continuous is the element of *reassurance* that is often involved:

I'll be seeing you on Thursday, so let's have a chat then.

By using the future continuous, the speaker is making it clear to the listener that the meeting has either already been arranged or will take place anyway. The speaker is not making the decision now, and no special effort will be required for it to happen.

A further difficulty is that there are a number of contexts where both forms are possible; although it changes the meaning slightly (or in some cases significantly, as in question 5 in the website page).

how to ... write and edit e-mails

60 – 70 mins

read aloud

- Dictating an e-mail address to someone is very common these days in real life, and your learners will probably be motivated to do this in English. You could start by writing on the board a website address and an e-mail address appropriate to your teaching context, e.g. the school's website / e-mail address, or one that has a few of the features mentioned in the **natural English** box. See if learners in pairs can read these aloud accurately, and feed in some of the language from the box as necessary. Go over the box together before learners work in pairs on the addresses in **exercise 1**. You can play the recording for them to check their ideas. Ask learners to read out their own addresses if they are prepared to divulge them!

vocabulary the language of editing

- Ask learners if they know any rules about how to write e-mails, then ask them to read the text to see if any are mentioned. Tell them not to worry about the errors.

- Do the first example together in **exercise 1**, then learners can work alone or in pairs on the rest. In feedback, check their pronunciation of the trickier items, e.g. *apostrophe, hyphen, italics*, and check the stress on *paragraph*. You may wish to point out that this language is useful too for learners taking exam classes such as Cambrige FCE and CAE.

- Ask them to talk through all the points in **exercise 2** one at a time.

Want to know more? Read the article *Twenty-first century English* (IATEFL 2001 Brighton Conference Selections) and **Language and the Internet** (2001) CUP, both by David Crystal.

edit an e-mail

- In **exercise 1** set the scene for this e-mail correspondence: two teachers, one in Sweden, one in the UK, who met some time ago on a course for teachers. You could ask learners to read the e-mails and summarize Stefan's e-mail and Caroline's response.

- Learners will need about ten minutes to read and proof-read the e-mails in **exercise 2**. Make it very clear that the errors are not grammatical; in fact, they all relate to the error types in the previous vocabulary exercise.

- Ask learners to look at Stefan's e-mail to find what phrase he uses to make a request. Ask them not to look at the **natural English** box, and see if you can elicit other polite requests and responses from them. They can then look in the box to check. See **language point** on the right.

- Once learners have listened and completed the gaps in the **natural English** box, do some controlled practice to help their pronunciation, especially intonation, on these requests. Check their pronunciation of *wondering* which is sometimes confused with *wandering*.

I was <u>wondering</u> if you could <u>help</u> me.

Do you think you could <u>possibly</u> give me a <u>hand</u>?

Is there any <u>chance</u> you could <u>do</u> this for me?

- Learners can then do **exercise 3** together. You could ask them to think up their own requests as well.

write an e-mail

- Learners are given suggestions for the requests, but it would be nice if they could think up their own requests. You could also encourage them to introduce themselves to Caroline with some kind of reminder of who they are, as Stefan did. You can do this activity in class, in which case you can monitor and help learners while they are actually writing, but if you prefer, ask them to do it for homework and exchange with another learner to write their response in the following lesson.

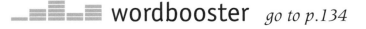 **wordbooster** *go to p.134*   This **wordbooster** can be used at any point in **unit four**.

ideas plus dictation

Ask learners in pairs to write down a couple of e-mail addresses they know well and a website address. Learners sit behind their partner and dictate the addresses to them. At the end, they check to see how accurately these have been noted down. A genuine dictation activity where accuracy is all-important!

exercise 1

1	tense	6 comma (not a) full stop
2	apostrophe	7 paragraph
3	spelt	8 brackets
4	double	9 italics
5	missing	10 hyphen

troubleshooting e-mail

Most learners nowadays will be very familiar with e-mail. However, if you have a few learners in your class who have never used it, there is no reason why you shouldn't use the text; it isn't technical and it may be useful to them in the future. They may not have a great deal to contribute to **exercise 2**, though, so ask them to listen to two learners who have experience. If none of your class is familiar with e-mail, you have to decide whether to drop the discussion and move on to the editing stage, which doesn't require any knowledge of e-mail, or ask them if they would like to know more about it. Any centre with e-mail facilities will be providing a great opportunity for learners to use English in a different medium.

exercise 1

They follow the rules for most things, but Caroline does not respond very promptly to Stefan's e-mail.

exercise 2

Stefan's e-mail

1 There is a question mark missing in the second line.
2 There should be an apostrophe in *I'm back*.
3 *English* should have a capital letter.

Caroline's e-mail

4 In line two, *how* should have a capital letter.
5 In line three, the brackets should be closed at the end.
6 *Appropriate* should be spelt with double *p*.

language point distancing

The requests in the **natural English** box are all quite polite or deferential. This doesn't mean that they are necessarily formal, however. The language chosen depends on the nature of the request: if the speaker thinks they may be disturbing or putting someone to some trouble, they may well use one of these forms, even if they are good friends. Compare asking to borrow a pen and borrowing someone's car. In the phrase *I was wondering if you could ...*, the past continuous is used with a distancing effect, to make the request seem less direct, and does not refer to past time. Other examples (not only of requests) would be:
I hoped ... (or) *I was (rather) hoping ... you could give me a hand tomorrow with moving.*
I was wondering if you'd like to come over this weekend.
Do you think ... ? before a request also makes it more deferential.

ideas plus e-mail

If you have e-mail / computer facilities in the place where you work, this activity would be fun done in real time on computers. Sort out who will work with whom first. You could also set it up as a homework exercise if learners have e-mail at home. Ask pairs to exchange e-mail addresses, send each other their requests and responses, and then print them out to bring to class in the next lesson. You could then correct them and return them to the learners.

extended speaking small screen survey

talk about different kinds of questionnaires

edit a survey

discuss answers to the survey

present a summary and analyse the results

collect ideas

- Ask learners if they have ever carried out any market research themselves or been interviewed in market research. Give them a few minutes to do **exercise 1** alone, and compare in groups. Some groups will have a lot to say in this activity, and other groups may have little to say: it really depends on your learners' experience. Most people will have done a magazine questionnaire, however.

edit a survey

- **Exercise 3** is simply a way of asking learners to read and absorb information. If anyone doesn't understand the background, clarify it at the end.

- Arrange the learners into groups of not more than four for **exercise 4**, and they will stay in the same groups for most of the rest of the lesson. Check the answers to this exercise before moving on. You could give the groups a time limit of ten minutes to complete this stage.

- Give learners a few minutes in groups to add their own questions in **exercise 5** while you move round the class and help where necessary. **Exercise 6** will require thinking time. Don't worry if this seems like a long period of silence: the learners are working and the subsequent discussion will benefit if they have had an opportunity to think through their answers beforehand.

> **exercise 4**
> 1 ~~Studies of Media~~ should be Media Studies
> I ~~was~~ wondering
> close brackets after *word processing*
> *Internet* only has one *t*
> 4 *In five / 5 years' time* NOT ~~by 5 years' time~~
> *you will be using computers* NOT ~~you are using computers~~
> 7 *computer games* doesn't have a hyphen
> 9 *How do you think TV or the Internet will develop?* NOT ~~are developing~~

do the survey

- During the discussion it is important that learners write down each person's answers clearly, as they will need the information in the next section. This could involve quite a lot of writing, which is why we have suggested learners take it in turns.

- Monitor the activity using the **feedback checklist** opposite, if you like.

present your summary

- Go over the instructions for the summary. Make it clear that the summaries are oral, so learners can make notes together, but discourage them from writing out a talk.

- Re-arrange learners in pairs for **exercise 9**. If possible, pair up learners who have produced summaries to different questions.

- Provide feedback on the discussion and presentations.

feedback checklist

During the **extended speaking** activity, note down examples of …

- **good language use**

- **effective communication strategies**
  (turn-taking, interrupting, inviting others to speak, etc.)

- **learner errors**
  (vocabulary, grammar, pronunciation, etc.)

- **particular communication problems**

Make sure you allow time for feedback at the end of the lesson. You can use the notes you make above to praise effective language use and communication or, if necessary, to do some remedial work.

---

ideas plus writing

Here are two ideas for writing.

1 Ask learners to produce a written version of their summary for homework. You could limit this to 100 to 125 words.

2 If the learners enjoyed working with the questionnaire, you could ask them to produce their own at a later date. Look at the examples of questionnaire types in **collect ideas**, **exercise 1** for suggestions. Learners could choose their own type in small groups, or could produce a questionnaire about the school or local environment or use of English outside class. It would be motivating if the class could use the questionnaire beyond the classroom, e.g. canvassing the views of learners in other classes or the staff in the school. Needless to say, you will need to help organize this.

test yourself!

Want to know more? Go to the **introduction** *p.7* for ways of using **test yourself!**

1 strange: weird, odd, peculiar
  surprising: amazing, astonishing
  annoying: irritating, infuriating
2 boost; restrict; ban; raise; expanding / getting bigger
3 question mark, apostrophe, hyphen, brackets, capital letter

1 I was wondering if you could possibly help me.
2 I don't know – it's a difficult issue.
3 I go there once in a while.
4 He doesn't have enough experience.

1 I'll phone you when I get in.
2 Don't come too early or I'll still be working.
3 Sophia's father dies at the end of the film.
4 I'll be married in a year's time.

five

wordlist

natural English

talking about test / exam results
I got eight out of ten / 80% in the test.
I only just passed / failed the test / exam.
I did (very) well / badly.
I got good marks.

so, anyway, so anyway
... the train was late. Anyway / So anyway, we had
  a burger and ...

expectations and surprise
She passed her test, as you might expect.
Inevitably, he ran out of petrol.
To my surprise / amazement, he threw ...
It was dark but for some reason, he didn't ...

spoken / written English
disconnect / cut off a phone
abolish / get rid of sth
reprimand sb / tell sb off
participate in / take part in
discover / find out
determine / work out
transpire / turn out
occupy / take up (time)
terminate / come to an end

introducing and focusing
The trouble is, ...
The thing is, ...
The problem was, ...

not that + adjective
I wasn't that nervous.
The food wasn't that good.

vocabulary

anxiety
scared stiff
petrified
relieved
upset
dread sth
look forward to sth
nervous
anxious
be in tears
cry
get on sb's nerves
nerve-racking
shake
tremble

feel uneasy
panic-stricken

adding emphasis
I did**n't** feel anxious **at all**.
I **did** get worried.
I was **really** petrified.
I was **much** more nervous.
It was **such** a relief.
I wasn't **that** nervous.
The spider was **absolutely** gigantic.
I was **so relieved**.

wordbooster

taking exams
cheat in an exam
prepare for an exam
fail an exam
sit / take / do an exam
retake an exam
get through an exam
turn up for an exam
an exam takes place
bluff your way through an exam
go on to another exam
make a mess of an exam

phrasal verbs
go on to another question
What's going on?
turn up for an exam
Something will turn up.
turn up the radio
get through (on the phone)
get through a packet of biscuits
I've got a test coming up.
come up behind sb

glossary
cheat
get away with sth
get caught (doing sth)
go over sth
What the hell ...? ⓖ
life-threatening disease
knit
disoriented

in unit five ...

life with **Agrippine**
cartoon oops!
natural English talking about test / exam results

listening what an experience!
listening driving anecdotes
natural English so, anyway, so anyway
grammar narrative tenses
natural English expectation and surprise

wordbooster
taking exams
phrasal verbs

reading a test of endurance
grammar modifying and intensifying adverbs
reading Excuse me, is it day or night?
natural English spoken v. written English

how to ... emphasize what you feel
vocabulary anxiety
natural English introducing and focusing
listening describing TV challenges
vocabulary adding emphasis
natural English not that + adjective

extended speaking taking exams
collect ideas listen to a woman's experience of
  exams
think back prepare and tell a personalized exam
  story
evaluate discuss the pros and cons of exams
writing summarize their opinion of exams

test yourself!
revision of the unit

life with **Agrippine**   25 – 30 mins

read for pleasure
nE talking about test / exam results

- You could start by eliciting or, if necessary, teaching the lexical items in **bold** in the first two questions. It is also worth pointing out that *get caught* will be followed by an *-ing* form if the next word is a verb, e.g. *She got caught cheating in her maths exam.* Learners can then discuss the questions in groups (note that they are framed in such a way that learners are not talking about *cheating* in the first person, but in general).

- When learners have read and discussed the cartoon and listened to the recording, you could spend a few minutes on the **glossary**. Items from the earlier questions are included, but also the useful phrasal verb *go over* sth and the phrase *What the hell ... ?* This phrase is very similar in meaning to *What on earth ... ?*, but is more informal and suggests greater anger. Learners can then test each other on all the items in the glossary.

- Look at the language in the **natural English** box. Most of it seems very straightforward, but in our experience learners often make mistakes with these phrases, e.g. *I got eight ~~from~~ ten* is quite common from certain nationalities; and other phrases are sometimes not part of learners' productive repertoire, e.g. *I did (very) well / badly.* You could also discuss how different educational institutions *score* exams in the country where you are teaching. Do they normally use marks, grades, or percentages? This does seem to vary from country to country.

- Learners can practise the language by talking about how well or badly they have done in various tests / exams. If necessary, you could give them examples: English exams, school or university exams, driving test, vocational exams, etc.

listening what an experience!

70 – 90 mins

talk about their experience of driving

listen to people telling anecdotes about driving

focus on narrative tenses and practise in context

tell their own driving story using narrative tenses and **natural English** phrases

lead-in

- For **exercise 1**, you could ask learners for a show of hands as to whether they are drivers or non-drivers, and then re-seat them so that they are paired up with people from the same group. The rest of the lesson does not require any knowledge of driving, so it should be appropriate for any learner. Check that learners understand *challenging* (= an activity which is quite difficult and requires determination, e.g. driving on mountain roads) in A question 3.

listen to this

- The aim of **exercise 1** is to help learners tune in to the task and check that they know the words *battery*, (*gas / petrol*) *tank*, and *wheels*, which are needed for an understanding of the recording. There may be a few more new items of vocabulary, but we would advise you not to get too involved in this, as the grammar in the lesson is quite challenging. Learners can work in pairs on the activity, and you can then elicit their answers and note the vocabulary on the board with phonemic script.

- Give learners a minute or two in pairs to discuss their ideas for **exercise 2**, once they have listened to the recording. Ask pairs to tell the class what they think; this will motivate them to listen and compare their ideas with the actual story. Notice that the speaker on the recording is American, and naturally uses American English vocabulary. See **language point** on the right.

- Play the recording for **exercise 3** when learners have read the sentences. You could let them compare their answers, but they may need to listen again. It is important that they understand this story because the grammar focus which follows is developed around the same context. The **natural English** box (*so, anyway, so anyway*) comes out of the recording, so go to the **listening booklet** on *p.18* and *p.19* where you will find a search exercise (5.2) for this language.

grammar narrative tenses

- This grammar section begins with a short text highlighting the key verb tenses in the lesson. If your learners are not familiar with the grammatical terminology you may need to take this stage slowly. First, they should identify the examples and do the matching in **exercise 1**. You might find it useful to copy the timeline onto the board or OHP so that you can use it as a focus in feedback. See **language point** on the right. You may want to look at the **language reference** on *p.159* and *p.160* before the lesson.

- **Exercise 2** will help learners with exercise 3. Focusing on the sequence of events in the driving story should make it easier for them to differentiate between the narrative tenses, particularly with the past perfect and the concept of something happening before a point in the past. Learners can work alone and then compare with a partner.

- In **exercise 3** remind learners that they cannot use the past simple and will have to use one of the other narrative tenses. Learners could work alone or in pairs. Monitor to check their progress, and take the opportunity to do some remedial explanation with individuals or pairs. If you find that several learners are having a problem with a particular concept or example, you may decide in feedback to go over the concept again, and to do one or more of the **cover & check** exercises in **language reference** on *p.159* and *p.160*.

- **Exercise 4** aims to contrast the style of two versions of a story, and to encourage learners to appreciate the effect of using a variety of tenses.

- For **exercise 5** it is important that they look at the picture first to set the scene.

it's your turn!

- This activity gives learners a framework for an anecdote, and provides an opportunity for them to use a range of tenses, guided by the questions. The storylines suggested in **exercise 1** are simply there to give learners ideas, but their own true story would be even better. You could suggest that the stories might involve learners in the class; you could bring in some pictures to stimulate ideas. If, however, one pair is having a lot of trouble thinking up a story, you should help them with suggestions. Discourage learners from writing the story, but they can make notes. Monitor all the pairs, offering help where necessary, and check that they are using different tenses.

- When most learners are ready, bring the class together and go over the **natural English** box. You could ask them to practise saying the phrases, stressing the underlined words. They should then think about where one of the phrases could be used in their story before moving on to **exercise 2**.

exercise 1

battery, bonnet, engine, headlights, gas / petrol tank, roofrack, wheels

exercise 2

He had just passed his test and he was driving across the USA on holiday / vacation.

exercise 3

All the answers are correct, <u>except</u>

- someone ~~stole the car~~
- he bought ~~a new car~~
- a policeman ~~thought it was a stolen car~~
- a policeman ~~took the car away~~

language point American and British English

Most of the language in the **student's book** is British English, but sometimes you will hear American speakers on the recordings, as in this case, and they use American English vocabulary. Here, for instance, the speaker uses *vacation* (GB: *holiday*) and *gas tank* (GB: *petrol tank*). There are a number of differences in British and American English in words connected to cars / driving. It is up to you to decide whether learners might find these interesting or useful, either in this lesson or as a revision activity in the next lesson. You could ask them to find equivalents in dictionaries.

British English	American English	British English	American English
petrol tank	gas tank	pavement	sidewalk
car park	parking lot	boot	trunk
motorway	freeway / highway	bonnet	hood
lorry	truck	bend in the road	curve in the road
windscreen	windshield	transport	transportation

Some monolingual dictionaries have useful labelled illustrations of American and British English vocabulary for cars.

exercise 1

1 past continuous: I was living   *was / were* + present participle (*-ing*)
  past perfect simple: they'd given   *had* + past participle
  past perfect continuous: I'd been working   *had been* + present participle (*-ing*)

2 <----------------------------->: I was living
  JAN <--------------------> JUNE: I'd been working
  X: they'd given

exercise 2

The correct order is: i c a e g b f d h

exercise 3

1 had been driving for two hours (emphasizes an activity continuing up to a point in the past, and indicates how long it had been happening)
2 someone had stolen the battery and drained the petrol /gas tank (past perfect clarifies that stealing happened before he returned, i.e. clarifies the sequence of events; this is true for 3, 4, and 5 as well)
3 someone had stolen the wheels
4 someone had stolen the car
5 had arranged for the car to be taken away (thinking it had been abandoned)

exercise 4

The version in exercise 3 sounds more natural due to the use of narrative tenses.

exercise 5

The barrier is in front of the first car.

language point past perfect simple and continuous

1 When you introduce these tenses, learners have a tendency to overuse them.

2 For many learners at this level the past perfect continuous will be new. In many languages there is no comparable form. A common problem is that learners use the past continuous (or equivalent of an imperfect tense) in place of the past perfect continuous. You can demonstrate how the difference can be significant by contrasting these examples with a timeline:

a *The police went to the hotel where Joe was staying and arrested him.* = he was still there

Joe was staying in the hotel

<------------------------------->

————————————————————X
the police arrested him

b *The police went to the hotel where Joe had been staying to see if there were any clues to his disappearance.* = he was staying there before, but had left before the police arrived

Joe was staying
in the hotel

<------------->

————————————————X
the police went
to the hotel

3 Learners sometimes think that the past perfect simple and continuous are only used for things that happened a long time ago.

Want to know more? Go to **Practical English Usage** by Michael Swan *pp.427–428*.

reading a test of endurance

60 – 80 mins

focus on modifying and intensifying adverbs and

use them by talking about challenges

read about a scientific experiment

focus on spoken v. written English in natural English phrases

discuss their reactions to the experiment

grammar modifying and intensifying adverbs

- For a suggestion about the beginning of this lesson, see **ideas plus** on the right. This activity would lead in naturally to **exercise 1**. First, look at the adjectives together; learners should know these words, but clarify any new ones, and check the pronunciation of items in phonemic script. They can then give their reactions to the situation to a partner, or in small groups. Meanwhile, you could copy the two groups of words (spaced apart) onto the board and add to them as the lesson proceeds.

- **Exercise 2** encourages learners to think about the concepts. Give learners a minute to compare their ideas, then elicit their answers. Add the adjectives to the correct group on the board, and learners can copy them into their **student's book** or notebooks. At this point, you might want to teach the terminology; *gradable* = adjectives which can be modified, e.g. *hot* can be described as *quite hot, rather hot, very hot*, etc. and *ungradable* = extreme adjectives, e.g. *boiling* cannot be ~~quite boiling~~ or ~~very boiling~~. If necessary, draw a cline across the board to illustrate this: you could use the one in the **language reference** on *p.161* illustrating the gradation from *boiling* to *freezing*.

- In **exercise 4**, give learners time to think, then elicit the answers and write *extremely* and *really* on the board in front of the group of gradable adjectives, and *really* and *absolutely* in front of the ungradable adjectives. Alternatively, if you have drawn a cline, add the adverbs in the appropriate place.

- After the **test your partner** exercise, move on to look at the meaning of the modifiers and intensifiers in **exercise 5**. Once they have decided where these go on the line, you will need to deal with some differences in meaning. See the **language reference** on *p.161* for details on *rather, fairly*, and *pretty*.

- **Exercises 6** and **7** provide contextualized practice of the language taught so far. Check that they understand *haunted* /ˈhɔːntɪd/ = a place where some people believe ghosts live. Monitor the group work and praise any good uses of the language at the end.

Want to know more? Go to intermediate **teacher's book, how to ...** introduce new language *p.143*.

read on

- **Exercise 1** asks learners to think about the most logical discourse structure for the narrative they are going to read, and it will help them to tune in to the article. Don't tell them whether their answers are the same as the text, but if there is anything completely illogical, you should deal with it.

- In **exercise 2**, the glossary provides a space for learners to note down two new words and their meanings. You could encourage them to do this with other texts you use, but it is advisable to restrict the number of words so that learners focus on what is most important for them. If possible, they should use dictionaries to check the new words, but you may find they can share knowledge with each other, and you can provide some explanations yourself.

- The **natural English** box provides a focus on more formal (latinate) verbs and more informal phrasal verbs and idioms. Look at the information in the box, then ask learners to work together to find the equivalents in **exercise 3**. You could suggest they keep a record of these and other similar items with their more formal equivalents in their notebooks. If written in two columns, learners can cover the items and test themselves. For a little oral practice, ask learners to practise saying the sentences from the text, substituting the latinate verbs for the phrasal verbs / idioms, either in pairs or as a class activity.

Want to know more? Go to **how to ...** teach reading (try it out: meaning consensus) *p.171*.

it's your turn!

- Give learners time to think of their reactions in **exercise 1**, then organize them into small groups. Monitor and collect examples of good and incorrect language use for feedback at the end. See if there is a group consensus about the experiment: how many would be prepared to do it and why? See also **ideas plus** on the right.

wordbooster *go to p.136*   This **wordbooster** can be used at any point in **unit five**.

exercise 2

nice and *frightening* go in A (they are gradable adjectives); *fantastic* and *awful* go in B (they are ungradable (extreme) adjectives)

exercise 4

you can use *extremely* and *really* with the gradable adjectives in A; you can use *really* and *absolutely* with the ungradable adjectives in B (so *really* can be used with both gradable and ungradable adjectives)

exercise 5

quite: fairly, rather, pretty
very: extremely, really
absolutely: really

---

ideas plus speaking

As a lead-in, you could ask learners to talk about extremes. Can they think of an occasion when they were extremely tired, hungry, or angry? Where were they? Why did they feel like that? How did they react? What was the result? Give them a minute to think, then tell each other in small groups. This will give them a little extra oral narrative practice and serve as a good diagnostic activity.

---

exercise 2

glossary: knit; disoriented
The order of paragraphs is: b, d, a, e, c

nE

Our phone's been cut off.
They got rid of the old system.
Joe was told off by the teacher.

exercise 3

para 1: *participate:* take part in; *explore:* find out;
   determine: work out
para 3: *transpired:* turned out
para 4: *occupied:* took up
para 5: *terminated:* came to an end

---

ideas plus extension activities

You could use the idea of the experiment in the text and ask learners to imagine that they had been through the ordeal themselves. Questions 1 to 4 will help them individually to plan their story. Learners then work in pairs on a role play. A interviews B to find out what happened to them during their month, what they did, how they felt, and what they missed, etc. They then swap roles.
You could also follow up this role play with a writing activity. You could give learners *a diary of the month*, which they complete. Learners write about what happened and how they felt at different stages of the month, perhaps focusing on the first day, the end of each week, and the last day.

how to ... emphasize what you feel

70 – 80 mins

vocabulary anxiety

* **Exercise 1** provides a number of vocabulary items, some of which are close in meaning. You could discuss the first pair of sentences as a class to check they know what to do. Then, put the learners in pairs for the rest of the activity, and let them have access to monolingual dictionaries to check the words they are unsure about. Monitor this activity and in feedback, clarify any problems with meaning and pronunciation (quite a few items here are given in phonemic script as they might cause problems). Make sure learners practise the phrases orally in pairs in **exercise 2**.

Want to know more? Go to **how to ...** develop lexis at higher levels *p.160*.

TV challenges

* Set the scene for this section on TV challenges. In many countries, programmes where members of the public are invited to do something very challenging are popular; if this is true for your learners, they could talk about these briefly. A video clip from one of these programmes would be a very motivating way to start this lesson. After looking at the first example in **exercise 1**, ask learners to think about the other challenges in the pictures, then have a quick feedback to check their ideas. At this stage, you may need to correct or feed in new language.

* Focus on the phrases in the **natural English** box. In **exercise 2**, learners can then go on to use these and the words and phrases expressing anxiety from **vocabulary** exercise 1. Give them a minute to think what to say before they tell the class. (These **natural English** phrases also occur in the recordings in the next listening activity.)

* Introduce the recording in **exercise 3**. These anecdotes include a number of the phrases taught in the lesson, and if you go to the **listening booklet** after they have listened once or twice, you can set them the task of underlining the phrases in the tapescript on *p.18* and *p.19*.

vocabulary adding emphasis

* There are many different ways of adding emphasis, especially in spoken English, but learners tend to rely on *very* much of the time. You can help your learners to enrich their language using these forms. **Exercise 1** illustrates two ways of adding emphasis to positive and negative statements. You could write these on the board and get learners to practise them, stressing the words in **bold**.

* **Exercise 2** encourages learners to think of different possible ways of emphasizing. Bear in mind that there are several possible answers in some cases, so as you monitor, only correct answers which are not good English, e.g. ~~I was very petrified~~. (Other possible answers are given in brackets in the answer key.) Pause the recording at appropriate points when you replay it for **exercise 3**.

* Most learners should be familiar with the rules governing *so* and *such* which occur in **exercise 2**. If this is not the case, go to **language reference** on *p.160* and *p.161* and do the **cover & check** exercises.

* The **natural English** box highlights one of the ways of emphasizing in exercise 2 (*not that* + adjective), and learners may be less familiar with this pattern. The way it is stressed is crucial, so it's advisable to focus on this in the recording, and then in subsequent practice. They can work in pairs on **exercises 4** and **5**. See **troubleshooting** on the right.

* In **exercise 6**, learners have the opportunity to use all the language they have studied in the lesson. You could demonstrate this with a true example of your own first. Monitor their discussions in **exercise 7** and give feedback to the class on their language use.

it's your turn!

* The final activity is a light-hearted and relaxing end to the lesson. Learners may come up with some amusing ideas and silly prizes; so much the better. If one pair doesn't have any ideas, you could split them up to work with other pairs who are having more success. Then everyone will have something to say in the mingling activity. You could have a vote on the best idea at the end.

exercise 1
1 These both mean *very frightened*.
2 These are different: if you are relieved, you're happy because something unpleasant has stopped, or not happened; *upset* means sad or angry.
3 These are opposites. *Dread* means to be worried about something that is going to happen; *look forward to* means to be happy and excited about a future event.
4 These can be similar, but *anxious* is slightly stronger in meaning.
5 These are similar in meaning.
6 These are different. A nerve-racking situation is one that makes you very anxious and worried. If sth / sb gets on your nerves, it irritates you.
7 These are similar when you are describing how your body moves when you're frightened.
8 These are different. *Uneasy* means you are worried or unhappy about what might happen; *panic-stricken* means you are so anxious about something that you can't think clearly.

exercise 1 possible answers
2 a bungee jump
3 to get in a booth with a spider
4 to ride on a bobsleigh
5 to walk a plank with crocodiles on either side

exercise 3
Lucy's challenge was the bungee jump (picture 2). David's challenge was to get in a booth with a spider (picture 3). Lucy didn't do her challenge, but David did.

exercise 1
at all emphasizes **wasn't anxious** and **did** emphasizes **get worried**

exercise 2
1 even (far, much)   4 that (too, very, at all)
2 really (absolutely) 5 absolutely (really)
3 such   6 so (incredibly, extremely)

exercise 4
1 it wasn't that good   3 it wasn't that funny
2 it isn't that expensive 4 it isn't that difficult

ideas plus personalization

Ask learners to choose three or four phrases they have just studied, and think of a personal experience for each one, e.g. *I was petrified when I was in a plane during a thunderstorm; I'm taking my driving test next week – I'm dreading it; I got lost on holiday when I was a small child, and my parents were very relieved when they found me.* They could write them down. When they've finished, tell learners to get up and mingle, and describe their experiences to other people. The listeners should ask questions about their experiences. You could demonstrate this yourself with a learner before they mingle.

troubleshooting providing extra challenge

If you want to provide a little extra linguistic challenge for your learners, you could introduce some useful lexical chunks which provide some kind of explanation when used after the structure *not that ... + adjective*.

The food wasn't that good,   **considering** the price.
considering that it was so expensive.
when you consider / think how much it cost.
given that it's such an expensive place.
in view of the price.

Ask learners if they can think of alternatives to *consider ...* in the example sentence in the **natural English** box on *p.65*. If you can't elicit any, introduce these. Encourage learners to use them in **exercise 4**, e.g. *Did you enjoy the film? Yeah, but it wasn't that good,* **considering that** *it was directed by Almodóvar.*

ideas plus speaking homework

If your learners have access to tape recorders, you could suggest they go home and plan a short anecdote about a nerve-racking experience they had (perhaps another topic from the pictures in **TV challenges**). They should make it last about two minutes, try to include some new language from the lesson, and rehearse their story. Then they make a recording, listen to it critically, and see if they can improve it. In the next lesson, they can then tell their stories in small groups as a revision activity, or if your class is small, you could collect in their recordings, listen to them and, at the end, record your reactions – giving plenty of praise as well as a few suggestions. This would be very motivating for learners to listen to at home.

extended speaking taking exams

60 – 80 mins

listen to someone's experience of exams

describe their own experience of taking exams

talk about the advantages and disadvantages of exams

write their opinions of exams

collect ideas

- **Exercise 1** can be done individually or as a small group brainstorming activity. Tell learners that *exams* should include tests too, e.g. driving test, swimming certificate tests, etc. Do a quick group feedback on their ideas. This activity may give learners ideas for what to talk about in **think back**.

- The speaker in the listening activity in **exercise 2** describes her experience of a set of exams in chronological order, and includes incidental anecdotes and opinions. We feel this provides a useful model for learners' own stories, but they should not feel obliged to keep to the format if it is not applicable. Play the recording for **exercise 3**, once learners have read the questions. They could compare their answers before feedback.

exercise 2
She is talking about her university finals; she had to do eight exams altogether.

exercise 3
1 false	2 false	3 true	4 false	5 true

think back

- Remind learners about the different kinds of exams and tests they brainstormed in **collect ideas** exercise 1. If a learner is having problems thinking of an experience, go and help them with suggestions. Encourage learners to describe different exam / test types, although if they all talk about their school leaving exams, their experiences will still be different from each other. Direct them first towards the story framework, which is there purely to give them some guidance and ideas, but stress that they do not need to talk about every issue there, especially if some are not relevant. Before they start to plan, look at the **checklist** together. It is very important that they do not just write out their story and read it aloud if they are to practise oral fluency. Their story should take at least a couple of minutes to tell.

- After they have had time to plan (perhaps a few minutes), look together at the **language reminder**. See **language point** on the right.

- Reorganize the learners into small, compatible groups for **exercise 5**. Meanwhile, monitor and make notes on language use. You could give them a time warning when you want to bring the activity to a close. Try not to let the activity go on too long so that some learners are not listening to or telling a story. If one group finishes early, split them up to go and listen to other groups who haven't finished.

- Bring the class together, and do feedback on language use. Be sure to praise the learners for good use as well as correcting and teaching language points that you noticed. If there has been a particularly good anecdote, you could ask that learner to tell the class about it, though not necessarily the whole of their story.

evaluate

- Our experience of using this **extended speaking** activity with learners was that some became really quite heated and involved when they came to the discussion in **evaluate**, and it proved to be very interesting and challenging. However, this section might be of less interest to certain groups. If you decide not to do it, you could ask them to write their anecdote for homework instead.

- In **exercise 6,** it is important that learners reflect on the experiences they described in order to make a link between the stories and the more abstract discussion. They will find a number of interesting features in common, often to do with fear, anxiety, a sense of anticlimax, confidence or lack of it, etc. Give learners thinking time, and when they start the discussion, monitor again and collect language for feedback.

write your opinion

- Some learners may find it useful to do a short writing activity for homework, either these discursive paragraphs or their personal anecdote. Collect them in the following lesson, and give feedback.

feedback checklist

During the **extended speaking** activity, note down examples of …

• **good language use**

• **effective communication strategies**
(turn-taking, interrupting, inviting others to speak, etc.)

• **learner errors**
(vocabulary, grammar, pronunciation, etc.)

• **particular communication problems**

Make sure you allow time for feedback at the end of the lesson. You can use the notes you make above to <u>praise</u> effective language use and communication or, if necessary, to do some remedial work.

---

ideas plus collect ideas role play

A more interactive way of using the recording is a role play. Put learners into A/B pairs, and tell them that one of them will be an interviewer or listener, and the other will be the woman in the recording. Tell the interviewer to read the questions in the story framework, and listen and tick the ones they think are relevant to the recording. Student B should listen and try to remember the content, making notes if necessary. Give them a short demonstration of what to do, playing the role of the interviewer yourself with one of the learners as the woman in the recording, perhaps asking the first couple of relevant questions. Be sure to react with interest, surprise, etc. Then learners role play in pairs.

Want to know more? Go to **how to …** teach reading, *p.172.*

---

language point think back *managed to / could*

Learners often make the mistake of thinking that *could* can be used to mean *be able to* in all contexts. It can't. If we use *could* for <u>general</u> ability, we can use it in both positive and negative forms in the past:

I could swim by the time I was four.
I couldn't type until I was in my twenties.

When we are referring to ability on <u>one specific occasion</u>, *couldn't* is possible, but *could* in the affirmative form is not used. *Managed to* is often used instead (*was able to* is also possible).

I tried hard, but I couldn't lift the box.

I tried hard, and in the end, I ~~could~~ *managed to lift the box.*

---

ideas plus evaluate discussion

If your learners enjoy more formal discussion, you could ask them in pairs to agree to adopt opposite points of view on exams. They should plan their arguments alone (or with a different partner who is on the same side). They then discuss the issues in pairs or groups, trying to counter one argument with another. This can be a useful oral preparation for writing discursive essays, as in the First Certificate exam, Paper 2.

test yourself!

Want to know more? Go to the **introduction** *p.7* for ways of using **test yourself!**

1 scared, nervous, anxious, worried, nerve-racking, dread (v)
2 sit / do / take; pass, fail, get through, retake, prepare for
3 absolutely awful / fantastic, etc; extremely nice / stressful, etc; pretty awful / nice, etc.

1 They want to **get rid of** that law.
2 He **turned up** two hours late for the meeting.
3 Do you think she'll **get through** the exam?
4 Why did he **tell** the children **off**?

1 It was such a stressful experience / it was so stressful.
2 When she arrived, I knew I had seen her before.
3 I'd been driving for two hours when we ran out of petrol.
4 I got good marks in the test – 8 out of 10.

six

wordlist

natural English

worth / value
What's ... worth?
It's worth ...
It's gone up / down in value.
It's good value.
It's worth a fortune.

talking about needs
I couldn't live / survive without ...
... would be absolutely essential ...
I'd have to take / have ...

you get
What you get in (France) is ...
You get lots of ...

apparently, it appears / seems that
A Was it an accident?
B Yes, apparently ...
        it appears (that) ...
        it seems (that) ...

getting attention
Excuse me, have you got a moment?
Sorry to bother you, but could I ...?
Can you spare a minute or two?
Excuse me, are you in a hurry?

passives in news reporting
He's known to be ...
She's believed to be ...
It's thought that ...
It's said that ...

vocabulary

feelings and emotions
over the moon ⑥
really fed up ⑥
thrilled to bits ⑥
heartbroken
let down
really ecstatic

collocation
extremely dangerous
seriously injured
badly damaged
surrounding area
latest information
terrorist attack
under control

the fighting could escalate
get out of control
on fire

expressing opinions and interest
I feel quite strongly.
I can see both sides.
I'm very much against it.
It doesn't bother me much.
I wouldn't like to say.
I'm not really bothered.
I'm not in favour of it.
There's no easy answer to that.

wordbooster

dangers and disasters
warn / warning
explode / explosion
escape (v, n)
accuse / accusation
kidnap / kidnapping
arrest (v, n)
injure / injury
attack (v, n)
survive / survival
capture (v, n)
damage (v, n)
threaten / threat
destroy / destruction
evacuate / evacuation

prepositions
accuse sb of sth
arrest sb for sth
protect sb from / against sth / sb
evacuate sb from somewhere
on the run
at random
in danger
in need of

glossaries

appreciate in value
hostile
wound
bodyguard
get beaten up ⑥
casualties

do you get it?

25 – 30 mins

> **listen** for pleasure
> **nE** *worth / value*
> **vocabulary** feelings and emotions

- Good news, bad news jokes seem to occur amongst different language groups, so it is possible that the format will be familiar to your learners. Give students a minute or two to discuss the question, then move on to look at and discuss the pictures in **joke time**, pointing out the glossary words first.

- Play the recording, and let the learners react in pairs using the responses in the speech bubbles, or their own reactions. If anyone doesn't understand the joke, you could ask other learners to explain it. Let them listen again with the recording if they want to.

- Go over the language in the **natural English** box. Focus on the pronunciation of *worth* and *value* and ask learners to practise saying the sentences. See **language point** below.

- The vocabulary slot, **feelings and emotions**, contains some useful natural, informal phrases for expressing reactions to good and bad news. Learners could work together and/or use dictionaries to find out the meanings. They should use phrases beginning *I'd be ... (heartbroken)* when they are talking about the different situations.

Want to know more? Go to introduction: **life with Agrippine / do you get it?** p.5.

> **nE** possible answers
> 1 good value for money   2 it's worth; go up in value   3 worth a fortune
> **feelings and emotions**
> good news: over the moon, thrilled to bits, really ecstatic
> bad news: heartbroken, really fed up, let down

---

language point *worth*

Learners met the form *worth* in the **how to ...** section in unit two *p.29*, but for many it's not part of their productive vocabulary. It is important to highlight the pronunciation and the different structures, e.g. *it's worth see**ing**; ten dollars' worth **of** lottery tickets*.

You can illustrate the meaning of *worth* like this:
*What **did** the painting **cost**?* = What price did you pay for it?
*What's the painting **worth**?* = How much could you sell it for?
You could also explain that *worth* is used in connection with money, effort, and time, e.g. *it's (not) worth the effort / the expense / spending time on it*.
Worthwhile means enjoyable, useful, or satisfying enough to be worth the effort, e.g.

*It's an old car and it's always breaking down. I was going to have it repaired but it's just not **worthwhile** / **worth it**. I think I'll get rid of it.*

---

reading trouble spots

70 – 90 mins

talk about events in the news and trouble spots

read about a foreign correspondent's kit, and talk about it using **natural English** phrases

focus on vocabulary collocations

read about training and surviving in trouble spots

discuss how they would feel as a foreign correspondent

lead-in

- As a lead-in to **exercise 1**, explain to learners what a *trouble spot* is (= a place where there is often political violence, or war). Ask them to give you **one** trouble spot in the world (but not more, or you will pre-empt the discussion). Give them a moment to think of their answers to the questions, then put them into small groups for the speaking activity in **exercise 2**. Monitor to check that all the groups are on the right lines; at the end, do a quick class feedback. See **troubleshooting** on the right.

- In **exercise 3**, learners will be able to find unknown vocabulary items in the picture by looking at the accompanying text. An alternative would be to tell learners to cover the text and look at the pictures with a partner, identify as many as possible, and say why they would be useful. They can then read to check their answers, although the text does not explain the purpose of all the items in the picture. Go over the answers at the end as a class. Don't spend too long on the vocabulary in this section, though, as there is more new language coming up. If necessary, explain *bribe* /braɪb/ = something (usually money) given in return for help; the transaction is often illegal.

- You can make a link between the **natural English** box and the text by drawing your learners' attention to the first line: *My ready-packed bag is a great comfort – I couldn't manage without it.* Once learners have completed the gaps and practised the sentences, give them a minute to think about their answers to 1 and 2. They don't need to limit themselves to items from the picture.

vocabulary collocation

- **Exercise 1** focuses on different types of collocation. Do the first one together, then learners can work alone or in pairs to complete the exercise. See **language point** on the right. When you go over the answers, it is also worth taking time to record the collocations on the board and ask learners to make a note of them, e.g. *vitally important*, *extremely dangerous*, etc. Give learners a couple of minutes to study and memorize the collocations, then test each other in pairs.

- **Exercise 2** provides an opportunity for contextualized practice of the collocations. Learners can either work in pairs, or alone and then compare. Go round and monitor, correcting their writing and suggesting possible answers if necessary.

Want to know more? Go to **how to ...** develop lexis at higher levels *p.160*.

read on

- **Exercise 1** asks learners to try to predict sentence endings from the key sentences given. This will allow them to tune into the text before they read and process the information. Don't worry if the learners' predictions are not exactly the same as the text. They will be motivated to read the text afterwards to check their ideas. Don't go over the answers, but you could ask learners in class feedback what they think the endings are.

- In **exercise 2**, learners should be able to deduce the meaning of the glossary words from context and the partial definitions, so discourage dictionary use at this point.

- Learners need to process a range of information in the text for **exercise 3**, and searching for a range of information is more challenging than most true / false or comprehension questions. You could suggest that learners either underline the relevant information or make notes. To increase the level of challenge, tell learners they can make very brief notes (not just copying out the whole sentences), then shut their books and tell their partner the answers in their own words. Quickly check the answers as a group at the end.

Want to know more? Go to **how to ...** teach reading *p.167*.

it's your turn!

- Learners will need a couple of minutes to think about the questions in **exercise 1** before comparing ideas in groups. Monitor and collect examples of good language use or errors for feedback at the end.

 **wordbooster** *go to p.138*　　　This **wordbooster** can be used at any point in **unit six.**

nE

I couldn't **manage** without **my personal stereo**.
Malaria tablets would be absolutely essential in the Amazon.
I'd have to **have my diary with me**.

troubleshooting world knowledge

Learners vary enormously in the amount they know about world or national events, and you may have some extremely knowledgeable people in your class alongside others who know very little. Be prepared for either situation; learners certainly aren't being assessed on their world knowledge here, and don't need any to complete the lesson successfully. However, here are three ideas:

- Ask learners to listen to / watch the news the night before class (in their mother tongue if necessary) then in the lesson they can start by comparing in groups what they learnt. It is all useful practice in English, and you could ask them to make a note of any vocabulary they might need as well.
- Find out who is interested in current stories in the news, and who isn't, and pair them up. Those who are interested can tell their partners what is happening.
- Use a very short video clip of the previous night's news. One idea would be to show it without the sound, on fast forward, so that learners see the images and with a partner, try to decide what the reports are about.

If learners are in an English-speaking country, they can talk about news in that country or their own.

exercise 1

1 extremely (*totally* is impossible, because it only collocates with extreme adjectives)
2 seriously   5 surrounding   8 under
3 badly   6 latest   9 escalate / out of
4 completely   7 terrorist   10 on

exercise 2 possible answers

Last night, the roads leading out of the city were extremely dangerous. The airport was badly damaged by mortar attacks and two other reporters were seriously injured. The latest information we have is that the political situation has got out of control and the villagers in the surrounding area are worried about terrorist attacks.

language point adverb / adjective collocations

The adverb / adjective collocations in numbers 1 to 4 of **exercise 1** are common in English but sometimes overlooked. Familiarity with collocation helps learners to produce natural English, and these combinations are often tested in Cambridge exams such as FCE, CAE, and CPE.

Some adverbs have a restricted collocational range with adjectives, e.g. *vitally* is only common with *important*; some have a wider range, e.g. *seriously* collocates with *ill*, *injured*, *hurt*, *wounded*, *affected*, *concerned*. Some adverbs have a very wide range of collocation, e.g. *extremely*. As a learner training activity, you could ask learners for homework to find typical adverb / adjective collocations by looking up these adverbs in a monolingual dictionary and noting the examples given: *badly*, *fully*, *completely*, *strongly*, *seriously*, *totally*, *vitally*. In the next lesson, elicit what they discovered (there may be differences between dictionaries), and put them on the board for learners to record. They can be revised through a 'test your partner' activity.

exercise 2

1 hot and cold climates
2 aren't allowed to go
3 getting in
4 organizations that have knowledge of the region

glossary

hostile: unfriendly and dangerous
wound: injury from a knife or gun
bodyguard: person whose job is to protect sb

get beaten up: be attacked / physically assaulted
casualties: people who are killed or injured in accidents or war

exercise 3

1 basic and advanced first aid; how to treat gunshot wounds and burns; how to prepare for extreme hot and cold climates; how to get out of danger; the latest information about the region
2 50 journalists lost their lives; as a result, training for journalists improved a great deal
3 you have to change from one set of bodyguards and fixers to another; you need to make the right contacts to be safe
4 if captured by a losing army, the fixers may be punished

listening have you heard?

discuss TV news in their country

listen to an interview with a TV journalist

focus on the past simple and present perfect passive

use the grammar and **natural English** phrases to develop news stories

lead-in

- Before you start the lesson, look at **troubleshooting** on the right.
- As with the reading section earlier in the unit, you could brief your learners about this lesson in advance and ask them to watch the news on TV the night before; you could even give them the questions in **exercise 1** to prepare. If you do this, they obviously won't need much thinking time before moving on to **exercise 2**.

listen to this

- The four short extracts in **tune in** are taken from different parts of the recording. They give learners an opportunity to get used to the voice of the speaker as well as reducing the information load when they get to the full passage.
- When learners have read each of the sentences in **exercise 1**, play the extract so learners can complete **exercise 2**.
- The recording for **listen carefully** has been split into two sections as some learners may find it an information overload in a single passage. Of course, if you want to raise the level of challenge, you could play both parts at once.
- If you follow the procedure in the **student's book**, play the first part and elicit answers to **exercise 3**. The journalist talks quite quickly, but the comprehension task itself is not demanding.
- Play the second part of the recording. Learners can compare with a partner before you check the answers. If you sense they have found it difficult, you could play the passage a second time before eliciting answers.
- Move on to the **natural English** box, which focuses on the use of the common expression *you get / you don't get*. Ask learners to find the two examples of it in tapescript 6.3 on *p.21* of the **listening booklet** and tell you what they think it means.
- The **listening challenge** shifts from TV news in Italy to TV news in Australia, and the speaker has a distinct Australian accent. When the learners have listened to the passage and answered the questions (you could ask them if they heard the expression *you get* in the passage), you could let them listen again with the tapescript in the **listening booklet** on *p.20* and ask you questions about it.

grammar past simple and present perfect passive

- Learners discuss the use of both passives and the past simple versus present perfect later in this section, but if you think your class are up to the challenge, you could start by asking them why they think they are going to study this particular grammar at this particular time (because the present perfect and passives are frequently used in news reporting).
- Tell learners to read sentences 1 to 8 in **exercise 1** to make sure they understand them. Then look at the questions and example together, before they prepare their answers individually.
- **Exercise 2** is best done in small groups as they are likely to generate more examples of stories from around the world.
- Learners can continue in groups for **exercise 3** or you could create pairs. Monitor the discussion to assess how much they understand about the reasons for using passives in general, and the present perfect here, in particular. (If you did this at the beginning of the section, you will just need to check they can identify the forms in the sentences.)
- You could check **exercise 4** in open class before creating pairs or small groups to discuss **exercise 5**.
- The decision to make use of the **language reference** at this point really depends on how well they have coped so far. If they clearly need reinforcement, go there now; if not, move on to **exercise 6** and give the **cover & check** exercises on *p.162* and *p.163* for homework.
- The language in the **natural English** box is extremely high frequency, but *apparently* is a word that few upper-intermediate learners seem to know or use. You could get learners to read the examples in **exercise 7**, silently or aloud in pairs, and then extend them by asking the second learner in each exchange to think of a different ending, e.g. (first example) *Yes, it seems that he didn't get very far*. They can then work on the other exchanges from the stimuli given, and continue to practise until they are fluent and confident. Ask different pairs to act out their exchanges for the class, but make sure each pair maintains a good pace; this will bring the lesson to an end with a real sense of achievement.

exercise 2

1 eight 2 eight 3 non-stop 4 Italian

exercise 3

1 You can watch the news from 7.00 to midnight.
2 Eight o'clock is a good time for news because Italian families sit down to supper then.

exercise 4

1 different
2 a different programme
3 very glamorous
4 important

nE

... so what you get in Italy is ...
... so you get really a non-stop news service ...

exercise 5

There is international news because it is a multi-racial society and people are interested in news from their country of origin. One channel is devoted to ethnic programmes, and news is in different languages on that channel.

exercise 3

1 have been cut off
2 have been evacuated
3 have been killed /... injured
4 has been badly damaged
5 have (just) been released
6 has been kidnapped
7 has been reported
8 has been accused

The passive form is used because we are more interested in what happened than who was responsible for what happened.
The present perfect is used because a past action or event is being described, but we are not given more detailed information, such as the time and place the events occurred.

exercise 4

story six

exercise 5

1 the past simple passive
2 we switch from the present perfect to the past simple when the time and place of the event are established, or when more detailed information is given; the passive is used because we still don't know who was responsible for the kidnapping
3 because we are now describing something occuring in the period of time from the past up to the present

exercise 6

1 was called out
2 were evacuated
3 spread
4 was brought
5 was injured
6 has not been discovered

language point passives

Passives present different problems for different learners. For example:

Japanese uses suffixes in place of an auxiliary verb, so learners do not always identify passives.

Spanish often uses a reflexive verb, e.g. *The house was built* in English is literally ~~the house built itself~~ in Spanish.

Russian learners have particular difficulty with progressive and perfect forms / uses of the passive.

Italian speakers have fewer problems with form, but the use is more restricted, so learners may not use a passive form in contexts where they are needed or preferred.

In other words, the issues that demand greatest attention will depend on the first language of your learners. If you are not very familiar with their language, speak to someone who is. If you are teaching in a multilingual context, be prepared to deal with different problems.

Want to know more? Read **Learner English**, Eds. M Swan and B Smith (CUP 2001).

how to ... be an ace reporter

60 – 70 mins

listen to vox pops from the news

practise ways of getting someone's attention through **natural English** phrases

focus on indirect questions

learn ways of expressing opinions and interest

interview five people to get their opinions

vox pops

- Begin by clarifying *vox pops* ◉ (= very short interviews with members of the public, broadcast on TV, radio, or in the press). Remind learners that they have listened to vox pops earlier in the **student's book**, e.g. **different opinions** unit three *p.36*. See **ideas plus** on the right for a possible lead in to the section. Learners can then discuss the topics in **exercise 1** in pairs before checking their ideas with the recording in **exercise 2**.

- The aim of the listening is to provide models of vox pops. Learners are therefore asked to focus on different linguistic elements: firstly, how the interviewer gets someone's attention, secondly, their use of indirect questions, and thirdly, the way the interviewees express opinions or interest.

- For **exercise 3**, tell learners to look at the **natural English** box for a minute, then do the listening task. After checking the answers, ask learners to practise the questions and answers together. You could do all the examples with the whole class first to work on their intonation.

grammar indirect questions

- For **exercise 1**, learners could use the tapecript, or if you prefer, go back to the recording and use it for dictation of the indirect questions. It would probably be useful to put these on the board as you go, then you can refer to them in the analysis.

- Learners can do the language analysis in **exercise 2** in pairs, or as a class activity. They can then work on the transformations in **exercise 3**. See **language point** on the right.

- In feedback on this exercise, focus on pronunciation and give the class the opportunity to practise saying the indirect questions naturally. You may need to provide a model yourself. This will help them in the pair practice in **exercise 4**, during which you should monitor and correct. Demonstrate first that **A** should ask an indirect question, and **B** should give a genuine answer.

Want to know more? Go to **how to ...** do informal testing (try it out), *p.149*.

vocabulary expressing opinions and interest

- Remind learners of the idiom *sitting on the fence* (= avoid saying which side of an argument you support) which they came across in unit four on *p.48*. You could draw a table on the board with three columns for learners to copy into their notebooks and fill in the sentences. They can work in pairs, then go over the answers as a class.

- When they do **exercise 2**, make sure they practise stressing the underlined syllables. You could also help them to sound more natural in some cases by adding *actually* either at the end or beginning of most sentences.

it's your turn!

- Learners now have the opportunity to put everything they have learnt into practice, using the framework in **exercise 2**. If they can choose a topic relevant to their learning context for **exercise 1**, so much the better; the suggestions are simply to supply ideas for those who need them.

- If your class is smaller than twelve, each pair can interview three or four people each. Give them time to plan their question.

- While learners are mingling and collecting opinions, monitor and make a note of language points for feedback. At this point, the interviewees won't know the topic and will have to respond spontaneously, which will be more challenging. Make sure that learners alternate between interviewing and being interviewed.

- If you are using the suggestion in **ideas plus** on the right, play the recordings at the end for feedback, otherwise write the notes you have made on the board.

- The posters provide a little writing practice and are a different way for learners to give feedback on the content of the activity. Learners' opinions could and perhaps should be written anonymously. You might want to display the posters on the walls for a few lessons.

exercise 2
1 banning smoking in bars and restaurants
2 having cosmetic surgery to look more attractive
3 the amount of housing being built in the countryside

exercise 3 These phrases are used in this order:
Excuse me, can you spare a minute or two?
Excuse me, have you got a moment?
Excuse me, are you in a hurry?

ideas plus using video

In order to stimulate learners' interest you could use some vox pop TV clips of the general public being interviewed in the street. These are quite common on consumer programmes or news reports, e.g. Sky News, CNN. If learners are studying in their own country, you could also use vox pops from local TV, but turn the sound down, tell them the topic and (in pairs, in English) they guess what each person's opinion might be. They then listen to confirm.

exercise 1
I'd like to know how you feel about the proposed ban ...?
Could I ask you what you think about people who have cosmetic surgery ...?
Could you tell me if you are worried about the amount of housing ...?

exercise 2
1 In indirect questions, the 'question' is introduced with another phrase: *I'd like to know ... / Could I ask you ... / Could you tell me ... .* The rest of the question is then in the affirmative form, not a question form.
For inverted *yes / no* questions, e.g. *Can you ...? Is he ...?* you need to add *if*.
2 Indirect questions sound more polite, as long as the intonation is appropriate.

exercise 3
1 what you feel about free school meals
2 what you think about football hooligans
3 if you agree with random drug testing
4 if you are concerned about genetically modified food

language point indirect questions

In theory, learners at this level should know this structure, but using indirect questions accurately in speech can be difficult, even at higher levels. There are various problems:
- Learners tend to invert the verb and subject in the second clause, e.g. *I'd like to know where there is a cashpoint.* NOT *I'd like to know where is there a cashpoint.*
- They also tend to omit *if* when the second clause is not a *wh-* question, e.g. *Could you tell me **if** the train is late?* NOT *Could you tell me is the train late?*

You can illustrate the word order and the use of *if* on the board if you have copied the sentences from **exercise 1**. Use a different colour to highlight word order, or write potential errors as above.
- Another issue is fluency. Some learners find these sentences quite a mouthful, so you will need to spend a little time helping them with rhythm and intonation. Provide an oral model.
- Finally, learners need to know that indirect questions tend to appear softer or more polite.

exercise 1
strong opinions: I feel quite strongly about that; I'm very much against it; I'm not at all in favour of it.
'sitting on the fence'; I can see both sides; I wouldn't like to say; There's no easy answer to that.
lack of interest: It doesn't bother me that much; I'm not really bothered, to be honest; I'm not all that interested in it.

ideas plus recording learners

If you have access to a video camera, you could get learners to record each other doing the vox pops. This could be done among the class, or learners could go out to the public areas in their place of study and interview English-speaking staff or learners. This activity could also be done with a tape recorder, and could be very motivating.

extended speaking radio news report

75 – 90 mins

listen to news reports

discuss how to update stories

write a news bulletin

read the news aloud

role play vox pops

collect ideas

- This **extended speaking** activity takes learners through the process of producing a news report. Because it is quite long and has a series of different stages, we suggest reading through the learners' material very carefully before you begin the lesson.

- In **exercise 1**, learners look at the pictures; this is to arouse interest, stimulate discussion, and help them to predict the content of the listening activity. Do a quick class feedback, so that they can compare their ideas at the end. Don't say if their suggestions are the same as the recording.

- In **exercise 2**, play the recording and pause after each story to allow time for the learners to make notes. You could ask them if they want to hear it a second time. Let them compare in pairs and also discuss whether their predictions were correct. Then go over the answers (see key on the right).

- **Exercise 3** gives learners practice in intensive listening. Play the tape once, then play it again with pauses if you wish to give learners time to amend the bulletin.

update the stories

- In **exercise 4**, make it very clear what the learners are going to do, and in particular, make clear the time of the old report (one o'clock), and the time of their report (six o'clock).

- Organize the learners in pairs. If you have an odd number, have one group of three and each of them can invent a different story. First, the pairs need to decide which story each person is going to develop. Give them a few minutes to work on their own. If you have a group who lack confidence and ideas, you could suggest that the pairs work on the two stories orally, together. In that case, in **exercise 5**, they could discuss their ideas with a different pair. While learners are comparing with their partner, monitor so that you can give learners any help they might need, and check that their stories are developing in an appropriate way.

prepare a bulletin

- It's very important that learners understand all the information in the **checklist**. Ask them to read it and ask you any questions about it they don't understand, before they start writing. Remember, if you adapt the activity in any way, you may need to adapt the checklist as well. Give learners a time limit for this writing stage (ten to fifteen minutes), but be prepared to revise your timing while they are working, depending on how much progress they are making.

read the news

- If your lesson is an hour, you could stop at this point. Ask learners to look at the advice from newsreaders in **exercise 7** for homework, and practise reading aloud on their own. In the next lesson, let them rehearse together, before going on to **exercise 8**. Otherwise, bring the class together after they have finished writing and look at the newsreaders' advice. If you wanted to spend more time on reading aloud, you could do a little practice first, using the recording of the *one o'clock news* from the beginning of the lesson on *p.77*. Tell learners to look at the tapescript in the **listening booklet** on *p.22*, and in pairs, think where they would pause, and whether there are any difficult words to pronounce. Then they listen to see if they marked the pauses correctly. Finally, they can read that story aloud at the same time as the recording.

- In **exercise 8**, if you have a small class, each group can read or play their recording. With a large class, divide them into sub-groups to read to each other.

- **Exercise 10** provides a possible update of the stories, which learners may be interested to listen to. Stress that there is no correct answer, and that their own stories are equally valid.

role play

- This vox pop activity is optional. If learners have been very motivated by writing their news reports, they may be keen to collect these vox pop interviews, possibly in the next lesson. This is an activity that can be planned alone or in pairs. Follow the procedure for **it's your turn!** on *p.68*.

feedback checklist

During the **extended speaking** activity, note down examples of …

- **good language use**

- **effective communication strategies**
  (turn-taking, interrupting, inviting others to speak, etc.)

- **learner errors**
  (vocabulary, grammar, pronunciation, etc.)

- **particular communication problems**

Make sure you allow time for feedback at the end of the lesson. You can use the notes you make above to <u>praise</u> effective language use and communication or, if necessary, to do some remedial work.

exercise 2
story 1: **Who?** two prisoners **What's happened?** they escaped from prison **What's the situation now?** they are still on the run
story 2: **Who?** Dino Walker, the Canfield goalkeeper **What's happened?** he has been arrested **What's going to happen?** his football club is going to make a statement later today
story 3: **What's happened?** there has been an explosion **Where?** in a house in Denton **Why?** we don't know

exercise 3
from Moorhouse Prison <u>last night</u>; <u>extremely</u> dangerous; have not given any <u>details</u>; recent <u>stories</u>; a <u>large</u> explosion; the cause of the explosion is not <u>clear</u>

nE
1 She's said / believed to be very rich.
2 It is believed / thought that the children are out of control.
3 She is known to be very mean.
4 The President is believed / thought to be unwell.

---

troubleshooting nE adapting material

Although the passives in the **natural English** box on *p.77* are very useful, you may decide you don't want to burden your learners with more input at this stage, in which case you could leave it out. Alternatively, you could do it at the beginning of the section, where it won't interfere with the flow of preparation for the **extended speaking** activity.

---

test yourself!

Want to know more? Go to the **introduction** *p.7* for ways of using **test yourself!**

1 threat, survival, explosion, injury, accusation
2 seriously injured, badly damaged, completely destroyed, extremely dangerous
3 accuse sb of; protect sb from / against; arrest sb for; evacuate sb from / in; in / out of danger; under / out of control; on fire; in need of

1 I couldn't do / live / manage without my medical supplies in the jungle.
2 The house has gone up in value since June.
3 Could you tell me if all the tickets have been sold?
4 I'm not (at all) in favour of hunting.

1 A doctor was arrested last night …
2 Several people have been injured …
3 Sorry to bother you, …
4 I'd like to know if you agree …

seven

wordlist

natural English

what / how / where on earth ...?
Where on earth have you been?
Why on earth did she go?
What on earth are you doing?

degrees of willingness
I'd be willing to (do) ...
I wouldn't mind (doing) ...
I'd be a bit reluctant to (do) ...
I'd find it hard to (do) ...

that appeals to me
... really appeals to me.
... doesn't appeal to me (at all).
What appeals to me is ...
That would appeal to ...

putting people at ease
Hello, it's ..., isn't it?
It's very nice to meet you.
Do have a seat.
Can I take your coat?
Did you have any problems getting here?
Did you find us OK?

linking reasons together
There are several reasons why ...
First of all, ...
Secondly, ...
And another thing is that ...

ending an interview
Thank you very much for coming.
It was very nice meeting you.
I'll let you know ...
I'll be in touch ...

vocabulary

voluntary work
volunteer / voluntary
charity
raise
prize
donate
fund-raising
the disabled
conservation

success and failure
cope with sth / sb
handle a situation
a fiasco
make a success of sth
achieve a target
succeed / success

wordbooster

conservation
endangered species
buried
reptile
captivity
site
remains
feed
the wild
dig sth up
breeding

uncountable and plural nouns
knowledge
experience
training
research
accommodation
equipment
proceeds
remains
facilities
expenses

glossary
be worried sick
be supposed to
hitchhike
get mugged
have a go at sb ☺
shiver
sweat
ward
laundry
be touched (by sb's actions)

who cares?

life with Agrippine   25 – 30 mins

read for pleasure
nE *what / how / where on earth ...?*

- Give learners a minute alone to plan their ideas, then brainstorm together. Some learners may not have many worries about their parents; this might depend on their age. Do a quick group feedback.

- The question in **cartoon time** aims to personalize the topic rather than test comprehension. Most teenagers and parents seem to have a problem with this, so your learners should have plenty to say.

- When you play the recording, you could draw your learners' attention to the mother's tone. At the beginning of the conversation she speaks in the same low key for the first couple of sentences, suggesting barely controlled anger. As she becomes more exasperated, her voice range widens on *But why didn't you ring?* You could ask learners to comment on her tone at different stages.

- Before learners test each other on the **glossary**, you need to decide whether you want to explore the meaning of *be supposed to* more fully. If so, you can go to **language reference** *p.164* and do the **cover & check** exercise. Otherwise, deal with this point at the end, or at another time.

- Make sure that learners practise saying the phrases in the **natural English** box with appropriate intonation. You can use the recording as a model or provide your own, stressing *earth* in each case. If you like, remind learners that they met *Wh + the hell ...?* in unit five glossary, which is stronger than *What on earth ...?* and more informal.

Want to know more? Go to introduction: **life with Agrippine / do you get it?** *p.5.*

---

ideas plus role play

This cartoon lends itself well to acting out. If your class would enjoy this, put them in pairs, one as Agrippine and one as the mother. They can either listen to the recording again to capture the atmosphere, or listen and shadow read, i.e. read at the same time as the recording, or they can simply practise reading it together. Go round and monitor to offer advice on their performance. If you like, change either role from female to male. Then ask learners to shut their book, and see what they can do from memory. It doesn't matter if they don't recall it exactly; they just need to improvise the parts they don't remember. Give them one more look at the book to refresh their memories, then they get together with another pair to act out their version.

---

reading caring for others

talk about being a patient

focus on the present perfect and past simple

talk about what you would volunteer to do using grammar and **natural English** phrases

read about a teacher in China who was cared for by her learners

describe what you would do for friends or family

lead-in

- **Exercise 1** leads in to the topic of the lesson and provides a chance to personalize. You could demonstrate by talking about yourself for a minute before learners talk in pairs.

- For **exercise 2**, learners should only think about what to say, not start speaking. They will come back and talk about these situations after they have studied the grammar. If there are other situations which are obviously relevant to your teaching context, include them.

grammar present perfect and past simple

- The sentences in **exercise 1** relate to the context of the lesson, e.g. *I've never done anything like that before* could be used to talk about any of the situations in **lead-in** exercise 2. Give learners time to choose the correct forms, perhaps going over the first one together to check they know what to do. Ask them also to justify which form they chose in that example. This will encourage them to think about the reasons for their choices.

- When they work in pairs in **exercise 2**, go round and listen to their answers and explanations. This will enable you to assess how well they are coping with the grammar, and whether you need to use the **cover & check** exercises in **language reference** on *p.165* at this point, or later for revision. Give them the opportunity to practise saying the correct sentences with a partner. See **language point** on the right.

Want to know more? Go to **how to ...** do informal testing *p.148*.

- Choose one of the situations from exercise 2 of the **lead-in**, e.g. *help a child who has problems with reading*, and use it to contextualize the language in the **natural English** box. Check that learners know the meaning of *I'd be a bit reluctant to do that* (= hesitate before doing something, because you don't want to do it) and *wouldn't mind doing* (= wouldn't object to). Use the situation about the child to elicit responses from the learners.

- In **exercise 3**, learners will be putting together the tense work and the **natural English** phrases to talk about the situations. Give them a minute to think what they are going to say, then tell a partner. Alternatively, do it as a mingling activity with the whole class. Monitor and make a note of language points for feedback afterwards.

- In **exercise 4**, learners listen to short vox pops after giving their own reactions. These reinforce the language taught, and provide natural listening practice. The last speaker has a strong London accent.

read on

- Put the headline of the article on the board: What do they think the article will be about? Which country do they think it might take place in? Then follow the instructions in the **student's book**, or use the suggestion in **ideas plus** on the right.

- **Exercise 2** is a way of checking general understanding of the paragraphs, and is a typical Cambridge examination test type. Pre-teach *end up* ⑥ = arrive / come to be in a situation which you didn't expect.

- **Exercise 3** may be a quick pair reaction. You could ask whether they would be prepared to help their teacher like this.

- Learners are asked to recall the information in the text from memory in **exercise 4**; this should provide a challenge. If you prefer, you can write the following on the board and ask learners to try and remember which ones the students performed for her: provide a cooked meal, sit and chat and entertain her, do her laundry, help her have a bath, wash her feet, shampoo her hair, stay overnight, and wash her. Finding the answers will test their scanning skills.

- With **exercises 5** and **6**, you could opt to do one or the other, as they will both provide speaking practice. Some learners may have a lot to say about hospitals in their country, and may be prepared to share experiences. As we have said before, you don't want to push learners to be too personal; but at the same time, some will be very happy to talk about something that is very significant for them.

Want to know more? Go to **how to ...** teach reading *p.167*.

it's your turn!

- This activity provides an opportunity to use the language from the **natural English** box on *p.82* (degrees of willingness) as well as the ideas in the article. If you like, refer learners back to it. It should be quite light-hearted. If you prefer you could replace the classmate with a neighbour.

exercise 1
1 I've never done (at any time in my life; we don't know when)
2 I've just done (present perfect with *just* for recent events)
3 I haven't done (talking about a period of time leading up to now; recent past)
4 I've done (completed action before now; we don't know when)
5 both answers are correct, and have a similar meaning; the continuous form can emphasize the ongoing nature of the activity
6 I always wanted (completed at a definite time in the past, i.e. when I was younger)
7 I've always hated (in my life, up to now)
8 I did (completed at a definite time in the past); I haven't done (talking about a period of time leading up to now; recent past)

exercise 4

	topic?	willing to do it?	why?
Gareth	1 help a child to read	yes	he had problems as a child
	2 walk a dog	no	doesn't like dogs, doesn't want the responsibility
DeNica	1 clear waste land	yes	satisfying; she had nowhere to play as a child
	2 babysitting	no	would find it very difficult
Derek	1 babysitting	yes	all children are noisy – that's fine; would be fun

exercise 1
glossary 1 c   2 d   3 a   4 e   5 b

exercise 2
1 how I ended up in hospital
2 life in a typical hospital
3 taking care of my diet
4 providing physical help
5 emotional support

exercise 4
provide a cooked meal; sit and entertain her; wash her feet; wash her hair; stay overnight, and watch over her

language point lubricators
In **exercise 1** we have deliberately included a number of very common spoken English phrases:
to be honest   as a matter of fact   actually   in fact
You could point these out to learners as very useful, high-frequency phrases which they can use to make their English sound more fluent and natural. They are all used to emphasize what you think or believe. You could also remind learners that *actually* doesn't mean *at this moment*.

ideas plus jigsaw reading
This text lends itself well to a jigsaw reading procedure. Divide learners into groups of five, seated together. (If necessary, have one or two groups of four, and one person in each group should read two paragraphs.) Give one paragraph to each learner to read. It is important that they have a time limit so that they don't read the other paragraphs. They can refer to the glossary. All learners then shut their books and in turn describe what they read to their group. They can ask each other questions if necessary. At the end, they can all read the whole text to check if anything was different or omitted. This is an interactive way to use a text, and it can also make the final reading stage more motivating.

listening was it successful?

60 – 80 mins

focus on charity / fund-raising vocabulary

talk about prizes using natural English phrases

listen to people describing charity events

focus on vocabulary describing success or failure

discuss a questionnaire using vocabulary from the lesson

vocabulary volunteer work

• Before you start the lesson, look at **ideas plus** on the right.

• Don't pre-teach any of the target items in **exercise 1**. Learners should be able to complete the text if you put them in pairs and they use their shared knowledge, the context, first language (some items might be similar in form and meaning to words in their own language, e.g. *volunteer* and *conservation*), and intelligent guesswork. Clarify any problems when you check the answers.

• Before learners work on **exercise 2**, practise the pronunciation of items given in phonemic script, and any others in the text you anticipate might cause problems, e.g. *disaster, sponsored,* or *various*. You could also refer learners back to the advice from newsreaders for reading aloud in unit six on *p.79*. After that, they can work in pairs while you monitor and correct where necessary.

lead-in

• Give learners some time to think about **exercise 1**, before exchanging information in **exercise 2**. At the end, ask one or two people with interesting experiences to tell the whole class, and elicit the names of charities that individuals would consider supporting, which leads conveniently to the language in the **natural English** box.

• When you go through the **natural English** box, you could personalize the language with examples you have just elicited, e.g. *The Red Cross **appeals to you**, Carlos, because you have worked in a hospital; **What appeals to you**, Yuki, is the World Wildlife Fund, because you like animals.*

• Introduce **exercise 3** giving one or two examples of charities which are local to your teaching situation, e.g. raising money for a children's home, a hospital, sports ground, etc. Read through the list of possible prizes together. Learners can then discuss them using the **natural English** phrases.

listen to this

• Ask learners to look at the picture and describe or guess the charity event being depicted.

• Play part 1 of the recording. This should confirm some of the suggestions the learners have just made. Note also whether learners are using the phrase *raise money* in their answers to **exercise 1**.

• You could quickly explain that a *marquee* /mɑː'kiː/ is a large type of tent often used for outdoor events and celebrations. Play the rest of the conversation and let learners compare their answers for **exercise 2** with a partner. As with previous recordings, you could play the conversation a second time if you sense that learners have missed or misunderstood some of the important information.

• The **listening challenge** is a slightly more complex story. Play it as suggested, or try **ideas plus** on the right.

• **Exercise 4** gives learners an opportunity to relate the stories to their own country / culture.

vocabulary success and failure

• Give learners about five minutes to read through the questionnaire in **exercise 1** and choose the correct words in **bold**. Check the vocabulary first, using the **language point** on the right if necessary.

• Put learners in small groups for **exercise 2**. Monitor the discussion and makes notes for class feedback at the end. Pay special attention to whether they have used vocabulary from the lesson correctly, but also note down other examples of good language or important errors that warrant attention.

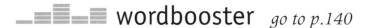 **wordbooster** *go to p.140*   This **wordbooster** can be used at any point in **unit seven.**

exercise 1

1 raise	3 voluntary	5 prizes	7 conservation
2 volunteers	4 fund-raising	6 donated	8 the disabled

ideas plus warmer

As a lead-in to the lesson, you could ask learners in small groups to brainstorm the names of different national and international charity organizations. International charities that most British people know include: Oxfam, The Red Cross, Médécins Sans Frontières, Mencap, Amnesty International, and the World Wildlife Fund.

exercise 1

It was a charity disco to raise money for a minibus to take young people to a training centre.

exercise 2

1, 2, 3 all three things were more expensive than expected
4 young people couldn't afford to go
5 older people didn't go because they weren't interested in a disco

exercise 3

It was a monthly lottery which was very successful. However, the people who won were always friends and relatives of the chairman. It was discovered that he chose the winners and stuck their winning ticket to the inside of the drum so that he knew where to find it.

ideas plus prediction

In **exercise 3** you could play the first part of the story (the 'successful' part), but stop the tape just as it gets to the introduction of the 'con trick' i.e. after '... one of the members noticed that the winning ticket always belonged to a close friend or relative.' Check learners have understood the story so far, then ask them to predict how the trick was done in pairs. Elicit one or two suggestions, without confirming or rejecting any, then play the last past of the story.

exercise 1

1 coping	3 fiasco	5 achieve
2 handle	4 make	6 succeed

language point *cope (with) / handle / deal with*

These items are often very similar in meaning.

Handle and *deal with* are synonymous in most contexts when they mean to *control a situation* (often one that has a problem), e.g. *He handled / dealt with the distribution problems efficiently.* Remember that both items have separate meanings as well: *Don't handle* (= touch) *the food without washing your hands; We deal with* (= do business with) *that company quite a lot.*

Cope (with) refers more to the ability or inability of someone or something to keep going under difficult circumstances, e.g. *While her business partner was in hospital she coped very well. He's on his own with three children and I think he finds it difficult to cope.*

how to ... have a successful interview

60 – 70 mins

what <u>not</u> to say or do

- This short reading activity comes from the Internet and is a typical attachment that is sent to amuse people around the world. It is intended as reading for fun, so avoid getting involved in dealing with vocabulary in the text. Learners should just read and react. You may need to demonstrate the meaning of *arm wrestle*.

greet and make small talk

- Learners can brainstorm with a partner in **exercise 1**, and compare with another pair. Elicit their ideas in open discussion afterwards, but avoid passing judgement or you will pre-empt the content of the listening activity.
- Play the recordings in **exercise 2**, and let learners react with a partner, then as a class. You can ask them to point out ways in which the second interview is more welcoming.
- For **exercise 3**, learners have to listen intensively for accuracy. Are the phrases in the **natural English** box **exactly** the same as the ones they hear? First ask learners to look at the phrases, then play the recording, pausing briefly to allow time to tick the ones which are the same. Replay the second recording if necessary.
- Go over the answers. If you think learners need help with the responses, you could elicit them and write them on the board (see answer key).
- **Exercise 4** gives learners controlled practice of the conversation. See **ideas plus** on the right.
- **Exercise 5** may well provide some interesting cross-cultural discussion. In some contexts, interviewers may take a very different stance, and the whole nature of the interviews may be quite different; there is no right or wrong answer to this. Monitor and ask learners to tell the class anything interesting at the end.

grammar *do, will,* or *would*

- This is a very short focus on grammar. See **language point** on the right. **Exercise 1** can be done as a class activity or in pairs.
- For **exercise 2**, you can do an example together first, reminding them that they have <u>not</u> been offered the job yet.

sell yourself

- This exercise aims to help learners structure and prepare their speech, which they will find very useful in the **extended speaking** activity. If they can plan in advance what they are going to say, it will give them more confidence for the interview. (In fact, this is what many people would do if they were going to a job interview in real life.) Monitor while learners are planning. They could make notes alone, practise saying their *speech* to themselves, then put the notes away and tell a partner from memory.

end the interview

- Finally, learners practise ending an interview. It is important that they bring interviews to an appropriate end, otherwise the listener will not know when to leave; we included this **natural English** box because in our research data, many learners failed to do this. Give learners time to practise.
- This activity can be done in pairs, or individually as suggested here, so that learners can look at their partner's work afterwards and make comments and suggestions. If you prefer, give this task for homework, so that learners can talk about it the following day.

exercise 2

The second interviewer is more welcoming because: he checks the woman's name, and gets it right; he greets her politely; he offers to take her coat and offers her a seat; he begins with relaxing small talk – about the weather, whether she had any problems getting there; he thanks her for coming; he starts the interview positively by saying that he is impressed by her CV. He is generally much friendlier in tone.

exercise 3

Hello, it's Catherine Walker, isn't it?
Can I take your coat?

nE possible answers
That's right.
Yes, nice to meet you, too. / How do you do?
No trouble at all.
Thanks.
Thanks very much.
Yes, I know this area quite well.

ideas plus bringing dialogue to life

Here is a technique from drama training which can make dialogue practice more fun and life-like. Learners have to imagine that the speakers are famous people, e.g. a national politician, business person, film star, etc. In this case, they are interviewing someone for a job as a personal assistant. The interviewee can be famous too if they like. Once each pair has decided their two characters, they practise the dialogue in role. They can also extend the conversation, keeping in role, for other learners to listen to.

exercise 1

a would   b do / will
(See **language point** on the right.)

language point *do*, *will*, or *would*

The difference between *will* and *would* in these sentences is quite subtle. It is true to say that if someone has accepted the job, they are much more likely to use *will*, e.g. *Will I have to do shift work?* However, in the case of someone being interviewed who hasn't yet got the job, native speakers might switch between real and hypothetical forms, i.e. *do / will* and *would*. The important point is that anyone who uses *would* is going to sound more tentative, a bit more polite and less *pushy*: they are not assuming that they will be offered the job. This is perhaps a useful piece of information for non-native learners, who may have to overcome communication barriers with intonation errors, and any extra linguistic softener that they use may have a positive effect on the listener.

nE
1
A <u>Thank</u> you very <u>much</u> for <u>com</u>ing.
B Not at <u>all</u>.
A As I <u>said</u>, I'll let you <u>know</u> as soon as <u>poss</u>ible.
B That's <u>great</u>, <u>thank</u> you.
2
A <u>Right, well</u>, it was <u>very</u> nice <u>meet</u>ing you.
B Yes, <u>thank</u> you.
A <u>So</u>, I'll be in <u>touch</u> by the <u>end</u> of the <u>week</u>.
B Excellent. Many <u>thanks</u>.

ideas plus recapping

Learners will be going on to use all the language learnt in this section in the job interviews in the **extended speaking** activity, so we suggest you don't give them another role play here. However, it would be useful to bring the lesson to an end by asking learners to think for a minute about what they have discussed in the lesson about interviews: how to behave, how to put people at ease, how to structure ideas, use of the tentative form *would*, and the way to end an interview. You could then elicit from the class what they have learnt, and tell them that they are going to do an extended interview in the next section.

extended speaking interviewing

read adverts for
voluntary work

choose a job and
prepare to be
interviewed

interview a candidate,
then be interviewed

evaluate both
interviews

collect ideas

- The activity will work best at the interview stage later in the lesson if the jobs chosen are fairly evenly distributed amongst the learners. In this first section, it will help if you can try to steer learners away from all choosing the same job. Give learners plenty of time to read the adverts and think about the different jobs in **exercise 1**. *Respite care* is explained in the glossary, but you may also need to explain *board and lodgings* (= food and accommodation). Once they have had a chance to look at the jobs, have a quick show of hands; if some people are undecided, then encourage them to choose the jobs which are under-represented. You may even decide to allocate the jobs evenly yourself in order to minimize class management problems later.

- If the class does not divide neatly into pairs for **exercise 2**, you can create one or two groups of three at this stage. Learners could write the reasons together, or they could do it individually first, then share their ideas with their partner(s). You could remind them to give reasons for wanting the job, as well as reasons for being good at it.

first interview

- If you have one or more groups of three (an odd number in the class, and / or an odd number wanting to do different jobs), the interviews will take longer, and one person will have to be an observer during each interview. See **troubleshooting** on the right.

- Before learners prepare their roles, read through the **checklist** with the whole class. It is very important that the interviewer prepares their role, and doesn't just read aloud from the card. Careful thought will produce much more satisfactory and natural interviews. During this stage, both interviewer and interviewee have plenty to think about, and they can also mentally rehearse questions and answers. While learners are preparing, go round and offer any help they need.

- For the interviews, re-arrange the seating so that interviewee and interviewer are facing one another. You could demonstrate how to begin the interview with the interviewee arriving, and the interviewer standing up to greet them.

- During the first interview, monitor and make notes. Notice in particular how effectively learners are carrying out the instructions, making the candidate feel at ease, listening and responding spontaneously to each other, and not just reading out notes. Wait until the learners have done their own evaluations after the second interview before giving your own feedback.

second interview

- Give learners time to prepare again, and during the interview, make notes for feedback.

evaluate

- Explain to the class that you want them to discuss their own and each others' performance, and direct them to the questions in **evaluate**. Give them time to think (a minute or two), then let them talk in twos or threes. Monitor so that you can assess how effectively they have evaluated their performance, and check they are not being overcritical; if they are, intervene and be encouraging. At the end, bring the class together and give them general feedback from your notes, especially on the global issues.

feedback checklist

During the **extended speaking** activity, note down examples of …

- **good language use**

- **effective communication strategies**
  (turn-taking, interrupting, inviting others to speak, etc.)

- **learner errors**
  (vocabulary, grammar, pronunciation, etc.)

- **particular communication problems**

Make sure you allow time for feedback at the end of the lesson. You can use the notes you make above to <u>praise</u> effective language use and communication or, if necessary, to do some remedial work.

---

troubleshooting first interview managing the class

If you have an odd number of learners, you can still work in groups of three, but when the first interview is conducted, the third student will be an observer. In this case, you need to give the observer a task. They could look at the questions in **evaluate** at the end of the section and either make notes or try to remember what they observe. Tell them that they will contribute their feedback at the end, after all the interviews. Then swap roles and do the other interviews.

test yourself!

Want to know more? Go to the **introduction** *p.7* for ways of using **test yourself!**

1. plural nouns: proceeds, remains, facilities, expenses
   uncountable nouns: knowledge, experience, training, research, accommodation, equipment
2. breeding, endangered species, in captivity, the wild, reptiles, feed, cages and enclosures (names of reptiles also possible)
3. volunteer / voluntary, donation, fund-raising event, the disabled, prize, lottery, proceeds

1. Where on earth have you been?
2. I wouldn't be willing / prepared to do that.
3. I'll be in touch as soon as possible.
4. Did you have any problems finding us / getting here?

1. I wouldn't mind working with snakes.
2. I haven't seen her lately.
3. Do you think you can cope with this job?
4. If they offered you the job, would you accept it?

---

eight

wordlist

natural English

all over the ...
He dropped them all over the floor.
You get them all over the world.
They were all over the place.

making threats
Put ... or I'll ...
Tidy ... otherwise I won't ...

apologies and excuses
I'm sorry I didn't mean to ...
I didn't do it on purpose.
I didn't realize ...
I wasn't aware that ...

linking events in a sequence
At first ...
As time went by ...
The situation deteriorated (when) ...
Things got much worse (when) ...
Eventually things came to a head (when) ...

repeated comparatives
... is getting more and more popular
... got louder and louder
... got worse and worse

vocabulary

ways of walking
stroll
limp
stagger
crawl
march
tiptoe

expressing anger
get angry / lose one's temper
get one's own back / get revenge
have a row / quarrel
control one's temper / keep calm
irritating / get on one's nerves
swear at sb / shout abuse

wordbooster

neighbours
my neighbour opposite / down the road
the person in the flat above / below
my next-door neighbour
the flat downstairs / upstairs
the basement
across the corridor
next door but one
in the top flat

word building
complain / complaint
behave / behaviour
prove / proof
deteriorate / deterioration
threaten / threat
compromise (v, n)
suspect / suspicion
remind / reminder

glossary
doubt
do sth up
pull out
speck
in retrospect

do you get it?   25 – 30 mins

> **listen** for pleasure
> **nE** *all over the ...*
> **vocabulary** ways of walking

- Give learners a minute to think about the questions in **with a partner**, then compare ideas. See **ideas plus** below.
- Check that learners know the word *snails*, then ask them to work out what is happening in the pictures. This could be done in pairs or as a class.
- If necessary, explain the joke, or better still, get a learner to explain it if someone in the class doesn't understand it.
- In the **natural English** box, notice the stress varies in the *all over the* ... phrases. Get learners to practise saying the phrases, stressing the underlined words. They can work in pairs on the practice exercise, and again, ask them to produce the phrases in their answers to each other and in a feedback stage at the end.
- The vocabulary slot, **ways of walking**, includes verbs describing different ways of walking. You could start by demonstrating the meaning of the verbs *stroll, limp,* etc. if you think most of the verbs will be new. If you think learners will be familiar with some of them, they could do the exercise, and deduce the meaning of the words they don't know, e.g. *tiptoe* is guessable from the word form. Go over the answers, then do the **test your partner** activity for fun.

> **nE** possible answers
> litter: all over the place   people who can speak English: all over the world
> graffiti: all over the walls   an untidy person's clothes: all over the floor / place
> fast food restaurants: all over the place / world
> **ways of walking**
> *stagger* = walk unsteadily, almost falling over
> probable answers
> 1 tiptoe   2 stroll   3 stagger   4 limp   5 crawl   6 march

> **ideas plus** speaking
> An alternative lead-in to this section would be to put learners into small groups and tell them they have two minutes to brainstorm as many excuses as they can for being late. You could make it a competition to see which group makes the longest list. This is a useful way to revise vocabulary: *miss the bus / train*, etc. *oversleep, get held up in traffic, my watch was wrong, my alarm didn't go off, the car broke down, there was a transport strike*, etc.

listening confrontation

discuss which situations annoy you, and make threats using **natural English** phrases

talk about what makes you angry using vocabulary expressing anger

listen to a radio report about anti-social behaviour and say what you would say or do

focus on apologies and excuses and use these in different situations

invent your own situations and role play them

lead-in

- Ask learners to look at the pictures of anti-social behaviour, and describe what is happening in each one, either as a class or in pairs. They will probably find that there are a few words they don't know, and this will create a need for new lexical items, e.g. *put your feet up on the seat, spray* (n) and (v), *graffiti, spray can, drop litter / a wrapper, double park a car.* Feed these in at an appropriate point, writing them on the board for learners to note down.

- **Exercise 2** should provoke a little discussion, especially if learners give their reasons which you can encourage them to do. You can either let them compare with another pair, or tell the class which annoys them most and why.

- Use the short recording in the **natural English** box, or if you prefer, dictate the sentences yourself, using the tapescript on *p.28*. Focus on intonation when learners practise the phrases, as this is crucial in delivering the threat. Look at **language point** on the right.

- You could ask learners in pairs to apply the phrases to the anti-social behaviour, and they can make up their own consequences!

vocabulary expressing anger

- For **exercise 1**, learners can work alone first, then compare with a partner or in small groups. If possible, provide dictionaries to help them with meaning. See **language point** on the right.

- When you go over the answers, check that learners can also pronounce the phrases correctly, particularly the items in phonemic script. Point out that *swore* is the past tense of *swear.* Then give them a minute to study the phrases before working in pairs for **test your partner.**

- **Exercise 2** is an information gap activity. Learners can stay in the same pairs, and you can ask them to cover the exercise above and complete the gaps. They can then check their answers quickly before they do the speaking activity in **exercise 3**. **A**s should read their questions to **B**s, who should respond spontaneously (with their books shut). Then repeat the activity with **B**s reading their questions to **A**s. Monitor and note any errors for feedback.

listen to this

- Either explain the context of the listening yourself, referring learners to the picture to set the scene, or ask them to read the rubric in **exercise 1**. See **ideas plus** on the right. Play the **tune in** section and check learners' answers.

- If your learners aren't able to answer the questions about the first interviewee in **exercise 2**, go back and replay the recording. Let them compare their answers in pairs, and if necessary, listen again. If you monitor this pair work, you should be able to detect any specific problems they are having, and deal with them. Notice that learners are being asked to comment on the attitude of the second interviewees. At this level, they need to be aware of the mood speakers are conveying through intonation and choice of language.

- Before **exercise 3**, you could ask learners to guess what sort of anti-social problem Julia Weeks is going to come across next. Elicit a few answers, or ask pairs to think of a few possibilities. This will help to raise expectations and motivate learners to listen.

- **Exercises 4** and **5** give learners the opportunity to express their own opinions.

- The phrases in the **natural English** box include an example of ellipsis: *I didn't intend to,* and we can also say *I didn't mean to.* You could point out that *to* is necessary, but the verb or action may already be known or have been referred to, so is redundant. Highlight the meaning of *didn't mean to* = didn't intend / plan to; *on purpose* = deliberately; *didn't realize* = didn't know / understand. Check learners can pronounce the phrases. For **exercise 6**, let them think of what to say in each situation, then role play the situations with a partner. You could demonstrate the first situation with a learner in front of the class.

- In **exercise 7**, encourage learners to respond to their partner's apologies and excuses with phrases such as: *Oh, that's OK, it doesn't matter; Don't worry about it; Well, make sure it doesn't happen again!*

it's your turn!

- This activity gives learners the chance to make up their own situation, relevant to the learning context. Show them the example, then give them a couple of minutes to think of their situation. Monitor and check that everyone has thought of one, and if not, give any pair who is short of ideas some help, e.g. something happening in a restaurant, school, at a bus stop, on a train, etc.

exercise 1

a man on a train with his feet on the seat opposite
a young man spraying graffiti on a wall
a girl dropping litter / a wrapper
a woman double parking

nE

Put those apples back, or I'll tell your father!
Tidy your room, otherwise I won't let you watch TV!

exercise 1

1 b 2 d 3 e 4 a 5 f 6 c

✐: *get your own back; got on my nerves*

exercise 2

A lose, nerves, have, swear
B get, control, get, quarrel / have rows

exercise 1

She's outside a takeaway chicken restaurant, and she's
waiting for people to drop litter.

exercise 2

first interview
1 She dropped a wrapper in the street.
2 She was daydreaming; the paper is biodegradable
  in any case.
3 She picked it up and put it in the bin.
second interview
1 They let their children pick flowers in the park.
2 They did nothing.
3 They thought it was OK for the children to do that.
  The woman got quite angry and they had a row
  with the interviewer.

exercise 3

He double parked; his excuse was that he was going
to the dry cleaner's and wouldn't be long; he was
aggressive and not apologetic.

---

language point making threats

Or (also *or else*) and *otherwise* are used here to warn that something bad might
happen. In this case, they are not unlike *if* sentences. Compare:

If you don't stop that noise, I'll call the police.

Stop that noise, or I'll call the police.
        otherwise, I'll call the police.

Notice that after *or / otherwise*, we use *will*, not the present simple tense, as in
many other languages.

language point expressing anger

get your own back / get your revenge The first phrase is informal, and both phrases
mean that you do something bad in return when someone has harmed you in some
way. You could illustrate it with this example: there was a famous case in Britain of a
man who left his wife. To get her own back, she cut all the sleeves out of his
expensive suits, and distributed his wine collection to everyone in her village.

argument / quarrel / row These items can all be used to describe an angry
disagreement between two or more people. *A quarrel* is often a personal
disagreement; *a row* is a serious disagreement between people or organizations.
When it is between people, it can be noisy and is also slightly more informal than the
other two. *Argument* can also convey a less personal disagreement, one based on a
difference of ideas. The phrase *have a quarrel / a row / an argument* is very common.

ideas plus fifteen minutes of fame

An increasing number of radio and TV programmes feature the general public:
soliciting their opinions in the street, radio phone-ins, e-mailing live radio and TV
shows, 'reality TV' shows such as *Big Brother* and *Popstars* and *Pop Idol* (two shows
which were competitions to manufacture a pop group or solo artist). Do your
learners think these programmes are a good thing, giving the public a voice, or just
cheap programming which can make people look silly? This might make a good topic
for discussion with your class.

reading too close for comfort

70 – 90 mins

focus on different verb patterns and practise them

read a text about a *flatmate from hell*

practise natural English phrases to link events in a sequence

invent a story about a relationship that goes wrong

grammar verb patterns

- Before learners focus on the grammar, **exercise 1** tests their understanding of eight verbs which they may not be familiar with. Put learners in pairs to do this. The guide to meaning is in the context, so they need to read the sentences carefully, then support their deductions with a dictionary if available. (If dictionaries are not available, put learners in small groups to pool their knowledge.) Check the answers and clarify any problems of meaning.

- As an introduction to the grammar, you could go through the eight sentences from exercise 1 again and elicit the constructions that follow each of the verbs, i.e. *pretend* + verb in sentence 1, *claim* + *that* clause in 2, *admit* + *-ing* in 3, etc.

- Still in pairs, learners can then go on to complete **exercise 2**. This involves transferring information from the first exercise, and then adding other possible constructions for these verbs, along with the constructions for an extra four important verbs.

- Check the answers to exercise 2 and write the table of constructions up on the board. If you are working in a monolingual context and you are very familiar with the learners' first language, it is obviously sensible to spend most time on verbs which are followed by different constructions in their language and are therefore most likely to cause difficulty. See **language point** on the right.

- Give learners time to read the short text and think about **exercise 3** before putting them into pairs to discuss their responses in **exercise 4**. This prepares them for the longer text to follow.

- **Exercise 5** is a further opportunity for a personalized response to the text, within a framework which practises the different verb patterns from exercise 2. Learners could work on these sentences together, or they could spend time on them individually and then compare. You could let each pair or group decide for themselves how they wish to work.

Want to know more? Go to **how to** ... do informal testing *p.148*.

read on

- You could introduce the text with a short discussion. See **ideas plus** on the right.

- If you have used one of the ideas on the right, you might decide to move straight into the text (or you may have to because of time constraints). If you haven't used these ideas, give learners time to think about **exercise 1** before discussing the questions in **exercise 2**.

- When learners have completed **exercise 3**, check their answers to the glossary. It may seem unusual to move into discussion of the text in **exercise 4** and then return to a more detailed comprehension task in **exercise 5**, but we wanted to give learners a chance to react to the content of the text, and this doesn't require a detailed understanding. When learners discuss their response, you can obviously move round the class and assess for yourself how much they have understood and remembered. You could bring the class together and elicit a few of their reactions at the end.

- Some learners may be able to do **exercise 5** immediately, but give them an opportunity to scan the text again if they need to. Check answers when they have finished.

- Introduce the **natural English** phrases. The task of matching the phrases to similar phrases in the text gives learners a chance to check they understand the items. The last pair of phrases indicating that events reached a climax (*things came to a head* / *it was the last straw*) are both very idiomatic, and they may sound a little strange alongside the rest of your learners' language, which will be less idiomatic. You can judge for yourselves how well they are able to incorporate and use the phrases in the next activity. Quickly practise the pronunciation of the phrases from the text and the box, and you could also point out that the words in brackets at the end frequently follow the **natural English** phrases.

it's your turn!

- This is a light-hearted end to the section. Give pairs five or ten minutes to invent their stories. Tell them not to write them, although they can note down the link phrases to help them to remember the framework and development of the story. When they finish, they can take it in turns to tell the story to each other, just to demonstrate they can remember the story and tell it fluently. Then, mix the pairs, so that everyone has an opportunity to tell their story to someone who doesn't know it.

 wordbooster *go to p.140*   This **wordbooster** can be used at any point in **unit eight**.

exercise 1

1 pretended	5 denies / denied
2 claimed	6 resents
3 admitted	7 attempted
4 suspected	8 threatened

exercise 2

verb + (*not*) + infinitive *promise* (*not*) *to do*	**verb** + (*that*) ... *promise* (*that*) *we* ... *suggest* (*that*) *we* ...	**verb** + *-ing* *suggest doing*
pretend	claim	deny
agree	deny	resent
attempt	pretend	admit
threaten	agree	
offer	admit	
	suspect	

exercise 5 possible answers
You could pretend not to notice.
You could attempt to catch him stealing.
He could claim that somebody else had taken it.
He may deny taking the money.
He could offer to pay the money back (if he took it).
He could promise to pay you back.
He could agree to leave immediately.
You could threaten to call the police.

exercise 3 glossary
1 d 2 c 3 e 4 f 5 b 6 a

exercise 5

1 Michelle; Sophie	5 Michelle
2 Michelle; Sophie	6 Michelle
3 Sophie	7 Michelle
4 Sophie; Michelle	8 Michelle; Sophie

nE
At first / Initially
As time went by / ... as the weeks passed
The situation deteriorated / Things took a turn for the worse
Things got much worse / Things went from bad to worse
Eventually, things came to a head / It was the last straw

language point verb patterns

Some verbs can be followed by several different constructions, and this can be confusing, e.g. *suggest* + *-ing* form and + *that* clause. Many common verbs also have different constructions from the learners' first language; this accounts for a number of common errors, e.g. *He wants ~~that you go~~; She suggested ~~me to leave together~~*.

For these reasons, correct verb patterns often require considerable practice and reinforcement. One simple way is to produce a number of cards like these:

deny | pretend | stealing the money | that we go

suggest | attempt | to break the record | to be French

Give out cards to different learners, one verb and one ending each. One learner holds up a verb and another must hold up a card with a possible way to complete the sentence correctly, e.g. *deny + stealing the money*.

ideas plus prioritizing

What makes two or more people compatible? What shared attributes do people need to be able to share a flat happily and successfully? You could introduce the topic by asking learners, in pairs or groups, to make a list. In order to focus their discussion you could limit this to six points, and to make it even more focused, you could ask them to put the six points in order of priority.

Start by giving or eliciting one or two examples, e.g. share the same sense of humour or enjoy the same kind of entertainment.

how to ... write a letter of complaint

70 – 80 mins

talk about how to write a letter of complaint

read a letter and focus on letter-writing conventions

focus on natural English phrases

study ways of linking ideas

write a letter of complaint

style and layout of a formal letter

- In this part of the lesson, learners are looking globally at what constitutes the most effective way to get the desired result from a letter of complaint. See **troubleshooting** on the right.

- You could begin this section by asking learners to talk in pairs: Do they write letters in their own language or English? If so, who to, and what kinds of letters? What was the last letter they wrote? Do they ever write letters of complaint? They could answer the same questions about e-mail. Bring the class together to share their answers quickly. If someone has written a letter of complaint, ask them to tell the class the circumstances and result, or tell them about a letter you have written yourself. This will lead into **exercise 1**.

- This activity asks learners to consider the best way to achieve one's purpose. However, there is no single correct way to write a letter of complaint, so accept any reasonable suggestions. In **exercise 2**, encourage learners to give reasons for their ideas.

- Emphasize that the letter in **exercise 3** could have been written differently, but that it seems perfectly reasonable in view of the poor service and in this particular context. Other writers might be less polite and less clear and systematic, but the approach suggested here is less likely to antagonize the reader.

- **Exercise 4** deals with letter layout and letter-writing conventions. If you have an overhead projector, make a copy of the letter onto a transparency, which will be useful for feedback, or draw the outline of a piece of paper on the board, writing in the address, date, addressee's address, and initial and final greetings. For many learners, the idea of putting your address at the top of the page will be strange, and there may be numerous other differences. Again, it can be useful to contrast the way it is done in the learners' mother tongue and in English, as suggested in question 6.

- Go over the phrases in the **natural English** box. Learners can work in pairs on the sentence completion.

grammar linking ideas

- You can direct learners to the examples which show how link phrases are used in single sentences or two sentences. Alternatively, you could introduce them by writing these sentences on the board:

  (A) *He won the match _____ (B) he was injured.*

  (A) *We know the children are safe there. _____ (B) we still worry about them.*

  Point out to learners that the ideas in A and B contrast with each other, i.e. the words in the gap have the meaning *but*. Ask them which words or phrases could go in the gaps, and put any correct suggestions on the board. At this point you can highlight the fact that some linkers, e.g. *nevertheless* and *however*, link ideas in two sentences (separated by a full stop or semi-colon) and others link ideas in one sentence, e.g. *although, despite, in spite of*.

- For **exercise 1**, learners will need to work alone, then they can compare with a partner. Check they understand that the relevant linkers show a contrast between two ideas. Then elicit the answers.

- **Exercise 2** is a diagnostic test, and can be done in pairs. Check the answers then complete the table in **exercise 3** together. This will help learners to clarify the rules of use. Assess whether they still need more practice. If so, do the **cover & check** exercises in **language reference** on *p.168*.

write a letter

- You may decide to start this activity in class, and ask learners to do the writing for homework. However, it can be very helpful to use the class time to guide learners when they are in the process of writing. Learners can plan their letters together in **exercise 1**, which will help them to generate ideas. They may also wish to change the context of the letter of complaint from those suggested, which is fine, as long as they can think of a few points of dissatisfaction. While they are planning, monitor and help where necessary.

- **Exercise 2** suggests a framework for their letter. If you prefer, you could tell them to shut their books, and work out the framework on the board as a class. See **troubleshooting** on the right.

- After writing, you can ask learners to correct their letters in **exercise 4**, using the format and language they learnt in unit 4 *pp.51 to 52*; this will be useful revision and will encourage them to work from draft to a more polished product, which is necessary for a more formal letter of this type.

- Finally, learners often find it interesting to see how their peers have tackled a writing activity, so let them read each others' letters, if they haven't already done so (**exercise 5**). This can also be a good informal way for students to learn new vocabulary from each other. Take the letters in at the end for correction and feedback in the next lesson.

exercise 1
B

exercise 3
Yes, it is. The writer followed the advice in B, except that he described (briefly) how the problems affected him personally.

exercise 4
1 in the top right-hand corner
2 the address of the person he is writing to
3 because he doesn't know the name or gender of the person he's writing to
4 It is conventional to end a letter *Yours faithfully* if you don't know the name of the person you are writing to. (People don't always keep to the conventions, however.)
5 para 1: the reason for the letter
para 2: information about delays, i.e. the main complaint
para 3: dissatisfaction with the service and state of the train (secondary complaints)

nE
the carriages just got hotter and hotter

exercise 1
although the guard apologized ...
Despite the fact that the journey ...
However, there was no apology ...

exercise 2
1 Despite / in spite of
2 Although ...
3 Neverthless / However
4 in spite of / despite
5 although
6 Despite / in spite of

exercise 3
Although it was very cold ...
Despite / In spite of the fact that ...
Despite / In spite of feeling ...
In spite of / Despite the cold ...
It was very cold. Nevertheless / However, ...

troubleshooting cultural differences

People in different cultures do not necessarily approach complaints in the same way, and the content and organization of ideas in a letter may vary. Learners may find the letter provided on the page quite straightforward, while it will be contrary to the expectations of others. If you are in a monolingual teaching situation, it might be interesting to write a similar letter in the learners' own language, translate it into English, and then compare the differences between the letter on *p.98* and the translated one. Is the information organized in the same way? Is there any different information, or are any parts omitted? Is the tone similar, or does the letter approach the complaint in a different way? Learners may find this comparative approach revealing and memorable.

language point linking ideas

Link words are crucial for a number of reasons:
• Learners will come across them constantly when reading and to some extent listening, so need to be able to understand them immediately.
• At this level, learners are aiming for increasingly sophisticated ways of expressing themselves; linking ideas coherently is one way of achieving this.
• Link words play an important role in contextual guesswork. If learners can understand them, they can make deductions about other new words, e.g. *He offered to pay the restaurant bill despite being skint*.
(If *despite* suggests a contrast between the two ideas, then it would suggest that he didn't have much money.)

troubleshooting writing paragraphs

If you feel your class needs help with paragraphing, here are some suggestions:
1 Rewrite a text (a letter or a narrative) with no paragraphing. Ask them to look at where there is a change of topic or argument, or a new development. Guide them as to the number of paragraphs they should create.
2 Use a text like *Single White Female* in the **student's book** on *p.95*; preferably one they haven't seen, though. Type out <u>only</u> the topic sentences, i.e. the first sentence of each paragraph. In pairs, learners make notes about the possible content of each paragraph, guided by the topic sentences. They read the original to compare.
3 Give learners a jumbled letter with say, three main ideas (about ten sentences jumbled). Ask them to reorganize them into three distinct paragraphs, and to give a heading for each paragraph to justify their ideas. (This is best done if you type out the sentences, photocopy them, and cut them up: one per pair or three.)

extended speaking nasty neighbours

read part of a story and decide how it ends

listen to the ending

develop a story with your own characters

tell a partner your story

write your story

collect ideas

- The story in **exercise 1** recycles quite a lot of new language from the unit, but also provides a model which may help learners when they come to produce their own story later.

- The comprehension task gives you an opportunity to listen and check that the learners have understood the events so far. You can clarify the meaning of any vocabulary items if necessary, e.g. *nasty* (= mean or unpleasant). If you are satisfied with the way they are able to describe the events, put them into groups for **exercise 2**. Don't let the discussion go on too long (it's not the main speaking activity), but equally, don't bring it to an end before learners are agreed on their ending, and while they are clearly engaged in the activity. At the end, elicit ideas from the different groups, then play the ending (**exercise 3**). Ask for reactions from different groups to check they have understood. For example: *How is the ending different from yours? What do you think of this ending? Is it as good as yours?*

develop the story

- Now that learners have worked their way through an episode of *Nasty Neighbours*, they should have a clearer idea of what is expected of them, and they may have picked up one or two ideas. **Exercise 4** builds on this further by asking learners to brainstorm other causes of dispute. In our research we found that learners could often provide these by recounting personal experiences. While they talk, move round to make sure each group is able to add to the list.

- Point out the photos which learners must choose their characters from. In particular, explain that they can take notes, but at this stage they should not try to write out the full story. If in doubt about this, see **troubleshooting** on the right. Then go through the story framework. After that, give the groups a time limit for their stories, e.g. fifteen minutes, but as always, be prepared to be flexible with this if they finish sooner or need more time.

- When learners have completed their story, it is a good idea for each learner to rehearse it. This will help to ensure that a) they remember all the facts and get them right, and b) they are able tell the story fluently and in an interesting way. When you are satisfied they can do this, move on.

tell your story

- Put each learner with a new partner to exchange stories. Monitor and make notes while they are doing this. At the end, choose one of the best stories and ask one of the group to tell the rest of the class.

write your story

- Learners can do this for homework, and shouldn't find it too difficult as they already have a model to help them, a story framework, and the notes of their own story. You could collect them in the next lesson and correct them.

feedback checklist

During the **extended speaking** activity, note down examples of ...

- **good language use**

- **effective communication strategies**
(turn-taking, interrupting, inviting others to speak, etc.)

- **learner errors**
(vocabulary, grammar, pronunciation, etc.)

- **particular communication problems**

Make sure you allow time for feedback at the end of the lesson. You can use the notes you make above to <u>praise</u> effective language use and communication or, if necessary, to do some remedial work.

---

troubleshooting develop the story making notes

If you haven't already spent time with the class on note taking, and you think your learners may not fully understand what they have to do when 'making notes', you could spend a bit of time on this now. Using the earlier story about Beck and Carter, for example, you could build up notes on the board with the learners. The first paragraph might look something like this:

- Beck moved next door to Carter
- at first fine, then injury to cat
- Beck's dog?
- Beck angry: accused, but no proof

You could then ask learners to make notes on the second paragraph. You could give them a bit more guidance by telling them that they should be able to do this in four to five separate points, with each point not taking more than seven or eight words.

test yourself!

Want to know more? Go to the **introduction** *p.7* for ways of using **test yourself!**

1 stroll, limp, march, stagger, tiptoe, crawl
2 have a row, lose / control your temper, swear at sb, shout abuse, get your revenge
3 threat, complaint, proof, deterioration, reminder

1 Sorry, I didn't do it on purpose.
2 I wasn't aware that you were there.
3 He still played, despite being ill / despite his illness.
4 She denied doing it.

1 Put that down or **I'll** call the police.
2 The woman in the **downstairs** flat is French.
3 He suggested **that we take** a later train. / He suggested **taking** a later train.
4 At ~~the~~ first, we got on very well, but later ...

nine

wordlist

natural English

expressing great surprise
I nearly fainted / died.
I couldn't believe my eyes / ears!
I couldn't believe it!

whenever, wherever, etc.
whenever you feel like it / it suits you
wherever you want
whatever you like

reacting to ideas
That's very original.
That could be very successful.
Maybe you should avoid anything to do with ...
I'm not sure that would work very well.
My (main) worry is that ...

the + comparative, the + comparative
The older you get, the happier you become.
The more money you earn, the more you want.
The sooner we leave, the better.

superlative + ever
It's the best talk I've ever been to.
That was the funniest film I've ever seen.
She gave me the most useful advice I've ever had.

vocabulary

books and publishing
title
publish
come out
hardback
softback
front / back cover
index
contents page
a copy (of a book)

advertising
take / last
logo / slogan
notice / advert
invent / make up
persuade / convince
advertising / publicity
brand / make

wordbooster

literal and figurative meaning
sink (v)
stream (v)
float (v)
flood (v)
wave (n)
leak (v)
the deep end
out of one's depth

affixes
fat-free, sugar-free, alcohol-free
home-made, hand-made
locally-grown, home-grown, organically-grown
non-iron, non-stick, non-slip
water-proof, bullet-proof, sound-proof

glossary

loo ⓢ
faint (v)
blurb
sequel
take the plunge
tackle a problem
grab sb's attention
commit suicide
get across an idea

life with Agrippine   25 – 30 mins

read for pleasure
nE expressing great surprise
vocabulary books and publishing

- This cartoon is about books and book signings. Before reading the cartoon, learners could look at the **books and publishing** vocabulary, and ask and answer the questions about their **natural English student's book**.

- Give learners a minute to compare their ideas to the questions in **cartoon time**. Then play the recording.

- In the **natural English** box, the phrases all express great surprise, so the intonation is significant; the voice range is wide. When you play the recording, draw learners' attention to this, and you can use the tape as an intonation model for your learners to imitate. Learners sometimes feel a bit self-conscious about this, but you can tell them that this intonation is perfectly natural in English. They can then invent their own surprising news to tell a partner.

nE
When I <u>saw</u> my re<u>sults</u>, I nearly <u>fainted</u>.
When I saw <u>Mary</u> with that <u>boy</u>, I nearly <u>died</u>!
I <u>could</u>n't believe my <u>eyes</u> when I opened the <u>box</u>.
I <u>could</u>n't be<u>lieve</u> it when I heard the <u>news</u>.

books and publishing
1 **natural English**; Oxford University Press
2 2003
3 softback
4 front cover: the title, the authors' names, the level (upper-intermediate), a picture of Agrippine, and sky with clouds; back cover: the blurb (see glossary), a picture of Agrippine, a list of all the **natural English** components, the website address
5 contents pages on *pp.2* to *5*
6 you'll have to count these

listening making a sales pitch

focus on advertising vocabulary

talk about the advantages of buying things on the Internet using **natural English** phrases

listen to people making a sales pitch for an e-business

discuss which idea is best and why

present an e-business idea to a partner and react using **natural English** phrases

vocabulary advertising

- Do the first example in **exercise 1** on the board to check that learners know what to do. Make it clear that sometimes more than one answer is possible. Learners can work alone or in pairs, and use dictionaries if available. See **language point** on the right.

- The items given in **exercise 2** often present pronunciation problems for learners; this short exercise gives them controlled practice.

- Learners may have different answers for **exercise 3**, especially if they are a multilingual group. Asking them to think about the differences will give them time to process the items, which may help them to remember them. With a monolingual group you can discuss whether any of the items are false friends, e.g. *notice* and *publicity* are false friends in some romance languages. The *Oxford Advanced Learner's Dictionary* (2000 edition onwards) includes special notes for *persuade / convince* and *take / last* in the feature, *Which Word?*

Want to know more? Go to **how to ...** use dictionaries with learners (lexical information), *p.177.*

- For a little revision in a later lesson, pairs could produce a short gap-fill exercise with their own sentences for three or four of the items in exercise 1. They can pass them to other pairs to complete.

listen to this

- In **exercise 1**, look at the **natural English** box first with learners, then ask them if they have used or noticed this language before. Give them a minute together to think of some advantages of buying goods on the Internet, e.g. you can find whatever you want; you can do it whenever it suits you; you can buy goods wherever you are.

- In **exercise 2** there is a synopsis of the content of the recording. This is in fact from a real TV series, and the final entries were broadcast over a week.

- Let learners read the sentences in **exercise 3** so that they are familiar with the ideas before they listen. After they have listened to Michelle Richie in the **listening challenge** (**exercise 4**), you might like to try the suggestion in **ideas plus.**

- Once learners have discussed their reactions in **exercise 5**, giving their reasons, they could have a class vote. (In fact, Joe Rajko was one of two winners, and his website is at youreable.com if your learners would like to visit it.)

it's your turn!

- If your learners need more help, you could put them in A pairs or B pairs first for **exercise 1**, to prepare their presentation together. Give learners time to absorb the information and rehearse telling it, eventually without looking. It doesn't need to be a completely faithful rendition. Monitor and help where necessary.

- Go over the language in the **natural English** box. They will need this in **exercise 2**.

- Reorganize the learners into A / B pairs to do their presentations. These are quite small scale, and will help to prepare them for the more challenging presentations they do in the **extended speaking** activity.

exercise 1

1a logo	1b slogan
2a notice	2b advert
3a make up / invent	3b invented
4a persuaded	4b convinced
5a advertising	5b publicity
6a make	6b brand

language point words with overlapping meaning

last / take *Take* describes the amount of time you need to do something, e.g. *It took an hour to clean the flat.* *Last* describes the duration or the length of time something continues, e.g. *The turbulence on the flight lasted for ten minutes.*

logo / slogan *Logos* are designs or symbols; *slogans* are words.

notice / advert *Notices* give information; *adverts* try to sell you things in the media.

invent / make up These can be synonymous when referring to stories, songs, slogans, i.e. words and ideas. However, new products are invented, not made up, e.g. *Mobile phones were invented relatively recently.*

persuade / convince These can be interchangeable, although *persuade* has the sense of making someone agree to do something by reasoning, e.g. *I persuaded him to accept the job.* *Convince* means to make someone believe something is true, e.g. *she convinced me that the government was wrong about the transport policy.*

publicity / advertising *Publicity* involves attracting attention through the media, e.g. *David Beckham attracts a great deal of publicity.* *Advertising* means trying to sell products and services through the media.

make / brand Pieces of machinery or equipment such as cars or washing machines are *makes*; a *brand* is something non-mechanical, e.g. a brand of coffee, toothpaste, etc.

exercise 2

Joe Rajko wants to provide a service for disabled people and their families, friends, and carers.

exercise 3

1 no, 15%
2 no, disabled people, their family, friends, and carers
3 yes
4 no, you can find information about it
5 yes
6 yes

exercise 4

Her website is *mykindofholiday.com* which gives information about holidays and travel. It will give you different options for hotels, car hire, exhibitions, places to eat on holiday, etc. It can give information about different types of holiday at a range of prices. Travellers will have a place on the website to chat to each other, give tips, etc.

ideas plus reading aloud

The music on the recording builds up the tension in the presentation and makes the sales pitch sound exciting. If you have an outgoing class with a sense of fun, you could try this. First, get learners in threes to practise reading one of the sales pitches aloud. Monitor and help with pronunciation. Then, in each group, one person should read the presentation, while the other two provide the 'sound effects': it could be very gentle drumming, or humming, or making da-da-DA! noises, as they build up to a crescendo. They swap, and a different person reads the script. The best groups could perform for the class.

ideas plus e-businesses

If you have an imaginative class, or one with a fair amount of Internet or business experience, they could devise their own million-pound idea together. They could be selling services or products. In this case, learners could work in small groups, using the listening as a model, and produce their one-minute sales pitch to the class. If you do this, you will need to allow a lot more time for this activity.

reading accentuate the positive

discuss TV adverts

focus on grammar of making comparisons

read a text about an advertising campaign for marriage

practise making comparisons using **natural English** phrases

interview others about their opinions on marriage

lead-in

- See **ideas plus** on the right.

- Without the use of video, you could introduce the topic by asking for names of famous products that are advertised on TV. Can learners describe one or two of these adverts, and give you the slogans, or perhaps name or sing the song that accompanies them?

- Put learners in pairs to discuss the questions. Conduct a short feedback at the end. This might include words or phrases you want to teach, some error correction, or just a summary of the adverts that are most popular and unpopular with your learners.

grammar making comparisons

- Learners will have met the *as … as* construction for making comparisons before, but will be less familiar with the use of specific adverbs for emphasis. For the majority of learners, this probably won't be part of their productive language.

- Learners can do **exercise 1** individually or in pairs, then you can check their answers.

- For **exercise 2**, it is a good idea to practise the phrases within the original sentences. Point out the weak form /əz/ and also the fact that the adverb in each sentence needs to be stressed. Listen to one or two examples round the class to elicit a good model, then give learners a minute to practise saying the sentences, individually or in pairs. See **ideas plus** on the right. Move round the class and monitor while they are doing this, and correct where necessary.

- Give pairs a couple of minutes to do **exercise 3** before they make comparisons in **exercise 4**. Again, go round the class and monitor their comparisons to check they are forming correct sentences, but don't comment at this stage on the content of their comparisons.

- Mix the pairs for **exercise 5** and listen to their comments.

read on

- Direct learners to the table for **exercise 1** and read through the statements and the example together. Give them five minutes to complete the other columns; they should produce at least one reason in each case, but they can add more if they wish.

- Form groups for the discussion in **exercise 2**. It is a good idea to discuss the ideas from exercise 1 first, then introduce the second part which substitutes *women* for *men*. Allow groups to select the two statements they wish to discuss. At the end bring the class together for a brief feedback, but don't confirm or reject any of their ideas at this stage (the text does this in the next activity).

- If you tell the class that the text answers the questions they have been discussing, they will be more motivated to read it. They can then work on the **glossary** for **exercise 3** and answer the question in **exercise 4**. You could check both exercises together, and ask them which answers they find most surprising.

- Before moving on, you could do further exploitation of vocabulary in the text. See **language point** on the right.

- The structure highlighted in the **natural English** box introduces another way of making a comparison, and with a monolingual group it may be interesting to compare how learners would express a similar concept in their language. Go through the examples. For the first, second, and last statements, you could also ask them if they agree. Get the class to scan the text for a further example of the construction, then put learners in pairs to complete the sentences in an appropriate way. At the end they can compare with another pair, or you can bring the class together to listen to some examples.

it's your turn!

- You could brainstorm one or two topics in **exercise 1** to give learners some ideas, e.g. What is the best age to get married? Don't give too many examples though, otherwise learners may find it difficult to think up their own questions. If any of the pairs are struggling, you can always give them some individual help while the others are working.

- When each pair has their questions, they can circulate and do **exercise 2**. Before they start, encourage learners to support their opinions with reasons and / or examples. During the interviews, monitor their discussions and collect examples of language use for feedback; some positive feedback and some relevant error correction.

ideas plus using video playback

If you have access to video playback, this is an ideal opportunity to use it. Record a selection of TV adverts, at home or at school, and play them to the class at the beginning of the lesson. You could turn the sound down and ask the learners for a commentary and reactions. Alternatively, play the ads with sound and ask some comprehension questions. Either way, it will help to bring the topic alive in the classroom.

exercise 1
a 1 b 3, 4 c 2

ideas plus mumble drills

Although oral practice is obviously more meaningful in pairs when any conversation is involved, there are occasions when learners can work alone, particularly to practise unconnected sentences. In fact, some learners like the opportunity to get intensive practice on their own, working at their own pace, and without any external pressure. Tell learners to repeat the sentences fairly quietly to themselves (hence the term *mumble drill*), then they won't disturb others. At the same time, you can still move round and listen, giving help where necessary. This type of activity is a change from the usual pairs practice of spoken input.

exercise 3 glossary
take the plunge, tackle a problem, grab sb's attention; commit suicide; get across an idea

exercise 4
all the statements are false
nE
the happier you are the longer you live
possible answers
1 fatter you'll get
2 better you'll feel
3 more you practise
4 more tickets you buy

language point lexical phrases

The text includes a number of phrases which some learners won't know or use, and yet they may not realize this as the phrases consist of individual words that are all familiar. For example:

call sb in = ask sb to come and help you with a problem

in a bad way = sb or sth is in a terrible condition or situation

for one thing ...; *for another ...* = two phrases commonly used together to introduce reasons for sth

in view of = because of

You could highlight these phrases and ask learners to explain the meaning; or you could underline the key word in each case (*call, way, thing, another, view*) and ask learners first to identify the whole phrase, then explain the meaning.

Want to know more? Go to **how to ...** develop lexis at higher levels *p.160*.

how to ... give a successful presentation

70 – 80 mins

focus on linking words and practise them

evaluate ideas which help in giving presentations

listen to advice on giving presentations

summarize the most important advice

grammar linking words

- If you have had experience of giving a short talk or presentation, you could tell the class about your experience (or one of them); this will serve as a model for the activity which follows and stimulate interest in the topic.

- Give learners time to think and plan in **exercise 1**, and be prepared to go round and help. Learners with no experience of giving presentations may be the ones who need most help; it may be difficult for them to imagine how they would feel.

- If you only have a third or a quarter of the class with experience of giving talks, form small groups for **exercise 2**. You should aim for at least one person in each group with an experience to talk about. You could ask the learner with the most interesting anecdote to tell the whole class, and encourage others to ask them questions about it.

- **Exercise 3** integrates the main language focus with recommendations for giving talks or presentations. Highlight the example clearly and ask learners to explain the meaning of *so that* (= *in order to* here). They can then complete the rest of the exercise, individually or in pairs. If they work on their own, give them a chance to compare with a partner before you check the answers. When you do this, you could ask learners to paraphrase the linking words. They will see short explanations for each one in their books in a moment, but it's a good idea if they can produce an accurate paraphrase themselves. With a monolingual group, you could also ask for a translation, but only if there is a clear equivalent in the learners' first language. See **language point** on the right.

- **Exercise 4** is an opportunity for some controlled practice of the sentences, some of which are quite long and difficult, but it is also a chance for learners to react to the ideas and voice their own opinions. You might wish to separate out these activities. Start with the controlled practice, and give feedback on the learners' rhythm and fluency; then mix the pairs and form groups for the freer, personalized response.

- **Exercise 5** should be straightforward if your learners were able to paraphrase the linking words earlier, but it is important they have a clear written record.

- Before learners work on **exercise 6**, you might like to highlight this use of *stick* (*to* sth) in question 1. Try to elicit the meaning (= keep), and point out that it is quite informal, and also frequent. Go round and monitor the pairs, and note down any points that may require clarification or consolidation. Bring the class together and listen to examples from the different pairs. You could invite different learners to comment on the examples they hear; are they logical, and do others agree with the idea expressed?

give your talk with confidence

- You could ask learners, in pairs or as an open class, to describe what is happening in each of the pictures. If they do that, they will probably use or perhaps learn vocabulary that comes up in the listening passage which follows, e.g. the verb *to lean on / against sth*; this will make the listening task a bit easier. Play the recording for **exercise 1** and check the answers related to the pictures.

- Play the recording again (**exercise 2**), and elicit the additional advice.

- Highlight the target pattern in the **natural English** box, then get learners to find the example of the structure in the tapescript in the **listening booklet** on *p.30*. At the same time, you could answer any other questions they might have about the tapescript. Then put them in pairs to practise the superlative + *ever* structure and listen to examples round the class when they have finished.

- It would seem natural to finish this lesson with a short presentation, but that is one of the main objectives of the **extended speaking** activity. At this stage, the important thing is that the learners have picked up some ideas that will really help them in the next section when they put theory into practice. See **ideas plus** on the right for a suggestion to make this final stage more memorable.

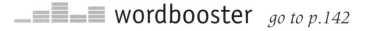 **wordbooster** *go to p.142*   This **wordbooster** can be used at any point in **unit nine**.

exercise 3

Put your main points in a logical sequence, otherwise the audience won't be able to follow.

Keep the notes short and simple so that you can read them easily at a glance.

Write your first two sentences and memorize them, as this will help you feel less nervous at the beginning.

Rehearse as much as possible in order to memorize the content and feel confident.

Have an extra copy of your talk in case you lose one.

exercise 5

1 so that   2 as   3 otherwise   4 in case

exercise 6 possible answers

1 (otherwise) the audience will get confused.
2 (so that) the audience go away with a positive impression.
3 (as) the audience will know if you are lying.
4 (in case) you drop them.
5 (in order to) feel fresh for your talk.

language point linking words

Some concepts in English are expressed in a different way in other languages, e.g. purpose clauses in Spanish use a preposition (*para*) followed by an infinitive (*He went there ~~for~~ to buy a film*). Some languages may have a literal equivalent for a concept in English, but then have different syntax after it, e.g. *otherwise* might be followed by the present tense (or a subjunctive); *in case* might be followed by *will* (or a subjunctive). Think about what happens in your learners' language so that you can pre-empt or highlight any problems.

exercise 1

stand behind something and lean on it
eye contact is important
use your hands to emphasize what you are saying

exercise 2

other advice includes:

be natural; practise in front of a mirror or in front of other people; look at individuals, especially if they seem unfriendly; don't cross your arms – it looks nervous / defensive

nE

... the best advice I've ever had was simply be natural.

ideas plus wall poster

Learners could transfer their ideas for the final exercise to a wall poster. If possible, give each pair a large piece of paper. On it, the learners are going to put their tips for giving presentations. They must decide what ideas to include and how they are going to organize it, but you could give them an example to start them thinking (and provide a structure for any pair that don't have ideas of their own). It could be in three sections:

section 1: maximum of three key pieces of advice (the most important recommendations)

section 2: maximum of three additional suggestions which may help

section 3: maximum of three things to avoid

Give each pair ten to fifteen minutes to discuss and write their poster, and then stick it on the classroom wall. When everyone has finished, they can walk round, read them all, and compare.

extended speaking advertise it!

listen to adverts and evaluate them

produce an advert in groups

present the advert to the class

collect ideas

- The aim of the first two activities in this section is to create interest in the subject, and to provide ideas for the learners' own adverts which they will produce later. When you play the radio adverts in **exercise 1**, don't spend too long on a detailed understanding of them; learners' reactions are more important, and they should provide a light-hearted start to the lesson. This listening aims to help learners to think about the atmosphere and tone of an advert.

- The advertising storyboard in **exercise 2** takes learners through the structure and development of an advert, and shows them the characters, the storyline, the voice over, and the slogan. This will serve as a framework for their own adverts. When they react in pairs, it doesn't matter whether they like the advert, find it funny, silly, or whatever; you just want to elicit a reaction. In many cultures, humour is an important aspect of advertising, but it may not be in the culture of your learners. Give them time to think about their ideas for **exercise 3**, then compare in pairs.

> **exercise 1**
> 1   the first advert is for washing powder; the second advert is for Network Q, which checks out used cars
>
> **exercise 3**
> We're calm, we're friendly, we're efficient.

produce an advert

- For **exercises 5** and **6,** organize your learners into appropriate small groups (not more than four per group). See **troubleshooting** on the right.

- Hand out any props once they have decided what to advertise, and look at the **checklist** in **exercise 7** together carefully. Be prepared for the fact that the discussion in groups will take a while to get going; they will have to brainstorm ideas and eliminate some before they can decide on the structure and situation in their advert. Monitor, and see if any groups are having problems coming up with ideas. Be prepared to feed in one or two ideas to help them. Groups may approach this task in different ways: some might start with quite a lot of basic discussion, mapping out the storyline carefully and planning their slogan, etc. while others may launch into dialogue writing once they have the characters.

- During the activity, you will need to monitor as suggested above, but you should also take notes of language used for feedback at the end.

- If one group finishes before the others, you can tell them to go on to the next section, **give a presentation**. It is unlikely that groups will finish at the same time; however, if you give regular time signals, e.g. tell learners they have ten minutes left, it should help them to hurry things along.

give a presentation

- You may decide to leave the presentations to the next lesson if you have run out of time. If so, the rehearsal stage will be even more necessary.

- Go round and help when learners are rehearsing, especially in any way which will make their advert or presentation easier to follow. This is the purpose of the rehearsal stage, and it will build confidence.

- You could ask learners if they would like to video or tape their presentations to go over afterwards. Voting at the end is optional.

- Finally, give learners feedback on the language points you collected during the monitoring, and of course, praise for their finished results.

feedback checklist

During the **extended speaking** activity, note down examples of …

- **good language use**

- **effective communication strategies**
  (turn-taking, interrupting, inviting others to speak, etc.)

- **learner errors**
  (vocabulary, grammar, pronunciation, etc.)

- **particular communication problems**

Make sure you allow time for feedback at the end of the lesson. You can use the notes you make above to praise effective language use and communication or, if necessary, to do some remedial work.

---

troubleshooting producing an advert

This is an activity in which your learners have complete freedom over the language they use; don't try to force them into using specific language from the unit. If they do, so much the better, but the language they will ultimately use in their advert is quite unpredictable, since it will depend on their choice of product, situation, and characters.

As this activity is very much in the learners' control, you may be worried that one group, for example, may not come up with an idea for an advert. This is a risk, of course, but remember that learners have already looked at several models, they are surrounded by adverts in their own language, and the guidelines and checklist in the materials are carefully staged. The most important thing for you to do is to organize the groups to ensure that you have one or two learners in each group with ideas to offer. One other thing you can do is to bring in some props: bars of chocolate, packets of soap powder, a flu remedy, etc. to stimulate ideas. These can then be used in the presentations.

test yourself!

Want to know more? Go to the **introduction** *p.7* for ways of using **test yourself!**

1 sink, float, flood, wave, leak, deep end, out of one's depth
2 I nearly fainted, I couldn't believe it, I couldn't believe my eyes / ears
3 sound-proof, water-proof, bullet-proof; fat-free, alcohol-free, sugar-free; hand-made, home-made

1 Come whenever it suits you.
2 That's the funniest joke I've ever heard.
3 Take it with you in case you need it.
4 The film isn't nearly as good as the book.

1 She's just as intelligent **as** her brother.
2 **The** more you work, **the** more you earn.
3 Leave early, otherwise you **will be** late.
4 Big companies do a lot of **advertising** on TV.

ten

wordlist

natural English

things like that / that sort of thing
They serve coffee, juice, and that sort of thing.
I need soap, shampoo, and stuff / things like that.
We discussed organic food, and issues like that.

expressions with tell
I can't tell X from Y.
Can you tell X just by looking?
Can you tell the difference between ...?

buying time to think
Let me think ...
That's an interesting question ...
I've never really thought about that.
I'll have to think about that.

adding ideas
In addition, ...
Furthermore, ...
Moreover, ...
What's more, ...
... as well.

clarifying your position
That's not what I meant.
That's not what I was trying to say.
No, what I meant was ...
What I'm trying to say is ...

vocabulary

memory
learn sth by heart
on the tip of my tongue
absent-minded
have a vague memory of sth
it rings a bell
my mind went blank

making judgements
immoral / wrong and unacceptable
a shame / a pity
ridiculous / stupid and absurd
a nuisance / annoying
harmful / damaging
upsetting / it makes you sad or angry
cruel / it causes pain and suffering
inevitable / it's bound to happen
justifiable / there's a good reason for it
illegal / it's against the law

wordbooster

animals
owl
zebra
bear
leopard
elephant
panda
snake
crocodile
scorpion
poison
bite
sting
covered in spots
fur
breed
skin
stripes
herd
in danger of extinction
beak
hunt

word building
capture / captive
attraction / attractive
cruelty / cruel
persuasion / persuasive
hunger / hungry
harm / harmful / harmless
justification / (un)justifiable
disgrace / disgraceful
sense / (in)sensitive
destruction / destructive
stress / stressful
protection / protective

glossary
absent-minded
tunnel vision
muffled
take (sth) for granted
disorientated
jostle sb

as nature intended?

do you get it?   25 – 30 mins

listen for pleasure
nE *things like that / that sort of thing*
vocabulary memory

- You could begin with the personalization activity, or for a different warmer, see **ideas plus** below.
- Learners can either describe the pictures together, or do it as a class activity. They should be able to identify a few examples of the couple's forgetfulness.
- Play the recording. If anyone hasn't understood the joke, explain it or ask a learner to explain it.
- The phrases in the **natural English** box are very common in spoken English, and if learners can use these, they will sound natural. You could ask them to identify where Michael used one of these expressions when telling the joke by looking at the tapescript on *p.34* (*things like that*). You may need to point out that *stuff* is a general (and quite informal) word meaning *things*; while *issues* is another general word meaning *subjects / topics* for discussion. Ask learners to repeat the phrases and then do the exercise alone or together.
- In the vocabulary activity, **memory**, learners are likely to know a few of the items, and they may be able to guess the rest. Go over the answers, and encourage learners to make a note of these useful phrases and idioms.

nE possible answers
1 that sort of thing
2 stuff like that
3 places / countries like that
memory
1 bell   2 vague   3 by heart
4 issues / topics like that
5 is full of clothes, toiletries, and stuff like that
6 *their own answers here*
4 absent-minded   5 blank   6 tongue

---

ideas plus memory games

1 Most teachers are familiar with *Kim's game*, in which you take into class a tray with about twelve to fifteen objects on it, e.g. a pencil sharpener, a packet of tissues, etc. and give learners two minutes to memorize the objects. You then remove the tray and they have to write them down; the winner is the person who remembers the most.

2 Another game is to make a list of fifteen items of vocabulary, ten of which you have taught in the previous week. Dictate the list, then learners tick the ones they think you taught them.

3 Finally, if you have a monolingual group, put them in pairs and ask them to draw one side of a coin or bank note of their currency without looking. One should draw, but they should both discuss what goes where (this is a communication activity). Their drawing ability is not being tested, but they may be interested to see how good their memories are for everyday objects when they compare with the real thing at the end of the activity.

lead-in

- Give learners a minute to think of someone to talk about; most learners can talk about an elderly relative, although it is important they only discuss this topic if it is not too sensitive. If you like, start by telling the learners about an elderly person you know. If they do not have anyone to talk about, you could ask them to comment on the photos. Do they think these people are representative of elderly people today? Which ones would they like to be?

grammar definite or zero article

- Give learners a minute or two to think about **exercise 1** before they discuss the points with a partner. While learners are thinking about **exercise 2** you could put the sentences on the board. Ask them to compare their ideas in **exercise 3**, then elicit the answers, adding the rules alongside the sentences as you go through for learners to copy. They can then work together or alone on **exercise 4**. Go to the **cover & check** exercises in the **language reference** on *p.170* if necessary.

- **Exercise 5** gives learners a chance to use the grammar and provide their own ideas for small group discussion in **exercise 6**. While they are writing, go round and monitor, correcting as required.

Want to know more? Go to **how to ...** motivate learners at higher levels *p.154*.

read on

- **Exercise 1** is designed to lead in to the text and get learners thinking about the topic. They will probably be able to anticipate some of the common problems, but may find out new things from the text when they read it. Monitor to see if you can feed in any useful words or phrases that they might need, e.g. *Elderly people might find it hard to ... / might have trouble ... -ing.* You could ask learners to shout out their ideas to the class after **exercise 2**. At this point you could also go over any language that learners needed, and put it on the board.

- Before **exercise 3**, you could write the headline of the text on the board, and check that learners understand *surgical gloves* (= thin rubber gloves used by doctors and dentists); *ear plugs* (= wax you put in your ears to protect you from noise); and *goggles* (show learners the pictures). They could also make an attempt to answer the question in the first line before reading. Let them compare their **glossary** answers in pairs.

- Learners can compare their ideas to **exercises 4** and **5** in pairs or groups. See **ideas plus** on the right.

- *Tell* is a very common verb with a wide range of meanings. In the examples in the **natural English** box, the meaning is *recognize* or *distinguish one thing from another*. Does the equivalent verb *tell* in the learners' mother tongue have this sense? When you move on to the A / B pair practice, check beforehand that learners can make an appropriate question, e.g. *Can you tell the difference between decaffeinated coffee and ordinary coffee?* If learners do know the difference, they should explain it to their partner.

grammar definite or indefinite article

- This section focuses on the use of *the* for referring to what has already been mentioned or is assumed, and *a / an* for something so far unmentioned or undefined.

- Learners can do **exercise 2** alone or in pairs. If you feel they need more practice, go to **language reference** and do the **cover & check** exercises on *p.171*.

- For some nationalities, the concepts relating to articles in this section are not problematic, e.g. for most speakers of Romance and Germanic languages and Greek. If this is the case, you could omit this part of the lesson. If you want to work on other rules to do with articles, you could go to the **workbook** unit ten. Otherwise, you can either stop the lesson at this point, or play the game in **ideas plus** on the right, which practises article use.

exercise 2

1 In sentence 1, we are talking about elderly people in general, and not a specific group of elderly people. In sentence 2, we are talking about a specific group of elderly people, i.e. the elderly people I know.
2 Because we are talking about young people in general, and not a specific group of young people.
3 *The elderly* means the same as *elderly people*.

exercise 3

~~the happy~~

exercise 4

1 Elderly people often keep ~~the~~ pets for company.
2 If you are rich, ~~the~~ life is generally a lot easier.
3 **The** young couple living next door to me are very friendly.
4 ~~The~~ most children like ice cream.
5 *correct*
6 ~~The~~ families don't live together as much as they used to.

exercise 3 glossary

tunnel vision b	disorientated a
muffled a	jostle sb b
take (sth) for granted b	

exercise 4

He wore the gloves, ear plugs, and goggles to get an idea of what it feels like to be a 75-year-old person.
surgical gloves: he couldn't distinguish the coins in his pocket; he couldn't tell the difference between silk and acrylic
ear plugs: everything sounded muffled; he felt cut off from Ms Parr and the photographer
goggles: it gave him tunnel vision; it made everything seem very bright
ear plugs and goggles made the world seem unsafe

nE

I couldn't tell the difference between a silk scarf and an acrylic one.

exercise 1

an experiment *2*
The goggles *1a*
the world *1c*
the coins *1b*

exercise 2

1 the 2 the 3 the 4 a 5 an

language point articles

In our research data from the **extended speaking** activity for this unit, we found that even at upper-intermediate level, learners of most nationalities had problems with the general versus specific rule for articles. Although most speakers of Romance and Germanic languages and Greek have article systems, this is one area where English rules often differ from their languages. Even where adjectives are used as nouns in other languages (as in *the rich, the elderly*), they are often in the plural form. It may be that you can treat this as a quick reminder of the rules, in which case, do these exercises and move on; if your learners have more problems, be prepared to spend time on it, and use the **language reference** and **cover & check** exercises on *p.170.*

Want to know more about language issues for specific nationalities?
Go to **Learner English**, Eds M Swan and B Smith (CUP 2001).

ideas plus exploiting the text for discussion

Exercise 5 elicits a more personal response to the text. Apart from a few words and phrases, learners should be able to understand the text at this level, so we feel it is more logical to ask learners to assess what new facts they have learnt. They may also have an emotional reaction to the text, which gives quite an insight into the problems of growing old. If you have a class who respond well to this type of subject, you could extend the discussion further. Ask them to consider what society and the government does to help the elderly, and whether they / we should do more. How could people help the elderly more than they do? As the world population ages, how will society cater for the elderly in the future?

ideas plus definitions game

Learners work in pairs, and have to define three words which they are given on a card, e.g. *the moon, capital punishment, junk food, kangaroos, the Nile, an ambulance driver, afternoon, kittens, a library, chewing gum.* You can choose your own items, but include a range of abstract nouns, plural nouns, countable / uncountable nouns, and proper nouns. In order to define the items accurately, the pairs should monitor their use of articles, and you can also correct these when they are writing their definitions. Learners can then read their definitions to all the pairs, who win points if they guess correctly.

listening there's no easy answer

listen to people giving their opinion on different topics

focus on vocabulary for making judgements

discuss different topics using the vocabulary and **natural English** phrases

lead-in

- With a monolingual group, you could do the first part of question 1 in **exercise 1** as a class, and elicit names of TV programmes where members of the public are invited to give their opinions. Afterwards, learners can discuss their opinion of these programmes in groups, and then discuss question 2.

- With a multilingual group, you could find out if any of the topics in question 2 are considered difficult or sensitive in their countries. This will be of general interest to members of the class, but may also be a warning to you of any topics which you might need to omit from the discussion.

- Listen to the groups discussing question 2. If there are any which immediately provoke strong opinions, make a note of it: there will be an opportunity for further discussion later.

listen to this

- The questions in **exercise 1** focus on the general tone of the recording, while allowing learners to tune in to the different voices. You could use the questions in the **student's book** here and for the rest of the section (**listen carefully** and **listening challenge**), or use the suggestion in **ideas plus** as an alternative.

- For **exercise 2**, you can either stop the recording at appropriate points to give learners time to write down their answers, or simply play it twice. Check their answers in both cases.

- If you think your learners have had enough listening for the moment, you could return to the **listening challenge** later in the lesson or in the next lesson.

vocabulary making judgements

- Introduce **exercise 1** and use the example to illustrate the fact that learners are looking for a synonym or paraphrase in the right-hand column for each of the phrases on the left. When you check the answers, practise the pronunciation of the items given in phonemic script.

- If you feel the need to consolidate or check the meaning, you could use the suggestion in **ideas plus** on the right. Use **test your partner** for some quick practice. The next activity provides freer, personalized practice of the vocabulary, and some of it also comes up again in **wordbooster**.

it's your turn!

- Before doing **exercise 1** you could bring forward the **natural English** box and introduce the language. Explain the function of these phrases, and throw out some quick questions so that learners can use them in reply, e.g. *Barbara, what do you think about mothers who steal food from shops for their children?*

- Look at the table for **exercise 1** together. Check the pronunciation of *live* /laɪv/ and ask someone the difference between *live* and *alive* (you cannot use *alive* before a noun). You may also need to highlight the phrase *out of season*, which learners will probably understand but wouldn't necessarily know or use, and also explain *body piercing* /ˈpɪəsɪŋ/ (= making holes in parts of the body so that you can wear jewellery there).

exercise 1

1 The presenter sounds calm.
2 The man sounds nervous and angry.
3 The woman sounds enthusiastic.

exercise 2

interview 1

1 testing cosmetics on live animals
2 it's wrong for animals to suffer for something as trivial as different smells in cosmetics
3 medical experiments on live animals
4 he thinks it's a different issue

interview 2

1 women having babies in their fifties and sixties
2 If we have the technology, why not use it? People are living longer nowadays anyway.
3 How will older parents cope as their children grow up and become teenagers?
4 She still thinks it's a good idea – we are healthier than we used to be.

exercise 3

The topic is raising the price of petrol to cut the number of cars on the roads. He is a doctor in a rural area so he thinks it's a very bad idea because he needs a car to see all his patients in the countryside. He doesn't think that money raised from petrol tax gets into hospitals or schools.

exercise 1

2 d 3 f 4 c 5 a 6 i 7 j 8 e 9 h 10 b

ideas plus prediction

If you would like some variety or feel that the passage in **listen carefully** might be very challenging for your learners, you could exploit it as a prediction exercise. Play the presenter's introduction of the first topic, and ask them to predict why the man in the audience might be against it. They may come up with two or three reasons. Then, ask them to predict what the presenter's next question might be in response to the answer they get to the first question. Again, this might mean two or three possible questions. Finally, how do they think the man might respond to the second question? When learners have done this, you could elicit some of their suggestions, put them on the board, then play the tape to see who came closest.

This procedure does several things: it should make the listening passage easier to understand as the learners will probably be prepared for both the questions and answers they are going to hear; and secondly, it can help to make the learners more motivated to listen; they want to see if their predictions were right. If, on the other hand, the learners were very inaccurate in their predictions, this is likely to make the passage harder to understand, and it may signal that one of the learners' main difficulties with listening comprehension is their inability to use the context to aid understanding.

Want to know more? Go to intermediate **teacher's book, how to ...** teach listening *p.150.*

ideas plus concept checking

You could give the class stimuli and elicit the most suitable response(s) using the phrases in the left-hand column. For example, if you said that children aged ten to twelve years old have to work in factories in some countries, you should be able to elicit: *it's cruel, it's immoral,* and probably *it's illegal.* Here are some more stimuli:

Everyone dies eventually. (*inevitable*); Some people can't afford to go on holiday. (*a shame*); Some drivers don't wear seat belts. (*illegal*); You have to wear a tie in some restaurants. (*ridiculous*)

how to ... write a human interest story

70 – 80 mins

talk about newspaper headlines

read an article about cosmetic surgery and analyse the arguments

focus on adding ideas through **natural English** phrases

study relative clauses

write a human interest story

look at issues behind a story

- The aim of the first activity in this section is to motivate learners by eliciting a reaction, and to encourage interaction. Although the eventual outcome of the lesson is writing, we have integrated speaking at various stages, especially when generating ideas about cosmetic surgery and when the learners prepare their human interest story at the end. You could start by asking them to define what they think a *human interest story* in a newspaper might be (a story that people find interesting because it tells them about the feelings of the people involved). You could also discuss which local / national newspapers or magazines specialize in this type of story. Then ask learners to think about the headlines in **exercise 1** and discuss them (**exercise 2**). If necessary, explain *walk away with* ⑥ (= obtain or win something very easily).

- Lead into the short article by looking at the photo in **exercise 3** and discussing it. At this point, see if they know *facelift* and *cosmetic surgery*. Then ask learners to read the article and complete **part 1** of the table in **exercise 4**, summarizing the arguments for and against. Check their answers at the end.

- While learners are thinking up their own arguments in **exercise 5**, monitor to help with language or ideas. At the end, you could elicit the class's ideas for and against, and put them on the board. This might also provide a record of some useful phrases, e.g. *people should be allowed to (spend their money however they want); it keeps you looking and feeling young; it isn't without risk.*

- Point out to learners that the phrases in the **natural English** box have informal equivalents in the text. You may wish to highlight the two sets of linkers, both formal and informal, separately on the board, so that you can show the difference in the position of the linkers in a sentence. See **language point** on the right.

grammar relative clauses

- See **troubleshooting** on the right, before starting **exercise 1**. Do the first couple of examples in exercise 1 together, then learners can work alone or in pairs on the rest. Monitor while they are working so that you can help any individuals who are having problems. Check the answers.

plan and write your human interest story

- This activity gives learners a chance to put into practice what they have learnt from this section. In **exercise 1**, learners have a new context around which to write their story, and one which most people will have an opinion about. Refer learners to the photo and text, and give them a minute to think about their answers to the questions. For a different idea, see **ideas plus** on the right.

- You could ask for a show of hands: do they sympathize mostly with Carl or his boss? If the class is divided you could match up pairs with different opinions to work together, as they will find it easier to think up the opposing arguments, although they would have to come to some agreement on the final tone of the article. Give them time to discuss their answers to **exercise 1**.

- Notice that certain key points about this type of article are highlighted in **exercise 3**. Bring the class together to look at the guidelines, and allow them a few minutes to talk about this with a partner if necessary. If you have time in class, or writing is a priority for your learners, carry on with the writing activity in the lesson, where learners can either write co-operatively, i.e. one article together, or work alone. In either case, this is the perfect opportunity for you to go round and help learners while they are in the process of writing. Otherwise, set it up as an out-of-class activity. If you or the learners have computer facilities, it would be fun to make their articles look authentic, i.e. using newspaper column format, large headlines, and a picture.

- In the next lesson, allow time for learners to read each others' work and comment on it. You can also take in the work for correction and feedback.

 **wordbooster** *go to p.142*   This **wordbooster** can be used at any point in **unit ten.**

exercise 4

Jean's reasons **for** cosmetic surgery: her husband is seven years younger than her; she didn't recognize herself in family photos

Bernie's arguments **against** it: the cost (the money was meant to be for his daughter's education); it is against the laws of nature

the benefits she felt: she has more confidence, she looks better and feels more energetic – a better wife and mother

nE

from the text, the link words are:

What's more, at 46, I found ...

*John **also** believes ...*

*... she feels more energetic **as well**.*

---

language point adding ideas

Furthermore and *moreover* are formal ways of adding information or arguments to what has been said; *in addition* is less formal but still more common in written English than spoken English.

What's more (and *as well as that / on top of that*) are informal ways of saying *in addition*, and follow the same syntactic pattern as the ones above, i.e. they are all used to link two separate sentences, usually with a full stop or a semi-colon preceding them.

Also and *as well* (and *too*) are common in spoken English, but you will need to point out to learners their position in sentences. *Also* usually goes in mid-position, between the subject and main verb, e.g.

*John **also** believes that ...*

*She's **also** thinking of having liposuction.*

As well and *too* usually go at the end, e.g. *She not only feels better, she looks great **as well / too**.*

---

exercise 1

1 whose	5 which / that
2 who	6 who / that
3 which	7 who / that
4 whose	8 whose

---

troubleshooting using the board to highlight grammar

You may prefer to work from the board to introduce this grammar point, in which case, write up the examples given in the grammar explanation before **exercise 1**. Ask learners in the first sentence whether *who performed the operation* is saying which surgeon we mean, or adding extra information about him; it is the former. Then ask learners about *who was only thirteen* in the second sentence: is it defining which person we mean, or adding extra information? (It is the latter.) Label the sentences as *defining* and *non-defining*, and point out the use of commas in the second sentence. Finally, you can ask the learners whether *that* can be used in both sentences. Again, clarify this point on the board. Give learners time to copy and ask for clarification if necessary.

---

ideas plus topics

If your learners had interesting story ideas for the unusual headlines in **look at issues behind a story**, **exercise 1**, or if there is a different topic they would prefer to write a human interest story about, that would be fine. Whatever motivates them to write is acceptable, within the bounds of decency!

extended speaking animals in society

60 – 75 mins

discuss and listen to the argument that children should have pets

prepare arguments on related topics

discuss the topics

write a summary of one of the arguments

collect ideas

- You could ask learners in advance to bring to class any photos of pets they have (or had when they were younger); this always helps to create more interest in the subject. If you have a pet or pets yourself, start by telling the class about it / them. In our experience this usually prompts quite a lot of questions, so when you put the learners in groups for **exercise 1**, encourage them to do the same. Make sure you have at least one pet owner in each group, even if it means creating quite large groups.

- Get the learners to read through the statements in **exercise 2** and ask you if there are any problems. Check the pronunciation of *unhygienic* /ʌnhaɪˈdʒiːnɪk/ but don't allow any discussion of the statements at this stage.

- Play the recording in **exercise 3**. You shouldn't need to play it twice, and there is no particular reason to spend very long on it.

- Learners can discuss **exercise 4** with a partner or their previous groups. See **troubleshooting** on the right for ideas on when to use the **natural English** box.

exercise 3
The speakers mention: a, c, d, e

prepare your argument

- Some people are interested in and concerned about the welfare of animals and their relationships with people; for others it is not a particularly relevant issue. For this reason, we have included a wide range of topics connected with animals in order to cater for different cultures and attitudes. There should be something of interest for everyone.

- Give learners plenty of time to read and think about the statements in each category in **exercise 5**. We have suggested one category each, but there is no reason why the learners shouldn't go on to discuss more categories later if there is sufficient time and interest.

- For **exercise 6**, put learners in groups of three or four with others who have chosen the same category. Learners can then spend a few more minutes alone preparing their ideas and adding their own statement. Don't worry if some learners are unable to think up their own statement; one or two additional ideas per group should be enough to keep the discussion going.

share your views

- Before the learners share their views, and if you haven't done so already, go through the language in the **natural English** box. See **troubleshooting** on the right.

- Nominate one person in each group to start the discussion, then leave the groups to talk freely. Monitor each group for several minutes and make notes of ideas and language use for feedback. You don't want to stop the activity while the learners are still clearly engaged in discussion, but it's actually more important not to allow the discussion to drag on when most learners / groups have obviously run out of things to say: if this happens, the lesson loses momentum and learners start feeling bored. It is a good idea to give the learners a warning that you would like them to wind up their discussion within a couple of minutes, and then stop it at an appropriate moment.

- You might decide again to nominate one person in each group to tell the class about their most controversial statement. At the end, conduct feedback on the learners' language and ideas.

Want to know more? Go to intermediate **teacher's book, how to ...** monitor and give feedback *p.156*.

write a summary

- Learners could write the summary for homework, using the linking words in the **student's book** on *p.120* to help them.

feedback checklist

During the **extended speaking** activity, note down examples of …

- **good language use**

- **effective communication strategies**
  (turn-taking, interrupting, inviting others to speak, etc.)

- **learner errors**
  (vocabulary, grammar, pronunciation, etc.)

- **particular communication problems**

Make sure you allow time for feedback at the end of the lesson. You can use the notes you make above to <u>praise</u> effective language use and communication or, if necessary, to do some remedial work.

---

troubleshooting collect ideas making the most of teaching opportunities

Later in this section there is a **natural English** box with useful language for when we feel we have been misunderstood, and we want to clarify what we mean. You may find, however, that some learners clearly want and need this language – and don't have it – during the initial discussion about children and pets. If that happens, bring the **natural English** box forward. There are no individual words in the expressions that learners won't already know (so the learning burden isn't great), but we feel the majority of learners are unlikely to produce these expressions for themselves. If you think it is unrealistic for learners to study them and then possibly put them to immediate use in a free speaking activity, you could suggest they just focus on one expression from each column rather than try to learn all four.

test yourself!

Want to know more? Go to the **introduction** *p.7* for ways of using **test yourself!**

1 as well, what's more, furthermore, moreover, in addition
2 it rings a bell, absent-minded, on the tip of my tongue, a vague memory, learn sth by heart
3 disgrace, cruelty, harm, justification, persuasion

1 I can't tell one from the other.
2 I like cola, juice, that sort of thing.
3 That's not what I was trying to say.
4 These animals are in danger of extinction.

1 Restricted vision is a common problem for elderly people.
2 I work with children whose parents are in prison.
3 Poverty is a problem which can't be solved quickly.
4 That policy is immoral and very destructive.

---

eleven

wordlist

natural English

exaggerating
I've got a million things to do.
I could eat a horse.
It cost a fortune.
It weighs a ton.
I've told you a hundred times.
I wouldn't do that in a million years.

imagining someone else's situation
In his / her shoes, I'd (probably) ...
In his / her position, I might ...
If that were me, I'd (definitely) ...

letter writing clichés
I hope you're well.
Sorry I haven't ... for a while but I've been ...
It was lovely to hear from you.
I was so pleased to hear that ...

reacting to ideas
That sounds like a great idea.
I've got mixed feelings about that.
I'm completely against that idea.

formal and informal language
I'm really sorry / I must apologize (for ...)
It's about ... / Further to ...
It's all my fault / We accept full responsibility.
I'll ring (your mother) / We will contact you.

vocabulary

describing character
understanding
(in)sincere
open-minded
kind-hearted
naive
courageous
brave
full of remorse
(un)trustworthy
vulnerable
(un)wise
easily led
reckless

wordbooster

phrases and phrasal verbs
cover up the truth
confide in sb
get mixed up with sb
ashamed of ...
end up (somewhere / doing sth)
out of the blue
turn up (= arrive)
by mistake

use your dictionary
I have no sympathy for ...
treat sb like a child
who's to blame
in the first place
I don't see the point of + -ing ...
Put yourself in his / her shoes.
to cut a long story short
in a bad mood

glossary

backside ⑥
stick to sth
get mixed up with (a group of people)
decent
harsh

right and wrong

life with Agrippine   25 – 30 mins

read for pleasure
nE exaggerating

- If you have a monolingual group, it should be interesting for learners to compare their ideas on which words are fashionable; there may be some differences of opinion. If you have a multilingual group, learners can work with someone of a different nationality and tell them about a few fashionable words in their language, translating them literally. If you have several learners of the same nationality, you could either group them together or apart. See **language point** below.

- In **cartoon time**, the words *brill*, *cool*, and *fab*, are all informal, so learners need to find informal equivalents in their language. If there isn't an equivalent concept where words meaning *great* have gone in and out of fashion, don't worry. You can do the second question as a class or in pairs. *Backside* is informal but not rude.

- In the **natural English** box, you will find that the sentences on the recording are longer, giving more context. If you like, you could use this as a dictation; learners make a note of each sentence beginning, then include them when practising orally. Either use the recording as a model for learners' pronunciation or provide the model yourself.

nE possible answers
Is that bag heavy? It weighs a ton!
Are you hungry? I could eat a horse!
What's your phone number? I've told you a million times!
Was that jacket expensive? It cost a fortune!
Would you do a bungee jump? I wouldn't do that in a million years!
Will you give me a hand? I've got a million things to do!

language point fashionable words
Unlike some languages, English does not have an academy which decides if a word is a recognized part of the language. In English, a new word is adopted as part of the language, and will be included in dictionaries, if it is used often enough.

- Here are some British English words which were fashionable in the 60s and 70s, and are still used today:

  hassle = something annoying that causes problems and complications, e.g. *I'll e-mail him – it's less hassle than writing a letter.*
  a rip-off = something that is not worth what you pay for it, e.g. *Tourist restaurants are often a rip-off.*

- Here are some words which were fashionable in the 60s and 70s, but are no longer commonly used:

  bread = money   *groovy, with-it,* = fashionable   *the fuzz* = the police
  Dictionaries will usually indicate that such words are old-fashioned.

- Here are some words (adjectives) which are fashionable today, and may or may not last:

  wicked = great, fantastic   *fit* = sexy, attractive   *top* = great, nice, e.g. *That's a top jacket!*

listening making the right decision

70 – 90 mins

lead-in

- Refer learners to the pictures in **exercise 1**, and make it clear that they have to imagine themselves to be the person indicated in each picture. Ask learners to describe what is happening in each one (but not what their reactions are). Go over the language in the **natural English** box, and explain the meaning as suggested, if necessary. Check learners' pronunciation of the sentences, and of *intervene* /ˌɪntəˈviːn/.

grammar past conditionals

- Learners need to read the situation in **exercise 1**, then tick the phrases they agree with. Don't worry if this conditional form is unfamiliar to your learners; they will be able to grasp the meaning of the sentences even if the form is new. (See **language point** on the right.) This first activity promotes a little discussion, and if you monitor it carefully, you should be able to assess whether learners have a grasp of the structure, and indeed, some may be using the forms in their discussion. This will help you to decide whether the point needs a quick revision with more opportunities for practice, or a more thorough treatment. Ask a couple of learners to say which statement they agree with at the end.

- Go on to the grammar focus in **exercise 2**. If learners are working in pairs, monitor and give help where necessary. Go over the answers at the end.

- You can give the model yourself for the pronunciation in **exercise 3**, or you can ask individuals to say a phrase until one of them produces a good model for everyone to copy. It can help if you isolate some of these weak forms and say them slowly for learners to repeat, e.g. /ˈwʊdəntəv/. Give learners time to work on this and try saying the phrases with a partner. You can also ask them to say the sentences in **exercise 1** for more challenge. Try to keep it fun and light-hearted, and correct where necessary. You could ask learners who find it easier to help others.

- **Exercise 4** gives learners a chance to personalize and adapt the sentences. Remember that you have the option of doing the **cover & check** exercises in the **language reference** on *p.173*.

listen to this

- The listening activity in **exercise 1** leads on from the short text in **grammar** exercise 1 on *p.126*. Play the first part and give learners time to try to predict the next part of the story. It is unlikely that they will predict the whole story accurately, but it will motivate them to listen. Ask one or two pairs to feedback their ideas, then play the whole story.

- **Exercise 2** doesn't have a 'correct' answer; it simply asks learners to listen and respond in a natural way. They may not understand the story in detail at this stage, but they have another chance to listen again and complete the sentences in **exercise 3**. Let them read the sentences first, see how much they can complete, then listen again. It may be too much to ask them to listen and write at the same time, so you could suggest they listen and look at the sentence beginnings, then write them out with a partner afterwards. Go over the answers at the end, replaying sections of the tape where they had problems.

- **Exercises 4** and **5** give learners more listening practice, and in addition, an opportunity to express their ideas using the structures. If this turns into a discussion on loyalty and becomes animated, so much the better. You may find that learners' use of the structure becomes inaccurate; you can make a note of examples for feedback at the end. On balance, though, an animated discussion with some attempts to use the language in context is a very positive result.

grammar mixed conditionals

- Mixed conditionals are perfectly understandable if you approach them from the point of view of the meaning you want to express. You may, for instance, wish to talk about a past event, and its present consequences, e.g. *If you hadn't married Frank, you wouldn't be in this mess now.* You could explain this on the board by using the examples given in the **language reference** on *p.173*, where it is shown in more graphic form. Ask learners to read the situation, then look at the sentences in **exercise 2** together, one by one. You can clarify that *she might go out with him* and *she would accept it* cannot be correct, as the grammar refers to the present time, but they both describe situations in the past. However, *he wouldn't be worried now* is correct, because both the grammar and situation refer to the present time. If necessary, go to the **language reference**, and do the **cover & check** exercises. See **troubleshooting** on the right.

- **Exercise 3** provides sentence beginnings for learners to complete in two ways. If they need more help, do the first one together on the board, then learners can continue in pairs. Go over the answers.

exercise 2

1 sentence (a) means in general; sentence (b) means on a specific occasion in the past
3 *if* + had + past participle, *would have* + past participle
4 sentence (a) is second conditional; sentence (b) is third conditional (or past conditional)
5 2 *wouldn't have* + past participle; 4 *'d (would) have* + past participle; 5 *might have* + past participle

language point past conditionals

Your upper-intermediate learners may have come across the third conditional before, and if so, this lesson will provide them with revision and opportunities to use the language in context. If it is entirely new for your class, take the presentation quite slowly, and make use of the **language reference** and **cover & check** exercises. Most learners can follow the logic of the forms given here, but they may find the concept more difficult with complex sentences containing negative *if* clauses, e.g. *If she hadn't accepted the invitation, she wouldn't have met Tom*. A common problem for learners, however, is manipulating and saying the forms quickly and naturally, using weak forms and contractions, which is why **exercise 3** is particularly useful for most learners. For some nationalities, there is a tendency to use *would* in both clauses, and a further possible confusion with *'d*, as it can be the short form of *would* or *had*. Highlight these forms on the board, e.g.

If you'd rung me last night, I'd have told you the result.
    had   **would**

exercise 3

1 The people in the car looked respectable / well-dressed.
2 She felt safe.
3 When they arrived at her village, she pointed out her house.
4 They carried on driving.
5 She felt nervous and started panicking.
6 Eventually they turned the car round and drove back to her village.
7 They said to her, *Be warned! You could have been attacked*.

exercise 4

He was in a pizza restaurant when he saw his friend's girlfriend, Laura, with another man. They were kissing each other. Mike didn't know what to do. The next day, he saw his best friend, Dino, but didn't tell him.

exercise 2

If Stefan had told Anna the truth in the first place, she wouldn't have gone out with him. / it would've been sensible. / he wouldn't be worried now. / he wouldn't have this problem with his ID card.

troubleshooting time management

If your class have found the lesson quite challenging, you may decide to omit this section on mixed conditionals and end the lesson here, or defer it till the next lesson. If you do this, it will give you an opportunity to start with a revision of third conditionals at the beginning of the lesson, and then lead in to the mixed ones.

reading a time to forgive

60 – 75 mins

read a series of letters between criminal and victim

write a short reply to one of them using **natural English** phrases

focus on vocabulary describing character

discuss issues connected with crime and prison

lead-in

- The topic in **exercise 1** may well be something that your learners have never thought about before, so give them several minutes to think about the issue and their reasons for saying *yes* or *no*. Put them in pairs or groups to compare their answers in **exercise 2**.

- It may concentrate minds if you give learners a time limit for **exercise 3**, e.g. one minute. You should warn them first that this is a memory test, so they should **not** write anything down.

- It may take some learners a long time to complete **exercise 4**. If others finish quite quickly, you could quietly ask them to underline the relevant part of each text which enabled them to put the letters in the correct chronological order. See **ideas plus** on the right.

- Check the answers, and elicit why the letters must be in this particular order.

- If the learners have found the letters interesting, they will want to react to the content. **Exercise 5** is an opportunity for a personalized response, but the discussion should also tell you how well learners have understood parts of the text. This may be more effective in groups rather than pairs, and you can move round and monitor the groups while they're talking. At the end, you may want to have some open discussion before moving on.

- The **natural English** box contains a set of letter writing clichés, which will be very useful to learners if they find themselves in a situation of corresponding regularly with someone in English; these really are commonly used phrases. You could go through the phrases in the box, then ask learners to find all the examples of them (with close variations) in the different letters.

- The written reply in **exercise 6** could be set for homework, expecially if you are short of time in class. (See **ideas plus**, **developing a text** on the right, for classes who do not respond well to discussion.)

Want to know more about exploiting reading texts? Go to **how to ...** teach reading *p.169*.

vocabulary describing character

- Put learners in pairs for **exercise 1**. Some of the words can be guessed quite easily even if learners have not met them before, e.g. *open-minded, kind-hearted, easily led*. Check the answers.

- **Test your partner** will help learners to fix the words in their memory, but it is also very useful for pronunciation practice, and some of these words are quite difficult to pronounce. Go round and monitor the pairs to check they are saying the words correctly.

- You will notice that some of the target items form opposites with specific prefixes, e.g. *unwise, insincere*. You could develop this further if you wish. See **language point** on the right.

- **Exercise 2** links the target vocabulary back to the characters from the prison letters and provides some personalized practice. Encourage learners to give reasons for their answers.

it's your turn!

- There is a lot to think about here, so give the class plenty of time to consider the issues in **exercise 1** and prepare their arguments and ideas. If you can allow them about five minutes, it will give learners time to make a few notes and rehearse some of their arguments silently.

- When they have prepared their ideas, go through the **natural English** box together. You could then ask each learner to think of a suitable place in the discussion where they can use each of the three phrases from the box. During the discussion in **exercise 2**, you can make a note of whether these phrases are being used appropriately.

- If your class do not respond well to discussion, or you think they may not have much to contribute on these particular subjects, you could use **ideas plus** on the right.

Want to know more? Go to **how to ...** motivate higher level learners *p.154*.

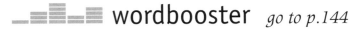 **wordbooster** *go to p.144*   This **wordbooster** can be used at any point in **unit eleven.**

exercise 1

1 a (Craig apologizes to Mrs Robinson)
2 f (Mrs Robinson responds to his request for forgiveness)
3 e (Craig responds to her forgiveness by saying she's very understanding, and talks about his education going *OK*)
4 c (she responds positively to the reference to his education)
5 b (it's Craig's last letter; he introduces the topic of the new prison and trying to get a job in the garden)
6 d (she responds to both of these new topics)

glossary

mixed up with; decent; harsh

---

ideas plus jumbled text

This task involves dividing a text into sections and mixing up the different sections. Learners then have to use clues in each section of text to piece the whole text together in the correct order. There are two main reasons for using this task type:

- Assembling a text in the correct order can be a very good test of understanding, either of the cohesive devices which show grammatical and lexical relationships between parts of a text, or as in this exercise, an understanding of the coherence within the texts. (See the answer key.)
- Most learners enjoy organizing jumbled texts occasionally and find them motivating.

Certain text types lend themselves to jumbling: sets of instructions with a logical development; a discursive text with arguments for and against a specific proposition; certain narratives. You normally need at least four or five distinct sections to make it worthwhile, and from a purely practical point of view, it helps if the text breaks down into a number of different paragraphs.

---

exercise 1

1	kind-hearted	5	full of remorse	9	wise
2	understanding	6	easily led	10	sincere
3	vulnerable	7	trustworthy	11	reckless
4	courageous / brave	8	open-minded	12	naive

exercise 2 possible answers

In the past, Craig was: untrustworthy, reckless, easily led; now he is full of remorse, appears sincere and wiser, and probably more trustworthy. Mrs Robinson is very understanding, kind-hearted, open-minded, sincere, and courageous. We have no clear evidence that either of them is vulnerable or naive, but it's possible that Craig was vulnerable, and some people might think that Mrs Robinson is naive.

language point

unwilling	disobey	unwrap	disapprove (of)	unpack
disloyal	unsatisfactory	dissatisfied		

---

language point prefixes

The prefixes *un-* and *dis-* can both be used before adjectives and verbs, and can have two meanings:

- to make a word negative, e.g. **un**wise, **dis**honest
- to reverse an action, e.g. *lock / **un**lock (a door);* *connect / **dis**connect (a plug)*

Ask learners which prefix could be used before these words, and what the meaning would be:

willing   obey   wrap   approve (of)   pack   loyal   satisfactory   satisfied

---

ideas plus developing a text

The text on *pp.128* to *129* consists of extracts from a series of letters. Working alone or in pairs, learners could choose one of the letters and complete it. Stipulate a minimum or maximum amount you want them to write, and move round and help where necessary with ideas they want to express. Learners can then walk round and look at each others' letters, or you could ask one or two learners to read out their letter to the rest of the class.

how to ... write an apology

70 – 80 mins

say sorry

- Start with the personalized speaking activity in **exercise 1**, or if you prefer, use one of the suggestions in **ideas plus** on the right. This warmer simply relates to the topic of the lesson, apologizing.

- Direct learners' attention to the photos of Darren and Nicola for **exercise 2**, but don't let them read the e-mail. Give them a moment in pairs to think what might have gone wrong, e.g. Darren might have forgotten. Conduct feedback, and encourage learners to use the past modal forms *could've* or *might've*.

- Once learners have read the e-mail in **exercise 3**, check their answers. You will probably need them to paraphrase the e-mail to see if they have understood the situation so far. Check that learners understand *gift wrap* (= wrap an item in pretty paper to give as a present).

- Let learners read the questions in **exercise 4**, then listen to the phone conversation. They can compare answers, and you can monitor to see how much they understood. If necessary, replay the recording or a part that learners did not grasp, then go over the answers. If you like, replay the recording while the learners follow the transcript in the **listening booklet** on *p.40*, and give them a chance to ask you questions about the language at the end.

- For the role play in **exercises 5** and **6**, student A needs to have the story of what happened clear in their minds, while student B needs to listen and react; they can decide whether to take it well or act offended. If you feel your learners need extra preparation, they could first think about what to say with another student who will play the same role first. You can make the phone conversation slightly more lifelike by asking learners to work with their phone partner back-to-back in the role play, or with one person talking over their partner's shoulder. Listen to the phone conversations, and in particular notice whether the learners use appropriate initial and closing phone greetings, and whether the apologies are acceptable. Give feedback at the end to the class on the language they used.

grammar reporting what people say

- For many learners, this grammar point will be relatively straightforward, and can be dealt with quickly. See **language point** on the right.

- Learners can work in pairs on the **grammar** exercise.

formal letter of apology

- You could introduce this section about differences between formal and informal written English with a brainstorming activity. Tell learners to shut their books, and ask them to make notes in pairs on possible differences between letters and e-mails. They could then compare with another pair. Then ask them to look at the two examples in this section, the e-mail on *p.132* and the letter on *p.133*. Finally, collate their ideas in a list on the board, highlighting any which are particularly problematic for your learners, e.g. where they are different from their own language.

- **Exercise 2** focuses on the structure of the e-mail and letter, i.e. the way in which the content is presented and ordered. Ask learners to complete the table, either alone or as a class. Again, you can compare the organization of the text itself with the way it would be done in their mother tongue. Are any unusual things included or missing, from their point of view?

- The role play in **exercise 3** gives a little oral practice of reported speech as well as a change of focus from writing to interaction. If you ask learners to swap roles they can both practise the construction.

- The language in the **natural English** box will be useful for learners when they write their letters, and is a text search activity. See **language point** on the right.

- You could let your learners choose which letter they would prefer to write in **exercise 4**. When they have finished, collect them in for correction and feedback.

exercise 4

1 *Classic French Cookery*
2 *A Hundred Most Beautiful Women*
3 At first she seems a bit angry and doesn't see the problem.
4 She thinks it's very funny.
5 He promises to ring his mother-in-law and apologize, and explain what has happened.

ideas plus songs

Many love songs describe things going wrong in a relationship and the need to say sorry: a very popular one with quite straightforward lyrics is Elton John's *Sorry seems to be the hardest word*. If you have a copy of the recording, you could use this at the beginning of the lesson, and either ask learners to listen and say what the song is about, or gap the lyrics, and ask learners to complete them. You can access song lyrics via a range of Internet websites, one of which is http://music.yahoo.com/launch/lyrics.html. Alternatively, if you teach in a monolingual environment, you could use a song in the learners' own language and ask them to rewrite the lyrics in English. It might be fun to see if they can then sing the song in English, perhaps while listening to the mother-tongue version.

exercise 1

He admitted he **had made** a mistake.
He explained they **had been waiting** for ages.
She told him she **had lost** the tickets.
She said she **would ring** me later.
He told me he **had been** there before.

exercise 2

1 Darren said there was a bit of a crisis.
2 He admitted he had done a very stupid thing.
3 He explained they had gift-wrapped both books in the shop for him.
4 He told her he had sent her mother the wrong book.
5 Nicola suggested he could swap them over.
6 He told her he was going to call her then.

language point reported speech

Reported speech is a grammar area which is often taught at intermediate level. However, our research data for the extended speaking activities at this level showed that learners were able to report speech in a number of appropriate ways without using the standard tense shift, e.g.

'I don't believe you.'   She says / said she doesn't believe me.
                         She said, 'I don't believe you.'

Other forms are also common, e.g. She was saying she doesn't / didn't believe me.

These informal constructions are very common in speech, but learners will still need to know about the tense shifts if they want to report something in a more formal written document, or in more careful, formal speech, for stylistic reasons. They will also need it in certain types of examination.

exercise 1

In a formal letter, the layout would be different: the address of both people would be given and the letter would be dated below the sender's address. The greetings (at the beginning and end) would be more formal; the vocabulary / phrases would also be more formal. Certain structures, e.g. passives, are more common in formal writing; there will be very few (if any) contractions in a formal letter; sentences will be more organized, etc.

exercise 2

apologize 1; admit responsibility 3; explain what happened 2; apologize again 5; say what will happen next 4

nE

It's about = *regarding ...*
It's all my fault = *I / We accept full responsibility*
I'll ring ... = *I / We will contact you to ...*

language point style

In this lesson, you will find three 'styles': informal spoken English, informal written English and formal written English. There are elements of style in the grammar point (see **language point** reported speech) and in the **natural English** box. If your learners are keen to focus on written English style and format, there are a number of easily accessible reference books (see below).

Want to know more? Go to **Oxford Advanced Learners Dictionary** (Study pages, B13–15); **Oxford Wordpower Dictionary** (S18–19); **Practical English Usage** by Michael Swan (section 317, letters).

extended speaking crimes and misdemeanors   60 – 75 mins

talk about a problem in a relationship

read a case study

discuss the case study

listen to another case study and react to it

evaluate your language skills

collect ideas

- This **extended speaking** activity includes two case studies. The lesson is developed in such a way that learners focus on one case study and become 'expert' in it, devote time to thinking through the implications of it, and then discuss it with other learners who read the same case study. The second part of the activity asks them to narrate: they recode their case study to a new partner (this is a distinct skill, and the stories need to be carefully and clearly told). Finally, learners have to respond spontaneously to the case study they have just heard: in other words, they move from a more planned response to an immediate one, which is more challenging. At the end, they evaluate their ability in the three activities.

- For **exercise 1**, see **troubleshooting** on the right.

- While learners are working together on **exercise 2**, monitor and see if there is one particularly interesting story that a student would be happy to share with the class at the end.

- For **exercise 3**, divide the class in two, and ask half to read case study A on *p.134*, and the other half to read B on *p.150*. They need to understand *to put something in writing* = write something in a letter or document as proof or evidence. They may need to read their case study more than once to make sure they understand and can remember the facts, so allow time for this.

- Go over the questions in **exercise 4**, which apply to (and are given with) both case studies. Check that learners understand *Where do your sympathies* /ˈsɪmpəθiːz/ *lie?* = Who do you feel sorry for? / Who is least responsible for what happened? Give them a minute or two to think about the questions but make sure they don't discuss them yet. The **language reminder** is likely to be particularly useful and may be worth putting on the board so that everyone focuses on it; in our data of learners doing this speaking activity, many learners used *should / shouldn't have done* (both accurately and inaccurately). It was first introduced in unit two on *p.24*.

analyse

- For **exercise 5**, organize learners into small groups of not more than four to discuss the <u>same</u> case study. Allow plenty of time for this; when we did this activity with learners they had plenty to say and the discussions continued for ten to fifteen minutes. While they are talking, monitor and make a note of language points for feedback at the end of the lesson.

- In **exercise 6**, subdivide the groups into pairs if possible, so that they can practise describing the case study. One learner can tell the story while the other follows with their book. Learners do not need to be totally accurate or give every detail, but they do need to tell the story clearly and coherently. (In our research, this proved less easy than it appears.) Explain why they are practising, i.e. that they are going to tell someone about their case study who hasn't read it. It is also important that they keep to the facts, and don't give their opinion.

- Tell learners to find a partner who read the other case study, i.e. put learners in A / B pairs. They should read the appropriate **checklist** in **exercise 7**, depending on who is to describe their case study first. This activity requires student B to listen very intently and then respond spontaneously, so the listening activity has a clear purpose and is also quite intensive.

- Monitor the pair work, noting down any areas where the stories are not clearly conveyed. When learners have finished and elicited their partner's reactions, they swap roles.

- Bring the class together at the end, so that they can exchange their views briefly and have a class vote.

evaluate

- This section asks learners to think about their skills in the different speaking activities in this section. This activity may be useful for you diagnostically. In subsequent lessons, you could, for instance, give learners extra practice in particular activities. For discussion, you could give pairs controversial topics to talk about for a minute each, prepared or unprepared. Narrating can be practised by asking learners to describe the story of a film, TV programme, or book they have seen / read recently.

- At the end, give learners feedback and correction on the language examples you have collected at various stages.

feedback checklist

During the **extended speaking** activity, note down examples of …

- **good language use**

- **effective communication strategies**
  (turn-taking, interrupting, inviting others to speak, etc.)

- **learner errors**
  (vocabulary, grammar, pronunciation, etc.)

- **particular communication problems**

Make sure you allow time for feedback at the end of the lesson. You can use the notes you make above to <u>praise</u> effective language use and communication or, if necessary, to do some remedial work.

---

troubleshooting collect ideas personal anecdotes

Some learners may have difficulty thinking up a relevant personal anecdote quickly, while others will have one (or several!) at their fingertips. It can help if you start by telling a story yourself, which does two things: it can give learners time to think, and it might trigger a memory of something that happened to them.

You can stress that when they tell their own stories, they do not need to say who the person involved was if it is likely to cause embarrassment, and of course, they should only reveal what they want to reveal. If some learners do not have a story or don't want to tell one, don't worry: tell them to work in a small group with learners who do. While they are listening, something might occur to them to talk about.

---

ideas plus evaluate dialogue writing

If your class enjoyed the case studies, you could extend the topic by asking them to work with a partner and write a dialogue between two of the characters, e.g. Jeff and Christopher, or Christopher's father and Jeff; Paula Lewis and her teacher, the teacher and the parents, Paula and her mother. This would give learners further practice in writing informal spoken English, recycle some of the vocabulary in the texts, and provide scope for creativity. They could then read or act out their dialogue for others.

test yourself!

Want to know more? Go to the **introduction** *p.7* for ways of using **test yourself!**

1 I've got a million things to do; I wouldn't do that in a million years; it weighs a ton; I could eat a horse; it cost a fortune
2 wise, vulnerable, reckless, courageous, naive, sincere
3 of, in, of, for

1 He's to blame.
2 He told Carol he would ring her later.
3 I'd be furious if I were him. / if I were in his position.
4 She shouldn't have taken the money.

1 If I **had** known, I would've told him.
2 I must **apologize** for the delay.
3 I don't see the point **of trying** to help him.
4 Maybe Chris **wouldn't have reacted** like that if Jeff had phoned him. / Chris **might not have** reacted like that if Jeff had phoned him.

twelve

wordlist

natural English

phrases with *mean*
What does that mean to you?
Does the name (Sanchez) mean anything to you?
That (present) means a lot to me.
(Success) means nothing to him / her.

phrases with *go*
Let me have a go.
It's your go.
I (ate all of them) in one go.
Go for it!

rephrasing an idea
So, what you're trying to say is …
So, what you're saying is …
So, what you mean is …

saying how easy sth is
It's (very) straightforward.
It's (dead / incredibly) easy / simple.
It's easy once you get the hang of it.
It's (a bit / incredibly) complicated.
The instructions are hard to follow.

fronting
The thing I like about … is …
The one thing that worries me is …
One thing I'd like to ask you is …

vocabulary

sleep and times of day
fall asleep
sunrise / dawn
dusk
noon
yawn
half-asleep
doze off
daydream
fast asleep
wide awake
insomnia
have a nap
snore

games
It's a good game.
win a trip / prize
make up your mind
consists of …
general knowledge (questions)
miss a turn
give sb a clue

wordbooster

collective nouns
audience
crew
jury
choir
crowd
series
pile
staff
public
congregation
herd
gang
set

attitude adverbs
surprisingly
miraculously
funnily enough
predictably
understandably
obviously
luckily
presumably
hopefully

glossary
twilight
sleeping bag
stretch your mind
appeal to sb
swot up on sth ◎
gamble
pay off (your debts)
mortgage

in unit twelve ...

do you get it?
joke Sherlock Holmes
natural English phrases with *mean*
vocabulary sleep and times of day

reading questions! questions!
listening describing a game
reading Millionaire hopefuls – go for it!
grammar reported questions

wordbooster
collective nouns
attitude adverbs

listening boost your brain power
listening a brain expert speaks
natural English rephrasing an idea
grammar *like, as, such as*

how to ... explain the rules of a game
natural English saying how easy something is
vocabulary games
listening people playing a game

extended speaking game shows
read about and discuss some TV game shows
design a game show
give a presentation
play a game
natural English fronting

test yourself!
revision of the unit

do you get it?   25 – 30 mins

listen for pleasure
nE phrases with *mean*
vocabulary sleep and times of day

- **With a partner ...** is intended as a light-hearted introduction to the section. For an alternative start, see **ideas plus** below.

- Play the recording and give learners a chance to react to the joke. (Amazingly, this turned out to top the polls of British people's favourite jokes on a website called laughlab.co.uk, which is doing a serious study on humour (referred to previously in unit two **do you get it?**). There is a comparative study of different nationalities' sense of humour, so it may be interesting to visit to see if the nationality you teach is represented. Site visitors can vote for the jokes they prefer.)

- Once learners have identified the phrase from the **natural English** box which is on the recording (*What does that mean to you?*), do the short exercise which goes with it. *Mean* is a very common verb with many meanings; the ones included in the box are very useful and not necessarily obvious to learners. You could look in a monolingual dictionary for other meanings if you want to extend their understanding of this verb. Some examples are: entail / have as a result, e.g. *He's missed the bus, which means I'll have to go and pick him up*; intend, e.g. *This message was meant for your eyes only*; be supposed to, e.g. *You aren't meant to eat that – it's just decoration*.

- In **sleep and times of day**, notice the phrase *fast asleep*, which many learners mistakenly think means *go to sleep quickly*, whereas it means *deeply asleep* (*fast* has the sense of *firmly / completely* here. The opposite is *wide awake*).

sleep and times of day
times of day: dawn, dusk, noon, sunrise, twilight
sleep: fall asleep, fast asleep, snore, have a nap, doze off
awake: yawn, daydream, insomnia, wide awake, half asleep

---

ideas plus vocabulary

You could start this lesson in a different way. Ask learners to do the **sleep and times of day** activity first. There are a few vocabulary items there which learners may be able to use when describing the pictures in **joke time**, e.g. *dusk, twilight*. You could also feed in a few phrases which learners may need for the descriptions, e.g. *night is falling; the moon is rising, the stars are coming out, the sun has set / gone down*.

---

reading questions! questions!

60 – 75 mins

talk about a popular TV game show

listen to the rules of the game

discuss how they would react as a contestant

read about a contestant's experience

study natural English phrases and reported questions

role play a phone conversation and use reported questions to describe it afterwards

lead-in

- Ask your learners to look at the picture in **exercise 1**. If they are all familiar with the game show *Who wants to be a millionaire?*, you could follow the procedure suggested in **troubleshooting** on the right. If not, the activities in the first three exercises will tune learners in to the topic and give them the information they need to put the text in context.
- For **exercise 3**, point out to learners that they should look at the symbols at the top of the scoreboard, as these are explained in the recording.
- **Exercise 4** is a personalized activity, which in fact follows the structure of the reading text. Once learners have answered the questions about themselves, they will be able to answer the same questions about the contestant in the article. Monitor the pair work activity, and conduct a quick feedback with the class so that they can see if their ideas are similar or not.

read on

- Follow the suggested procedure for **exercises 1** and **2**, which learners can do alone or in pairs. Go over the answers together, and any of their own words that they added to the glossary box.
- Focus on the verb *go* in the **natural English** box. Notice that *in one go* and *Go for it!* are both in the last paragraph of the article, and you could start by writing these two phrases on the board, showing where they occur in the text and asking learners to guess what they mean. This would lead naturally into the **natural English** box. (There is another interesting use of *go* in paragraph 3: *I went for younger people* = chose. You could point this out to your learners.) Notice that *go* is stressed in all four expressions, so check that learners are producing the main stress on *go* in the phrases.

grammar reported questions

- In **exercise 1**, learners can work alone then compare their answers in pairs. See **language point**.
- If your learners find this grammar quite straightforward, you could introduce an element of competition into **exercise 2**. Put them in pairs and give them one minute to unjumble all the questions, without writing the answers down. Allow a thirty-second extension if necessary. Once they have finished, do some oral practice of these questions to help learners pronounce them fluently.
- If learners aren't sure about the answers to the general knowledge questions, let them mingle and see if they can find out from each other.

it's your turn!

- This activity is a light-hearted end to the section which provides some practice of reported questions in a communicative context. Explain to the learners that they are going to work with a partner. One wants to be a contestant on the game show, and they are going to ring and try to get on the show, as the woman in the text did. Put them in pairs for **exercise 1** to decide who will be the contestant, and who will interview them. The interviewers should then look at the role card on *p.150*.
- Learners who are conducting the telephone interviews will need a couple of minutes to think of their two general knowledge questions. The contestants will have little to do at this point, so you could suggest they do a **cover & check** exercise from the **language reference** on *p.175*, or if you want to do the role play twice and reverse the roles, the contestant could spend the time preparing to be the interviewer, and look at that card.
- When learners are ready, seat them so that they are back-to-back, or one person is speaking over their partner's shoulder to simulate the phone conversation scenario. Monitor during the role play. Once they have finished, have a show of hands to see who has been successful. Repeat the role play if you like, then pair learners up with a new partner for **exercise 2** to report their conversations. Note their use of reported questions for feedback at the end.

exercise 2
Portugal

exercise 3
They can ask the audience, go fifty-fifty (take away two incorrect answers), or phone a friend.

---

troubleshooting Who wants to be a millionaire?

Have a show of hands to see how many of your learners are familiar with this popular TV game show. You then have a choice. You can ask learners who know the game to explain the rules to someone who doesn't, using the photo of the scoreboard and the symbols as a prompt. Another approach is to put learners in pairs or small groups, and ask them to write a short summary of the rules (in not more than 120 words). You can give them the first sentence of the recording T12.2 to start them off. Monitor and assist where necessary. At the end, let them compare what they have written with the recording and transcript on *p.42*, and they can adapt or lift useful language from the transcript to improve their summary. This would be useful for a class who want to aim for greater accuracy, or simply want more writing practice.

---

exercise 1 glossary
swot up on sth; gamble; mortgage

exercise 2
1 Yes; she likes to stretch her mind and she wanted the opportunity to win money.
2 She didn't have time to prepare.
3 Her friend, Wendy, and her boyfriend, Wayne.
4 During the show, she stayed calm, but by the end, she was in a daze.
5 She re-evaluated her life, paid off her debts, got a mortgage, bought a motorbike, and split up with her boyfriend.

nE possible answers
Go for it!   Let me have a go.
I ate all the chocolates in one go.   It's your go.

---

ideas plus vocabulary exploitation

The final paragraph of the text lends itself to a paraphrase activity, extending learners' use of vocabulary. You can approach this in different ways:

• Tell them to underline the following words / phrases: *chance, sort out, re-evaluate, split up with, part, on good terms, go for it*. They then have to rewrite the paragraph and find an alternative word / phrase for each underlined item. (The answers are in the text below.)

• Give them a copy of the following text, and without looking at the original article, see if they can produce a paraphrase or alternative word for the underlined words and phrases. They then compare with the original.
Here was an opportunity to organize and re-assess my life in one go. That meant separating from Wayne, my boyfriend of more than four years, because I felt our relationship wasn't going anywhere. We separated amicably. My advice to Millionaire hopefuls is – have a go!

Both activities can be done in pairs.

---

exercise 1
What's the capital of Peru? Do you have a criminal record? Are you related to anyone employed on the programme? What's the height of the Eiffel Tower?
a In reported questions, the word order in the subordinate clause is subject + verb, whereas in direct questions the word order is inverted. The verbs in these reported questions shift back a tense, e.g. *is > was; have > had.*
b Simple form *yes / no* questions require an auxiliary + verb, but these auxiliaries are not used in reported questions. Instead we use *if / whether* to report this type of question, e.g. *Are you related ...? They asked if / whether I was related ...*

exercise 2
He asked me what the highest mountain in Japan was.
She wanted to know how far it was from Paris to Vienna.
I was asked whether papaya was a kind of fruit.
I was asked how long ago the Berlin Wall came down.
She asked me whether the Swedish flag had more than two colours.

exercise 3
What's the highest mountain in Japan? (Mount Fuji)
How far is it from Paris to Vienna? (645 miles / 1037km)
Is papaya a kind of fruit? (yes)
How long ago did the Berlin Wall come down? (in 1989 – will depend when you read this how long ago it was!)
Does the Swedish flag have more than two colours? / Has the Swedish flag got more than two colours? (no)

---

language point reported questions

Although this grammar area may be familiar to some learners, it is not surprising if they make accuracy errors in fluent speech as there are a number of rules to bear in mind. The most common error is word order: learners often retain the question form in the subordinate clause, e.g. *They asked me ~~what was the capital of Peru~~.* or *She wanted to know ~~what did he think of it~~.* By this level, many learners will be capable of using *if* in reported *yes / no* questions, but few use *whether*, despite the fact that it is very common in both spoken and written English, so you could point this out and encourage them to use it. Note that question marks are not used in reported questions.

Notice that in more formal spoken and written English the tense shift rule is usually applied. However, in spoken English, we may decide not to change the tense, especially if we are describing something that is still true and has not changed, e.g. *She asked me if Brendan still works at the same bank.*

listening boost your brain power

60 – 75 mins

lead-in

- The puzzles at the start of the lesson (particularly the second one) require some *lateral thinking* (= using your brain to make connections between things that are not normally brought together). Some learners love these puzzles and work them out quite quickly; others find them frustrating. Try to assess your group's attitude. If there is clearly no enthusiasm, you might wish to omit the **lead-in** altogether, and introduce the lesson in a different way, e.g. by asking the learners if they think the brain increases or decreases in power as we get older. What evidence do they have for their opinions?

- Ask learners to read the puzzles with the help of the pictures and the glossary. Then put them in groups to work them out. The first puzzle shouldn't prove too hard, but the second one is more difficult. If your learners are getting nowhere, you could offer help at appropriate moments. See **troubleshooting** on the right.

listen to this

- For **exercise 1**, introduce the recording and play the first part. See **troubleshooting** on the right. Part of the reason for including these sentences is that they introduce learners to several key words from the passage that they will need to recognize at other points. You could also ask learners to repeat the phrases.

- As learners have to complete the notes in **exercise 2**, you may decide to stop the tape at one or two appropriate points to give them more time to do this. Alternatively, play the recording without stopping, but play it twice. Whatever you decide, tell the learners what you are going to do.

- When they have compared with a partner, go over the answers, and then introduce the phrases in the **natural English** box. Get learners to find the exact phrase used by the interviewer in the recording, then give them a minute to practise saying the phrases.

- Give learners time to think about **exercise 3**, then put them in pairs or groups for **exercise 4**. It doesn't matter whether the learners have a lot to say or just a little; but it is an opportunity to react to the text and reflect on the subject matter.

grammar *like, as, such as*

- Ask learners to complete **exercise 1** alone, then compare with a partner before you check the answers. See **language point** on the right.

- If you walk round and monitor while learners are doing **exercise 2** individually, you should be able to see which learners, if any, are having problems. If a significant number are experiencing difficulty, use the **language reference** with the **cover & check** exercises on *p.175*.

- The **listening challenge** normally follows **listen carefully**, but we delayed it in this section, otherwise there would have been a lot of listening in one section of the lesson. Placed here, it also serves as an appropriate introduction to **it's your turn!**, which ends the section.

- As the task for the **listening challenge** involves more note taking, you must decide whether to pause the recording at suitable moments, or play the whole section twice.

it's your turn!

- Give learners a minute to read through the different tasks in **exercise 1**, then match them with a partner, and ask each pair to choose three tasks to try out. Before they begin, you could suggest that pairs make a note of the ease or difficulty of each task in turn, and if they find something difficult, they should try to note down why it is difficult. If they wait until the end to do this, they may have forgotten things.

- When they start the activities, you should be prepared for some moving round and a certain amount of noise, but do your best to monitor what is happening and their use of language. You may notice an opportunity to teach one or two useful words and phrases, and perhaps revise and remind learners of the phrases they met in unit one of the book on *p.10*, e.g. *I found X quite tricky / challenging, I was hopeless at Y, I found it hard to do Z*, etc.

 **wordbooster** *go to p.144*   This **wordbooster** can be used at any point in **unit twelve.**

exercise 1

The man was wearing the woman's husband's clothes, which he had stolen in a suitcase from their car, and the woman recognized the clothes.

One Man was the name of a horse, much loved by people who go horse racing. The headline was on the sports pages of many newspapers the following day.

troubleshooting puzzle clues

If some of the groups are finding the second puzzle difficult, the following clues might help them:

- Point out the significance of the story appearing on the <u>sports</u> page, not a news page.
- Point out the significance of the fact that it is <u>not</u> a police matter.

exercise 1

the brain degenerates as we **get older**
rich in vitamins **and minerals**
these improve the blood flow to **the brain**
they make stronger connections between **brain cells**

exercise 2

Not true that brain degenerates as we **get older**. New cells **grow**.

But important to keep active in different ways:

1 Eat **balanced diet, vitamins and minerals / fresh fruit and vegetables**
2 Try **herbal extracts,** e.g. ginseng and gingko
3 Take lots of **physical exercise**
4 Do **brain exercises:** puzzles, memory tests, creative tasks, etc. to keep the brain active.

Good e.g. of a memory test: **think up 25 uses for an elastic band.**

nE

So, what you're saying is, ...

troubleshooting listening

Learners may find this listening passage difficult for several reasons:

- the medical expert has a distinctive Scottish accent
- she speaks quite quickly
- the subject matter is rather scientific, and some learners may be intimidated by this.

Don't say any of this to the learners, but after listening to the first part, ask whether they think the main recording may be difficult to understand, and if so, why? It might be interesting to see if they come up with any of the suggested difficulties above. After the next section, you can ask them if any of their fears were justified, or whether they had problems they hadn't anticipated.

exercise 1

1 b   2 c   3 a   4 a   5 d

exercise 2

1 as	5 such as
2 as	6 like
3 like	7 as
4 as	8 like

language point *like* and *as*

The exercise in the **student's book** highlights the distinction between *like* + noun / pronoun and *as* + clause when expressing similarity. You might also wish to tell your learners that in informal English, *like* is sometimes used instead of *as*, e.g. *He's retired now, but he still gets up at dawn like he did when he was at work*. This would not generally be considered correct in formal English.

how to ... explain the rules of a game

60 – 70 mins

discuss games using **natural English** phrases

focus on games vocabulary

listen to people playing a game

practise the rules of a game

explain the rules of a game and play it

lead-in

- Begin by setting the language in the **natural English** box in context: either ask learners to look at the pictures of games and see if they know them, or do the activity suggested in **ideas plus** on the right.
- Play the recording for the **natural English** box so that learners can complete the sentences. Go over them afterwards, and check learners understand and can pronounce *straightforward* = uncomplicated. Point out that *dead* = very, and is very informal, and *to get the hang of something* = learn how to do something, e.g. use a new computer. Learners will need to practise the phrases for fluency, so either use the recording as a model or give the model yourself. Give them a moment to think about the questions in **exercise 1**, then they compare their ideas in groups. Encourage them to use one or two of the **natural English** phrases.

vocabulary games

- The errors in **exercise 1** are ones that we picked out from our research data for the **extended speaking** activity for this unit. See **troubleshooting** on the right.
- Go over the answers to **exercise 1**, then you can ask learners to shout out the answers to **exercise 2**. Clarify the meaning of any items learners aren't familiar with, and encourage them to make a note of new items in their notebooks.
- Play the recording in **exercise 3**. Learners only have to follow the game, and see if it is one they know. (In English it is called *Twenty questions*.) Then ask them to order the rules as suggested in **exercise 4**.
- **Exercise 5** gives learners an opportunity for controlled practice, and there are some useful phrases in **bold** in the rules. Encourage learners to memorize them so that the phrases will become automatic; they may well need some of these phrases in the **extended speaking** activity. For an extra activity, you could organize learners into small groups at the end to play the game. One person should think of an object, one or two people should do the guessing, and another person should look at the rules and check that they are playing the game correctly.

explain a word game

- In this activity, learners have some controlled practice in explaining the rules of a game based on a written description. Describing a game is not as easy as it sounds, as our research data revealed, which is why we have suggested that in **exercise 2** they rehearse the rules with a partner so that they can check each other's description and build confidence. Monitor and help learners with accuracy and pronunciation during this activity, and if there are any queries, deal with them.
- Reorganize learners into new pairs for **exercise 3**, and monitor and note down any language points for feedback at the end.

play the games

- Depending on the time and the atmosphere, you may decide to play one game or both in groups. You can always use one or either game as a warmer in another lesson. The categories supplied in *Fives in sixty seconds* are all vocabulary areas which have been covered in the **student's book**.

nE
It's very straightforward.
It's dead easy.
It's easy once you get the hang of it.
It's pretty complicated.
The instructions are hard to follow.

ideas plus vocabulary warmer

Before they open the **student's book**, organize learners into small groups, and put these categories of games on the board: **board games**, **word games**, **card games**. Elicit an example of each one to check learners' understanding. Then give them two minutes in groups to brainstorm as many games in each category as they can. If a group doesn't know the name of a game in English, they can ask you. At the end, elicit their ideas onto the board. The winner is the group with the highest number of games. In the **student's book**, they will see chess, Monopoly, cards, and bowls. Here are some other games:
card games: snap, rummy, bridge, pontoon, poker, patience
word games: crosswords, twenty questions, What's my line? (guessing a job)
board games: scrabble, snakes and ladders, ludo, draughts, backgammon, Ma Jong

exercise 1
1 ... it's a very good **game**.
2 The contestants won a fantastic **trip** to the Bahamas.
3 ... you win a **prize**.
4 When you have **made up your mind / decided**, you throw the dice.
5 Each team in the competition consists **of** five people.
6 You have to answer **general knowledge** questions.
7 If you can't answer, you **miss** a turn.
8 I don't know ... can you **give** me a clue?

exercise 2
Monopoly, game, contestants, win, get the answers right, throw the dice, team, competition, general knowledge questions, miss a turn, give someone a clue

exercise 4
1 d   2 g   3 f   4 b   5 e   6 a   7 c

troubleshooting anticipating vocabulary difficulties

The approach we took with this vocabulary selection in **exercise 1** was to work from learners' errors. You could spend a few moments before the lesson thinking about the kinds of errors learners are likely to make with this area of lexis: are there other items they frequently get wrong, or phrases which they don't use? You could read through the rules of the game in **exercise 4** and try to anticipate what kind of errors learners might make if they were trying to produce these sentences themselves without the script, e.g. how might they say *take it in turns*, or *compete against*, or *the aim of the game is to ...*? You could then add a few more examples to exercise 1 on the board for them to correct at this stage, before they get to the ordering activity. They will see the relevance of the vocabulary you highlighted at that later stage.

extended speaking game shows

75 – 90 mins

collect ideas

- While the pairs are brainstorming **exercise 1**, you could start writing up names of game shows on the board in a column. After a few minutes, bring the class together and elicit more of their ideas. Write them on the board as well, along with the reasons for their success. Leave this information on the board as it may help weaker groups in the later activity.

- Ask learners to read the description of three more games in **exercise 2**. To check they have understood, you could put them in threes and ask one person in turn to shut their book and explain the rules of one of the games; the other two learners meanwhile can keep their books open to check that the description is accurate. Most of the vocabulary should now be familiar, although you may need to check words like *soundproof* and *booth*.

- You could bring the whole class together for **exercise 3**. Of particular interest might be your learners' assessment of whether a game will appeal to a wide audience or just a particular age range, as this will be an important factor for them to consider when they design their own game in the next activity.

design a show

- Learners now work in groups on their own game show. Go through the **checklist** carefully, and make it absolutely clear that learners have the freedom to invent something completely new, but equally, they can adapt a game they are already familiar with. For example, they may wish to adapt one of the games you wrote on the board earlier. An example of an adaptation might be to play a version of Mr and Mrs, using twins instead of partners, and possibly to have one set of twins competing with another set of twins.

- When the groups start the activity, don't be surprised if several groups take a while to get going and make significant progress. You can obviously help and guide learners if necessary, but this is the type of activity that often requires time to gather momentum.

- When the groups are nearing completion – this may take anything from ten to twenty-five minutes – give them a two-minute warning.

give a presentation

- It is important for the overall success of the activity that the groups are able to present their ideas clearly and fluently; hesitant or confused presentations will greatly undermine their sense of achievement. Rehearsal time is therefore essential and shouldn't be rushed. Make sure each learner knows exactly what they have to explain and can do it. Give individuals time to prepare their own part, then let each group rehearse the whole presentation and give each other feedback on parts that are successful and parts that could be improved.

- Before the presentations, go through the **natural English** box. These introductory phrases are very common and useful because they give learners a way in to their comment or question without appearing too direct or even abrupt.

- During the presentations make notes on good language use as well as any important errors for correction. You may also note down clear cases where learners didn't have a particular word or phrase that would have made their presentation more effective in some way. If it is language that may be of use to other groups as well, you could feed it in immediately so that others can use it in their presentations.

play the game

- It seems a natural ending to this particular activity for learners to play one of the games. We have suggested *Ten to one*, but if you think one of the games presented by the learners is equally practical (and everyone in the class clearly understands it), play that instead.

- Make sure when you play *Ten to one* that you get learners up on their feet, standing in a line.

feedback checklist

During the **extended speaking** activity, note down examples of …

- **good language use**

- **effective communication strategies**
(turn-taking, interrupting, inviting others to speak, etc.)

- **learner errors**
(vocabulary, grammar, pronunciation, etc.)

- **particular communication problems**

Make sure you allow time for feedback at the end of the lesson. You can use the notes you make above to <u>praise</u> effective language use and communication or, if necessary, to do some remedial work.

test yourself!

Want to know more? Go to the **introduction** *p.7* for ways of using **test yourself!**

1 audience, crew, pile, congregation, herd, jury, crowd, staff, gang, set, choir, series, public
2 doze off, fast asleep, have a nap, snore; (these are to do with being awake, but are related to sleep: yawn, half-asleep, daydream, wide awake, insomnia)
3 have a go, in one go, it's your go

1 He asked if I knew the answer.
2 He wanted to know how long the journey would take.
3 Does the name Jim Carter mean anything to you?
4 That game doesn't appeal to me.

1 He got a job **as** an engineer.
2 So what you **are trying** to say is, we don't need the money.
3 You take **it** in turns to answer.
4 If you don't know, **have** a guess. (*take* is also possible in American English)

unit one wordbooster

25 – 30 mins

This **wordbooster** can be used at any point in **unit one**.

sporting collocations

- Begin by making clear what collocations are before learners open their books (see **language point** on the right). **Exercise 1** can then be done alone or in pairs.
- Be prepared to accept or reject learners' own suggestions in **exercise 2**. They might like a couple of minutes to study the table before they test each other in **test your partner**.

collocation in dictionaries

- If your school or your learners don't have access to any learners' dictionaries, you won't be able to do **exercise 2**. However, you can still do **exercise 1** and point out how this important feature is shown in dictionaries. This might be an appropriate point at which to gently encourage learners to buy a dictionary of their own to bring to class.

Want to know more? Go to **how to ...** use dictionaries with learners *p.178*.

unit two wordbooster

25 – 30 mins

This **wordbooster** can be used at any point in **unit two**.

health and medicine

- Learners will probably know various different items in **exercise 1**, and there will probably be a few items no one will know. Point out the useful phrases for asking about new words, and let them see what they can teach each other. They can also use dictionaries if these are available. When you go through the answers in **exercise 2**, check pronunciation as well. See **language point** on the right.
- For **exercise 3**, learners get the opportunity to use the items, and in a small group there is a chance that everyone will have had several of the ailments. Make it clear at the start that if they don't want to talk about a medical problem, they should just listen.

tourist information

- The main reason for having these sentences in **wordbooster** is to focus on some very common sentence beginnings which learners don't always use, e.g. *Is there any chance of getting ...? What's the best way of getting ...? Do I have to ...? What's the best place to ...?* After learners have done **exercise 1**, you could highlight these beginnings on the board.
- Demonstrate **exercise 2** with a learner, then the class can work in pairs.

Want to know more? Go to **how to ...** develop lexis at higher levels *p.160*.

exercise 1
the following are <u>not</u> correct: **go** ~~ski~~, **take part in** ~~a team~~, **join** ~~a sport~~, **lose** ~~an award~~, **win** ~~the opposing team~~, **practise** ~~sport~~, **do** ~~table tennis~~

exercise 2
go windsurfing, **take part in** a competition, **join** an aerobics class, **lose** a race, **win** a cup / a race / a competition, **practise** heading the ball, **do** karate.

---

language point collocation

Collocation describes the way certain words are often used together. There are many different combinations:

- verb and noun, e.g. *take a photo* NOT ~~make a photo~~
- adjective and noun, e.g. *a pretty woman* NOT ~~a pretty man~~
- adverb and adjective, e.g. *seriously injured* NOT ~~very injured~~

You could write the incorrect collocations on the board (*make a photo*, *a pretty man*, *very injured*) and ask learners what is wrong with them. They should be able to correct these, and you can explain that they are collocation errors, i.e. using the wrong word combinations.

---

exercise 1 possible answers
latest: film / record / weather forecast
flick through: a newspaper / a magazine / a document

exercise 2 possible answers

1 dip into a book, magazine, report
2 know sth or learn by heart
3 skip a page, a chapter, the last part of the book
4 look up a word, the meaning
5 get / give sb the gist

---

exercise 1

1 earache
2 a sore throat
3 a cough
4 a bandage
5 eye drops
6 a pain in her arm / her arm hurts
7 a nose bleed
8 sunburn
9 a plaster
10 tissues
11 tablets / pills
12 ointment

---

language point health and medicine vocabulary

There are many potential problems with pronunciation of the items in **exercise 1**, mainly due to sound / spelling interference, e.g. *cough* /kɒf/, *bandage* /'bændɪdʒ/, *tissues* /'tɪʃuːz/, and many learners mispronounce *sore throat* /sɔː 'θrəʊt/ and *sunburn* /'sʌnbɜːn/. *Earache* should be fairly obvious from the learners' knowledge of *headache*. Give learners plenty of practice with the words, and suggest that they record the phonemic script as a memory aid.

These items also present problems of countability. *Earache* and *sunburn* are never countable, whereas *headache* always is. *Toothache, stomachache* (also *stomach-ache* or *stomach ache*), and *backache* can be countable or uncountable. There is a restricted number of items with *-ache* and any other complaints are usually described as *a pain in my / his / her ...* or *my / his / her (arm) hurts*.

---

exercise 1

1 What's the best way of getting to the river from here?
2 Do I have to book train tickets in advance?
3 Is there any chance of getting tickets for the concert?
4 How much does it cost to get in to the exhibition?
5 Can we get something to eat round here?
6 What's the best place to get souvenirs?

unit three wordbooster

This **wordbooster** can be used at any point in **unit three**.

personality phrases

- Learners will need some of this vocabulary in the **extended speaking** activity. Do the first example in **exercise 1** as a class, then learners can do the rest in pairs, using dictionaries if available.

- **Exercise 2** focuses on meaning and connotation. Certain lexical items are always intrinsically positive in meaning, e.g. *supportive*, some items always have a negative meaning, e.g. *a pain in the neck*, but others can be interpreted either way, depending on the speaker's attitude, e.g. *She's very ambitious* might be a criticism or an admiring comment. This feature may be present in your learners' mother tongue and it is something you could discuss with them.

- Before you go on to **test your partner**, check that learners can pronounce the items correctly.

paraphrasing

- Paraphrasing is an obvious communication strategy for language learners, as well as a common feature of native speaker discourse. For **exercise 2**, give learners a minute or two to check the meaning of their words, perhaps with other learners who are looking at the same words. They can use dictionaries if necessary. They should think about how to convey the meaning without using the words.

- When they are ready, match them in A / B pairs to see if they can guess the words from their partner's paraphrase. For an interesting idea on dictionary use, see the reference below.

Want to know more? Go to **how to ...** use dictionaries with learners (try it out) *p.177.*

unit four wordbooster

This **wordbooster** can be used at any point in **unit four**.

words of similar meaning

- Learners met and used *ban* and *allow* earlier, so you could begin by asking them to explain the meaning and find a word in **bold** in the sentences which has a similar meaning. They can then complete the rest of **exercise 1**, and compare with a partner before you go through their answers. You will also need to practise pronunciation.

- Learners should not assume that words which have a similar meaning in one context will be similar in meaning in all other contexts, or have the same collocational range: this is the purpose of **exercise 2**. Do the first one as an example. You may need to explain the meaning of *morale* (= level of confidence and positive feelings; you can have *high morale* or *low morale*). Practise the pronunciation /məˈrɑːl/, not to be confused with *moral* /ˈmɒrəl/.

- Put learners in pairs to discuss the rest of the exercise and then talk through the answers and use **test your partner** for quick practice.

making the most of your dictionary

- This section draws learners' attention to a dictionary feature which can help them with groups of words which are similar in meaning. This example comes from the *Oxford Advanced Learner's Dictionary*, but there is a similar feature in the *Longman Dictionary of Contemporary English*, called *Usage Note*. With a monolingual group, it might be interesting to consider how many words would be used in the learners' first language to fill the gaps in these sentences.

- If your learners have either of the two dictionaries mentioned above, you could ask them to find and discuss another example of *Which Word?* or *Usage Note*. If they don't have these dictionaries (but have others), ask them to find a different dictionary feature which will help them with a specific problem, e.g. words within the same general topic such as parts of a car, or information about American English.

Want to know more? Go to **how to ...** use dictionaries with learners *p.177.*

exercise 1

1 articulate 2 laugh 3 eccentric 4 neck
5 control 6 ego 7 life 8 supportive

exercise 2

1, 2, and 8 are always positive
4, 5, and 6 are always negative
3 and 7 may be positive or negative depending on context; here, 3 is a little negative, 7 is more positive

exercise 3

informal items: a good laugh, a pain in the neck, a big ego

---

language point using lexis to agree / reinforce meaning

Exercise 1 includes mini dialogues which illustrate a common feature of spoken English. The listener shows agreement by repeating or echoing what the speaker says, either directly, e.g. A *He's **kind**, isn't he?* B *Mm, **very kind**.* Or, as shown here, the listener paraphrases or provides a synonym of the speaker's words, e.g. A *She's **rather wild**, isn't she?* B *Yeah, **a bit out of control**.*

It is worth pointing out this feature to learners. It is also a very good way for them to broaden their vocabulary and at the same time, it provides an opportunity for pair practice in **test your partner**. Notice that the items are a mixture of single words and lexical phrases.

---

exercise 1

shy and *a very good sense of humour*

---

exercise 1

1 regulated; check	3 allowed	5 reduced; raise	7 expanding
2 ban; restricting	4 declining	6 boost; lack	8 censored

exercise 2

1 prices	3 your English	5 population figures	7 trees
2 morale	4 taxes	6 the weather	8 metal

---

exercise 1

1 opportunity; chance
2 possibility; chance
3 occasion
4 opportunity; chance

unit five wordbooster

25 – 30 mins

This **wordbooster** can be used at any point in **unit five** before the **extended speaking** activity.

taking exams

- Learners will already know some of these verbs, and others they can probably work out using the context and through a process of elimination. We would suggest, therefore, that you don't pre-teach any of the items from the list. Let learners work in pairs on **exercise 1**, using dictionaries if available, then discuss any problems when you go through the answers. You could also point out to the learners that they will need many of these items when they do the **extended speaking** activity.

- When everyone has completed the questions with the correct verb or phrase, you can continue with **exercise 2**. You can leave learners in their existing pairs, or create new pairs. For example, with a multilingual group it will be more interesting to match learners from different countries; with a group who come from the same country, you may want to divide the class by pairing up learners who drive with those that don't. If necessary, create small groups rather than pairs for this.

- At the end, ask learners to tell the class if they learnt anything interesting or unusual.

phrasal verbs

- In **natural English**, we do not generally lift out phrasal verbs and teach a group of them in isolation. We recognize their importance, but tend to include them on a regular basis alongside other lexical items (as in **taking exams** exercise 1). The reason for presenting a group on their own here is simply to give you an opportunity to examine some of the issues of meaning and grammar that apply to phrasal verbs in general. See **language point** on the right.

- You could start by clarifying some terminology. Write the example sentence (*The plane took off.*) on the board, underline _took off_, and ask the learners to identify the type of verb it is, i.e. a phrasal verb. Tell learners the verb is *intransitive*. Can they explain that? If not, tell them that it is a verb that doesn't need a <u>direct object</u>. You could point out that an intransitive verb may have other information after it, e.g. *The plane took off* **two hours late**, but it doesn't need an object so you can always finish a sentence with an intransitive verb (as in the example). Go through a similar procedure with the *transitive* example (verbs which do need a direct object).

- After this, go through the examples to show how dictionaries enter separable phrasal verbs.

- For **exercise 1**, go through the example given, then ask the class if they could put *continuing* for the second sentence. They should say no, and you can ask them what they could put; someone should come up with *happening*. Then let them complete the exercise individually or in pairs. Check the answers.

- Learners can do the first part of **exercise 2** just by looking at the eight sentences. You could check that first before they use dictionaries to see whether the two transitive verbs are separable.

- If learners don't have access to dictionaries, ask them in **exercise 3** to write down sentences including these phrasal verbs with meanings they already know. Learners can then listen to each others' examples; they may learn some new meanings.

exercise 1

1 take place
2 turn up; do / take
3 fail / make a
  mess of; retake
4 cheat
5 sit / take / do
6 prepare
7 come up
8 pass / get through;
  go on
9 bluff

exercise 1

1 b happening
1 c passes
2 a come / arrive
2 b will appear / will be found
2 c increase the volume
3 a make contact
3 b used / used up / consumed
4 a happening / taking place
4 b appeared

exercise 2

2c turn up (the radio); separable, e.g. *turn it up*.
3b get through (a packet of cigarettes); inseparable

language point phrasal verbs: grammar and meaning

There are two main issues concerning the grammar of phrasal verbs. Firstly, is the verb transitive or intransitive? And secondly, if it is transitive, is it separable? In practice, we find that the most common learner error is with the position of the pronoun when the verb is transitive, e.g. ~~I picked up it~~. Knowing a pronoun must always go before the particle (if the verb is transitive and separable), is probably the single most important rule learners need to know, i.e. *I picked **it** up*.

With *meaning*, learners shouldn't assume that if they meet a word form they already know, they will also know its meaning. Many phrasal verbs have more than one meaning, so it's vital to look at the context carefully. Learners also need to recognize that phrasal verbs have collocational restrictions. For example, *break out* can mean *start*, e.g. *War could break out at any time; The fire broke out on the third floor*. However, we cannot talk about a *hurricane* or *earthquake* ~~breaking out~~. Learners obviously cannot learn all the collocational possibilities of a phrasal verb at the same time, but when they meet a verb in a new collocation, they should note it down.

unit six wordbooster

This **wordbooster** can be used at any point in **unit six.**

dangers and disasters

- **Exercise 1** concentrates on the verbs in the table we think the learners are least likely to know, but when you check the answers you should also elicit the meaning of the other verbs and add your own explanations and examples where necessary. Practise the pronunciation of the verbs, paying particular attention to those for which phonemic script is given.

- Learners can complete **exercise 2** individually or in pairs, and check their answers using dictionaries if available. Go through the answers before learners test each other.

- If you want to explore some more adjective + noun collocations, and provide further practice of some of the nouns in the table, look at **ideas plus** on the right.

- **Exercise 3** consolidates the meaning of the verbs in some common collocations. Make clear to the learners that in some of the sentences there are more possible answers than spaces provided.

knowing your prepositions

- Many learners are not aware that good dictionaries will tell them if a word is commonly followed or preceded by a particular preposition. This exercise is, therefore, as much about raising awareness as it is about learning vocabulary.

- If dictionaries are available, get learners to make use of them to find answers to questions they don't know. If they are not available, put learners in small groups to pool their knowledge. You will then have to fill any gaps in their knowledge when they have done as much as they can. Most of the potentially difficult items were in the previous exercise (*accuse, arrest, evacuate*), but you will need to elicit or teach the meaning of *at random* (= not following any pre-arranged order), and possibly *on the run*, which is transparent in meaning but may be a new expression for some learners.

- Encourage learners to note down combinations as suggested, as they will then have a written record of the phrases and can test themselves at the same time. Many learners enjoy doing this and it encourages independent revision.

Want to know more? Go to **how to ...** use dictionaries with learners (try it out) *p.177.*

exercise 1

a kidnap b threaten c injure d survive e capture f evacuate

exercise 2

verb	general noun	verb	general noun
warn	*warning*	attack	attack
explode	explosion	survive	survival
escape	escape	capture	capture
accuse	accusation	damage	damage
kidnap	kidnap; kidnapping	threaten	threat
arrest	arrest	destroy	destruction
injure	injury	evacuate	evacuation

exercise 3 possible answers

1 The bomb exploded.
2 Nobody survived / escaped.
3 Terrorists attacked / injured / kidnapped / threatened the politician's family.
4 The police warned / arrested / captured / accused the young man.
5 The soldiers attacked / captured / damaged / destroyed / evacuated the building.

ideas plus probable answers

1 loud 2 serious 3 extensive 4 narrow 5 major 6 wild

ideas plus further practice

Some of the nouns in **exercise 2** collocate with specific adjectives. You could get learners to complete the sentences below with a suitable adjective, then use dictionaries to see if their adjectives are listed as common collocations. If you think this may prove too difficult, or dictionaries are not available, give them the adjectives in a box and ask them to complete the sentences. There is more than one possible answer for each question, but our suggestion for the most likely collocation is given in the answer key. You can decide which others are also acceptable, e.g. *lucky* for question 4.

1 We heard a _____ explosion.
2 It could be a _____ injury.
3 The damage to the building was _____ .
4 They both had a _____ escape.
5 Disease now represents the _____ threat.
6 She made _____ accusations, all of which are untrue.

exercise 1

1 of 2 for 3 from / against 4 from / in 5 on 6 at 7 in 8 in; of

unit seven wordbooster

The vocabulary in this **wordbooster** will be needed by certain learners in the **extended speaking** activity. You could do it at almost any point in the unit that is convenient for you.

conservation

- Put learners in pairs for **exercise 1** and do the first one as an example. This will demonstrate that learners are not necessarily looking for synonyms here, but words that can replace the words in **bold** in this particular context. You can let them use dictionaries, or you may want to see what they can achieve just using the context; it's up to you. Tell them, however, not to write their answers next to or just above the words in bold in the text; you will see why in a minute.

- Go through the answers and practise the pronunciation of the items in phonemic script.

- Explain **exercise 2**, and do the first one as an example, i.e. (reading aloud with the target words covered): *It's true that zoos keep animals in captivity, but one reason … .* Make sure learners cover the words, and have followed your instruction not to write them down next to or above the items in the text. Encourage them to keep practising until they can produce the amended text without hesitation. Ask someone to read the text to the class at the end.

uncountable and plural nouns

- Go through the rules for uncountable and plural nouns, i.e. uncountable nouns don't usually take a plural form and are always followed by a singular verb, e.g. *The information **was** very helpful.* Plural nouns take a plural form and are always followed by a plural verb, e.g. *You know I lost my sunglasses?* ***They were*** *under the sofa.* You could use the **language reference** on *p.166* and *p.167* for this, although it may be more effective if you get learners to shut their books while you work through the rules on the board. This will keep the learners' attention focused on you, and you can ask questions and elicit answers as you proceed.

- Put learners in pairs to correct the sentences in **exercise 1**, and remind them that some are already correct. Check the answers. The **language point** on the right may be helpful to you at some stage, although we don't feel it is necessary to go through these details unless learners ask you, or there is a specific problem.

- For **exercise 2**, tell them to allocate a page or two in their notebooks for each group, and write down the examples from the exercise on the appropriate pages. Then they can add further examples. It shouldn't be difficult to think of uncountable nouns, but they may not immediately think of other plural nouns, e.g. *shorts, tights, sunglasses, pants, jeans, pyjamas, headphones*, etc.

unit eight wordbooster

This **wordbooster** can be used at any point in **unit eight**.

neighbours

- On the face of it, this language may seem very easy for upper-intermediate learners, but when we piloted the **extended speaking** activity at the end of the unit (without any pre-teaching), we found that learners had a lot of difficulty describing where people or things were in relation to other people / things. For example, few learners were able to produce phrases such as *the person next door but one*, or *the person in the flat downstairs*. However, the meaning of the phrases should be transparent, so it is just a matter of mastering these relatively simple but natural ways of expressing specific concepts in English.

- Let learners complete **exercise 1** and then compare with a partner. You can clarify any problems at the end. See **language point** on the right.

- **Exercise 2** provides some controlled practice. Move round and monitor the pairs to check they are producing the target language fluently, then move on to **exercise 3**.

word building

- This exercise is quite straightforward, and the words should not present any problems as most of them have already come up in one form or another in previous parts of the unit. Check the answers when learners have finished, working individually or in pairs, then move on to **test your partner**.

exercise 1

1	captivity	6	feed
2	endangered species	7	dug up
3	breeding	8	buried
4	the wild	9	remains
5	reptiles	10	site

exercise 1

1 His knowledge of the topic ~~are~~ limited. (*is*)
2 Has she got enough work experience~~s~~?
3 *correct*
4 *correct*
5 We always provide ~~a~~ training for successful applicants.
6 We are doing more research~~es~~.
7 *correct*
8 Everyone loved the accommodation~~s~~.
9 *correct*
10 Do they have the funds to buy the new equipment~~s~~?

exercise 2

plural nouns: proceeds, remains, facilities, expenses
uncountable nouns: knowledge, experience, training, research, accommodation, equipment

---

language point uncountable and plural nouns

Some nouns can be countable <u>and</u> uncountable; some can be countable <u>and</u> plural:

Experience is <u>uncountable</u> when referring to knowledge and skills gained, e.g. *He has a lot of experience in banking*; it is <u>countable</u> when it means an event or activity, e.g. *Going to India was an experience I will never forget*.

Facility can be <u>countable</u> when it means a special feature of a machine or service e.g. *Computers have a spell-check facility*; it is <u>plural</u> when referring to the buildings, services, or equipment provided for a particular purpose, e.g. *The building has special facilities for disabled people*.

Expense can be <u>countable</u> when talking about something that makes you spend money, e.g. *Travelling to work is a big expense*; it is <u>plural</u> when referring to money that you spend for a particular purpose, e.g. *living expenses*, and most commonly, money spent at work which your employer pays back to you, e.g. *I can claim all my travel expenses at the end of each month*.

Dictionaries are indispensable for checking whether words are countable (C) or not (U).

Want to know more? Go to **how to ...** use dictionaries with learners (think!³) *p.177*.

---

exercise 1

1 down / across
2 next
3 opposite / upstairs / downstairs
4 corridor
5 opposite
6 door
7 penthouse / basement / top flat

---

language point overlapping meaning

You may need to explain *basement* (= room(s) below street level where people live), as some countries do not have a clear equivalent. Moreover, it should not be confused with a *cellar*, which is a room below ground level, with little natural light, and normally used for storage.

Other overlapping concepts are: *flat* (British English) and *apartment* (American English). However, this distinction has become less clear in recent years as *apartment* has become increasingly common in British English to describe either a holiday flat or a rather expensive flat (estate agents commonly use the word).

Top flat is a neutral term; *penthouse* describes a top floor flat which one would expect to be large and luxurious.

1	complaint	5	threats
2	behaviour	6	compromise
3	proof	7	suspicion
4	deterioration	8	reminder

unit nine wordbooster

This **wordbooster** can be used at any point in **unit nine** before the **extended speaking** activity.

literal and figurative meaning

- Learners can complete **exercise 1** in pairs and if possible use dictionaries. When you come to *sink*, contrast it with *drown* to check understanding. *Sink* = go down under the surface of water and not come up again; *drown* = die because you are under water and cannot breathe.
- Go through the example to illustrate the difference between literal and figurative meaning. If necessary, provide more examples:
  Thousands of people are starving. (literally, dying from lack of food)
  What's in the fridge? I'm starving. (used figuratively here to mean *very hungry*)
  He went mad. (literally, he went insane, or figuratively, he got very angry)
- Do the first question in **exercise 2** together, eliciting a suitable paraphrase for each word in the context: *stream* = a crowd moving continuously in the same direction; *flooding* = coming in large numbers. Let learners complete the rest of the exercise in pairs, then check their answers.

affixes

- The meaning of the affixes here is not difficult, so you could work from the board. Write down examples, elicit the meaning from the class, then ask for further examples of words containing the affixes. When you have finished, the learners can check in their books to see if their examples are included, and they can learn some new ones. If you want to add any further examples, make sure you don't include any that will serve as answers in the next activity. For *non-slip*, you could give *non-slip mat* as an example.
- Learners can do **exercise 1** in pairs.
- The prefixes in **exercise 2** are not particularly common, but they illustrate a feature of many prefixes, namely that they are often guessable, particularly if learners speak one of the Romance languages which have prefixes with similar meanings.
- As an alternative to **exercise 3**, you could explore more affixes. See **language point** on the right.

unit ten wordbooster

Some learners will need vocabulary from **exercise 2** in the **extended speaking** activity; but **exercise 1** can be used at any point in **unit ten**.

animals

- **Exercise 1** is simply an opportunity to extend a lexical set. Working in pairs or groups, learners will probably be able to label most of the pictures and complete the activity using dictionaries. It is worth highlighting the pronunciation, particularly *leopard* /'lepəd/, as this often causes problems.
- You could go through the questions in **exercise 2** eliciting or explaining the target vocabulary in **bold**, but it might be more fun to turn it into a game (see **ideas plus** on the right).
- While the learners are preparing their questions in **exercise 3**, you can move round and help where necessary. When they are ready, they can ask their partner, or you could make it a mingling activity. Conduct a short feedback at the end on their language and, perhaps, one or two of the more interesting questions.

word building

- Some of the words in **exercise 1** have already appeared in the unit in one form or another (*captivity, justifiable, cruel, harmful*), so there shouldn't be many items that will be completely new as both noun and adjective: *disgraceful* may require an explanation (it means *bad and unacceptable*, and is most commonly used to describe behaviour). Let learners use dictionaries if available to find or check any new forms.
- When you have been through the answers, practise the pronunciation, concentrating on word stress. The stressed syllables are underlined in the answer key.
- Learners can do **exercise 2** alone, in pairs, or as an open class, and you could extend this focus on word building with a further look at the relationship between suffixes and word stress. See **language point** on the right.

exercise 1

1 *sink* = go down under the surface of water (or mud) towards the bottom (v)
2 *wave* = line of water moving across the sea or ocean (n)
3 *stream* = a small river (n)
4 *leak* = a hole or crack which allows liquid to escape (v and n)
5 *float* = stay on top of water and not sink (v)
6 *deep end* = part of a swimming pool which has the most water in it (n)
7 *flood* = large amount of water on an area of land which is usually dry (v and n)
8 *out of one's depth* = when the water is too deep to stand in and your head is under water

exercise 2

1 a crowd moving continuously in the same direction; coming in large numbers
2 secret information that has got out
3 start with the most difficult jobs (to see if they survive or not)
4 strong sudden feeling that spreads
5 move as if on air, not touching the ground
6 doing things that are too difficult

exercise 1

b water-proof	f sugar-free
c locally-grown	g non-stick
d sound-proof	h hand-made; water-proof
e alcohol-free	

exercise 2

mini = small; *micro* = very small; *multi* = many; *pre* = before

---

language point affixes

e-   -wards   ex-

Write these three affixes on the board. Put learners in pairs and ask them to explain the meaning of each one, then find three words including the affix with this meaning.

possible answers
e- (= electronic): e-mail, e-fit, e-commerce, e-business, e-shopping
-wards (= in the direction of): forward(s), backward(s), inward(s), eastward(s), homeward(s)
ex- (= former or previous): ex-wife / ex-husband, ex-boyfriend / ex-girlfriend, ex-boss, ex-leader, ex-smoker

exercise 1

1 owl	4 leopard	7 panda
2 zebra	5 elephant	8 crocodile
3 bear	6 snake	9 scorpion

exercise 2

1 snake	6 snake, crocodile
2 scorpion	7 zebra
3 leopard	8 elephant, zebra
4 bear, panda	9 pandas, leopards (in some parts of the world)
5 panda	10 owl

---

ideas plus game

You could make **exercise 2** more competitive by setting a time limit and offering a prize. Put learners in pairs and allow them to use dictionaries. When one pair has finished, stop the game and get them to tell the class the answers. If there are any problems, the winning pair should explain their answers. You can also add your own further concept checks by asking for other examples of animals that have *stripes*, e.g. *tiger*, can *sting*, e.g. *a bee* or *wasp*, etc.

exercise 1

noun	adjective	noun	adjective
captivity	captive	justification	(un)justifiable
attraction	attractive	disgrace	disgraceful
cruelty	cruel	sensitivity	(in)sensitive
persuasion	persuasive	destruction	destructive
hunger	hungry	stress	stressful
harm	harmful / harmless	protection	protective

attractiveness and *persuasiveness* also exist as nouns, but they are rare

exercise 2 1 The most likely form is the stem, i.e. without *-ful*. Other examples: use > useful; hope > hopeful, care > careful; thought > thoughtful; tact > tactful. 2 The most likely forms of the noun are *-ity* and *-ion*. Other examples: creative > creativity; active > activity; productive > productivity; intuitive > intuition; preventive > prevention; informative > information

---

language point word stress

Ask learners to look again at the adjectives ending in *-ive* and the nouns ending in *-ion* in **exercise 1.** What do they notice about the stress on these words? (The main stress falls on the syllable before *-ive* in all but one example, and on the penultimate syllable with every example of *-ion*, e.g. *prevention.*) These are common patterns and will help learners to make a calculated guess at the correct pronunciation of other new words they meet with these endings.

unit eleven wordbooster

> This **wordbooster** can be used at any point in **unit eleven** before the **extended speaking** activity.

phrases and phrasal verbs

- This may seem a miscellaneous group of lexical items, but the learners will have an opportunity to use most of them again in the **extended speaking** activity at the end of the unit.
- Put learners in pairs or threes for **exercise 1**. Using their shared knowledge, the sentence contexts, and some intelligent guesswork, they should be able to answer most of the questions. At the end, check their answers and clarify any problems of meaning. See **language point** on the right.
- **Exercise 2** provides consolidation and encourages learners to keep a written record of the items as phrases, not just individual words, e.g. it's not worth learning *ashamed* without the preposition *of*.

use your dictionary

- Learners often have problems retrieving the meaning of a phrase from a dictionary (they don't know where to look for it), and many learners are not even aware that dictionaries include phrases as well as individual words. This section therefore has a dual purpose: to develop learners' awareness of phrases and their ability to identify them; and to make them more efficient in dictionary use.
- Highlight one or two of the phrases listed in the entry for *blue* (e.g. *out of the blue*) and explain the hierarchy of words to look up when trying to track down a phrase in a dictionary, i.e. noun first, then verb, adjective, or preposition. It is important to point out that this is not a rule, simply a guideline. Also point out that dictionaries differ in the way they enter idioms.
- **Exercise 1** concentrates on learners identifying phrases (see **language point**). Don't worry too much about the meaning at this stage; just see if learners, in pairs or threes, can identify word combinations which occur so frequently that dictionaries include them in bold and explain them.
- When you have checked and clarified the answers – still without explaining the meaning of the phrases – put them back in pairs or groups for **exercise 2**. Go over their answers, then let them find the phrases in a dictionary (if available) and check the meaning if necessary.

Want to know more? Go to **how to ...** use dictionaries with learners *p.176*.

unit twelve wordbooster

> This **wordbooster** can be used at any point in **unit twelve**.

collective nouns

- Highlight the fact that these nouns refer to a group of people or things and can be used with a singular or plural verb, i.e. we can view them as a number of individual people / things, or as one single entity.
- Working in pairs or small groups and with the nouns given in the box, we think learners can probably use their shared knowledge and the context to work out most of the answers. When you go through the answers you can clarify the meaning of new items and check their pronunciation; *choir* /ˈkwaɪə/ is different from what most learners imagine.
- **Test your partner** provides some straightforward practice and consolidation.

attitude adverbs

- These adverbs are important but are not often included in coursebooks. See **language point**.
- After doing one or two examples together, learners could complete **exercise 1** alone or in pairs. If dictionaries aren't available, encourage them to consult other members of the class for words they don't know. *Presumably* is used to introduce something which you think is probably true. Elicit their answers at the end and clarify any problems of meaning with further examples.
- Make it clear to learners for **exercise 2** that they must have logical answers in mind for each of their sentence beginnings. If any of the groups finish before the others, ask them to choose another adverb and write a suitable sentence beginning. Move round and monitor as much of the group as you can to ensure the tasks being set are achievable.
- When the groups complete the sentences in **exercise 3**, monitor their endings carefully. At the end, you could ask groups to read out some of their completed sentences.

exercise 1

1 up	5 up
2 in	6 out; up
3 up	7 by
4 of	8 up

language point explaining phrasal verbs

You can often explain the meaning of a phrasal verb with a more formal verb, but that doesn't mean the two verbs will be interchangeable in most contexts. For example, *turn up* = arrive and *cover up sth* = hide sth, but we cannot say, *When does the train ~~turn up~~?* or *The boy ~~covered up~~ behind a tree.*

Turn up is used about people, usually for one specific occasion (not about regular habits), and is often used when someone is earlier or later than expected, or doesn't arrive at all.

Cover up is not used to describe people hiding physically, but usually means intentionally concealing information and facts to avoid a scandal or prevent someone from getting into trouble.

exercise 1

1 have no sympathy for
2 treats him like a child
3 is to blame
4 in the first place
5 don't see the point of ... -*ing*
6 put yourself in her shoes
7 to cut a long story short
8 in a bad mood; don't take any notice of ...

exercise 2

The key word in each phrase will depend on the dictionary you are using. Likely key words are:

1 sympathy	5 point
2 treat	6 shoes
3 blame	7 story / cut / long
4 place	8 mood; notice

language point lexical phrases

Words may occur together in a fixed phrase, e.g. *to cut a long story short, in the first place*; or as part of a phrase with a limited number of variations, e.g. *in a **good** / **bad** mood, put yourself in **my** / **his** / **her shoes** / **place** / **position**.*

When words combine in these ways, learners should obviously try to recognize them, and record them as phrases in their notebooks. Some phrases are quite easy to spot (most learners will identify *to cut a long story short*), but sometimes it is difficult and you will have to highlight the fact that a particular combination of words forms a phrase or common collocation, e.g. *I have no sympathy for sb; I don't / can't see the point of -ing.*

collective nouns

1 herd	7 pile
2 crowd	8 public
3 staff	9 set
4 crew	10 audience
5 jury	11 series
6 gang	12 congregation; choir

exercise 1 possible answers

1 I found them in the sand.
2 I still prefer the old flat.
3 it wouldn't start.
4 there was a cancellation and we were given the room. / there was another hotel nearby.
5 he was very fed up.
6 I'd need to improve my English first. / I'd have to get a job / visa.
7 they've split up.
8 it'll stop raining by then.

language point attitude adverbs

These adverbs are important for two reasons:

- receptively, they can help learners to predict what is coming next
- productively, they are extremely useful in linking ideas together.

Presumably, *hopefully*, and *obviously* are among the most common thousand words in spoken English.

teacher development chapters

how to ... do informal testing

1   What is informal testing? Why do it?

There is a difference between **formal** and **informal** tests.

With a formal test:

- learners generally know the test is going to happen, so they can revise for it
- learners do it alone without external help, although dictionaries may be allowed in certain circumstances
- it is not marked by learners themselves, but by the teacher or other authority
- it has a mark or grade which usually carries some significance, e.g. to determine whether a student can enter a class or move up to the next class.

Formal tests are usually carried out at the end of a period of study, e.g. each term or year, and possibly at the end of each week or unit of the coursebook. But they don't have to be carried out formally. The same test can be done with no prior notice, by learners working individually or in pairs, marking their own answers, and with no particular status attached to the mark or grade. A formal test has now become an informal test.

Furthermore, there are many other ways in which you as the teacher are engaged in informal testing. Here are just a handful of examples:

- concept questions to check understanding of a language point (see *p.150*)
- comprehension questions to check understanding of a spoken or written text
- oral drills to test language forms and check pronunciation
- gap-fill exercises (and the like) to test grammar and lexis
- even controlled speaking exercises allow informal testing of language forms, concepts, and use.

the teacher

In other words, informal testing is taking place at many different stages in every lesson as part of the most common everyday classroom procedures. From your point of view, it provides continuous insights as to what the students have understood and learned, and this knowledge is essential in helping you to decide whether you can or should move on to the next stage in the lesson. And if the testing identifies a problem, you know you need a solution: you can retrace your steps and repeat a procedure; perhaps look at the problem in a different and possibly more effective way; or make a note of something that will need to be recycled and revised at a later date. This can be shown diagrammatically, e.g.

language input > check / test understanding
> move on > possible recycling > test understanding
> remedial teaching > test understanding > move on

Informal testing also gives you feedback on your own teaching. You shouldn't assume that if certain learners haven't understood something, it's your fault (any more than you should assume that if they have learnt something it is because of you). However, if you become aware that the majority of the class is having difficulty with a new concept, this information helps you to rethink your teaching approach.

the learner

Informal testing enables learners to check if they have understood something, and it helps them to see the progress they are making, which is obviously vital for their motivation. For certain learners, formal or informal testing may be needed to provide external motivation where internal motivation is lacking, while for others, it can serve as a useful reminder that language studied is not the same thing as language learnt. Successful language learning does demand recycling and revision, and informal classroom testing is a vital part of that process.

A glance back at the examples of test types opposite also illustrates the important role that informal testing plays in fostering communication. All the techniques mentioned set up interaction of some sort, either between teacher and learner, or between learners themselves.

> ### think![1]
> Carry out a quick piece of informal testing on yourself. Cover the section above, and note down:
>
> - three ways in which formal and informal tests are different
> - three examples of informal testing in the classroom
> - two reasons why teachers and learners need informal testing.
>
> Has this informal test given you any useful feedback?

2   Who tests?

Traditionally, the teacher is viewed as the authority figure in the class who tests learners either formally or informally. You are usually in the best position to assess whether the group as a whole, as well as individuals in the class, have all understood new concepts and can manipulate forms; and you have both the teaching techniques and the language skills to do this informal testing most efficiently. Nevertheless, learners are sometimes very aware of each others' difficulties, and in many situations they can effectively test each other informally. Equally they can test themselves.

learners testing each other

You will find a number of **test your partner** activities throughout the **student's book**, as in this example, where learners have to decide whether the verbs are followed by -ing form or infinitive.

---

5 Put these verbs / phrases in the correct place in the table.

keep	give up	be willing to	get used to
used to	practise	finish	mind
try	be prepared to	remember	regret
start	look forward to	take up	tend

test your partner

– Practise.

– Practise doing.

– That's right.

from upper-intermediate **student's book**, unit one p.11.

There are several benefits when learners test each other in pairs:

- more student-student interaction is created

- learners are in a position to check what they have learnt in a less stressful and less exposed context

- it leaves you free to monitor the pairs and assess how well the target language is being used

- it allows you to help individuals in areas where less peer correction takes place, e.g. pronunciation.

Activities where learners have to match definitions or illustrations with vocabulary items lend themselves to a peer testing stage, once the correct meanings have been established (see the example activity from the **student's book** below).

---

1 Match phrases 1 to 6 with responses a to f with a similar meaning. Put the ⓖ symbol next to the two most informal phrases.

1 Did you **get very angry?**

2 Did you **get your own back?**

3 Did you **quarrel** /ˈkwɒrəl/ **with** your sister?

4 Did you **shout abuse** /əˈbjuːs/?

5 Did you **control your temper?**

6 Did you **find it irritating?**

a Yes, I **swore** /swɔː/ at him.

b Yes, I **completely lost my temper.**

c Yes, it **got on my nerves.**

d Yes, I **got my revenge** /rɪˈvenʒ/.

e Yes, we **had a big row** /raʊ/.

f Yes, I managed to **keep calm.**

from upper-intermediate **student's book**, unit eight p.92.

One learner in each pair (the 'tester') uses the exercise to test their partner, so has the answers which the 'testee' cannot see. Learners can then swap and repeat the exercise. They can therefore support each other, give clues, feedback, and correction.

If you are in favour of the use of the mother tongue in class, there is no reason why learners in a monolingual context shouldn't test each other using **translation** (see p.150).

---

try it out sentence transformations

1 Divide your class into two groups: A and B. Give all the As a set of six sentence transformations to do, such as:

Did you enjoy yourselves last night?
Did you have _____?
I last saw Jimmy in 1998.
I haven't _____.

(You will find examples of these in grammar practice books, and a similar type of exercise with key words in First Certificate, Paper 3.)

Give Bs a different set of transformations to do.

2 When they have finished, go over the answers with each group separately, or give each group a photocopy of the answers (but don't go over all the answers as a class).

3 Form A and B pairs. A should read their first sentence, with the beginning of the transformation to their partner, who has to do the transformation orally without looking at A's paper. If B says something different from the correct answer, A should write it down. Do all of A's sentences, then swap, and B reads their sentences for A to transform.

4 At the end, the pairs look at any differences in their answers together to decide whether they are possible answers.

5 Have a plenary to clear up any differences. Sometimes more than one transformation is possible.

Students find the oral exercise very challenging, and the activity is a useful way to revise the use of grammatical structures and vocabulary.

---

learners testing themselves

There are many ways in **natural English** in which learners can test themselves in and out of class. Here are some examples:

- In the **glossary** activities accompanying texts, learners have to make guesses about unknown words in context. They can then use a dictionary to check, which encourages them to use a productive learning strategy built upon self-testing.

- In their own time, learners can test themselves on grammar. For example, they can study a section of grammar in the **language reference** then cover the left-hand side of the page and do the grammar exercise on the right (**cover & check exercises**). They can repeat these exercises several times.

- The **teacher's book** includes a wordlist for each unit. You can photocopy this for learners to test themselves on key vocabulary in the unit.

- At the end of each unit, there is a section called **test yourself!** This is an opportunity for learners to test themselves on some of the key language in the unit. (Equally, you could administer and mark this which would make it a formal test.)

The **workbook** with answer keys can obviously be used as a self-testing device. If you set exercises for homework, learners can check their own answers, and then rather than spending class time going over them, learners can take the opportunity to ask about the examples they found difficult.

3 Testing language informally

When introducing or revising new language, teachers draw on a range of techniques for checking learning, some of which are listed below. The ones you choose to use will obviously depend on several factors. Which is the simplest way to check this particular item? Which techniques work best with your class? Which are feasible with your class? Translation, for instance, is unlikely in a multilingual context.

You may have other ways of testing informally too. It is worth noting that many of these techniques can both teach and test, depending on when and how they are used. Timelines, for example, can be used to explain a concept, or to test one.

translation

Imagine this scene: you are teaching a class of Spanish speakers and the phrase *I could eat a horse!* comes up in a lesson. The teacher explains that this is an idiom which means *I'm very hungry*, and the meaning is not literal; it is an exaggeration. She asks the class for a translation. One says, *Tengo un hambre de lobo* (i.e. hunger of a wolf – an equivalent idiom) and the others nod in agreement and note it down.

Here, you have a piece of language, explained in English then tested through the mother tongue. It is a quick, time-saving technique, and you are satisfied that everyone has grasped the meaning accurately.

It is obvious that all language learners automatically search for equivalents. For low level learners this is appropriate and understandable, but as learners become more proficient they are less reliant on translation even though they may still find it reassuring to find an equivalent in their mother tongue.

The use of L1 for checking understanding is certainly useful if applied in moderation. Carried to extremes, though, it can have drawbacks.

- Where translation is the **only** means of testing, learners are missing the opportunity to process language through English itself.

- Constant use of translation into the mother tongue may lead to a classroom in which very little at all happens in English, which is clearly not desirable.

- Learners can develop an obsession with finding one-to-one equivalents, which can be frustrating.

- In multilingual classrooms, the use of the mother tongue can set up tensions, especially if you have a dominant group of one nationality who shout translations across the room, making other learners feel excluded.

Translation as a means of informal testing has been out of favour for some time, but used wisely it is a very effective tool.

think!²
How often do you ask learners to translate words, phrases, or sentences as a way of checking their understanding? At which levels do you use it? Do you think you will use it more, less, or about the same in the future?

concept questions

One way of checking understanding without resorting to the learners' mother tongue is by using 'concept questions'. These focus on the meaning of grammatical structures or vocabulary items. They are used alongside specific examples, and well-chosen questions are an effective way of assessing whether learners have grasped a concept. Look at this example of *manage to*, taken from a reading text a teacher is using with her class: *The box was heavy, but Josh <u>managed to</u> carry it upstairs.*

The teacher wants to check if learners are able to deduce the meaning of *manage to*, so she writes the sentence on the board and underlines *managed to*. She then asks:

T: Was it easy to carry the box?
Ss: No.
T: But did he do it?
Ss: Yes.
T: So what does *manage to* mean?
S1:   Something is difficult to do, but you do it.
T: Yes, you are successful.

The questions are in this case part of the technique for checking understanding, but could equally be used at different stages of a lesson, e.g. to revise vocabulary or grammar.

In order to design such questions you need to define precisely or paraphrase the meaning of the target item using simple language. From this breakdown, you create questions. Here is an example:

I <u>wish I'd gone</u> to the wedding. = I didn't go to the wedding, and now I'm sorry about it.

T: Did the person go to the wedding?
Ss: No.
T: Are they sorry now about that?
Ss: Yes.

Learners don't always get the answers right, of course, which is a signal for you to go back and clarify the meaning of the item. These questioning techniques are particularly useful in multilingual teaching contexts, but they are often used in monolingual contexts too, as a way of maintaining a high level of English use in the class and challenging learners to think about meaning. They do require some careful thought, however. Here are some guidelines.

- Dictionaries and grammar books are invaluable for clarifying concept before you plan your questions.

- It is important to avoid using the language item you are testing in the questions themselves. For instance, if you are testing the concept of the present perfect continuous in *She's been working there for years*, don't ask *<u>Has she been working</u> there for a long time?* Instead, you might ask, *Did she start working there recently?*

- Keep the language in the questions simpler than the language you are testing. For example, if you are testing *might* with intermediate learners in *She might accept the job*, avoid using *Is she <u>likely</u> to accept the job?* as *likely* will probably be unknown.

– Aim to cover all aspects of the concept, e.g. *a gadget* = an object you use + it's small + it makes life easier + it isn't really necessary.

Learners are sometimes puzzled by concept questions, as they can appear simplistic and slightly quirky. But most learners adapt to them, and they are a safer indicator of understanding than *Do you all understand? Good!*

---

think!³

Do you think these questions check the concept of the underlined items effectively? If not, how could they be improved?

1. *I've just broken my laptop.*
   Did I break the laptop?
   A long time ago, or a short time ago?
   Is the laptop still broken?

2. *They reluctantly agreed to help me.*
   Did they agree to help me?
   Did they agree immediately?

3. *He was supposed to meet Mary at six o'clock.*
   Did he arrange to meet Mary at six o'clock?
   Did he meet her at six o'clock?

4. *The answer he gave was ambiguous.*
   Was his answer clear?

---

go to **answer key** *p.153*

---

timelines and clines

Timelines are most commonly used to underline or consolidate concepts of time and aspect. For example, this simple timeline shows the difference between *for* and *since* when used with the present perfect:

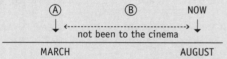

A: I haven't been to the cinema since March.
B: I haven't been to the cinema for six months.

Some learners find this kind of diagram very helpful and memorable; others find them less effective. If your class are not familiar with timelines, you will need to deal with the first one or two carefully, pointing out how time, events, and duration are represented.

Timelines can also be used to test meaning rather than just illustrate it. Here is an example from the **student's book**.

---

1. Read this short story and answer the questions below.

> A horrible thing happened to me earlier this year when I was living in New York. I'd been working for a TV company for six months and I then went away on holiday for two weeks. When I got back, they'd given my job to someone else, so I moved back to Los Angeles. What a nightmare!

---

1. Underline the examples of the past continuous, past perfect simple, and past perfect continuous. How are they formed?

2. Match the three underlined phrases with the two dotted lines --- and the cross **x** on the timeline below.

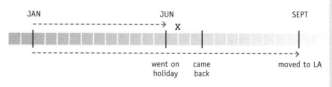

from upper-intermediate **student's book**, unit five, *p.59*

---

think!⁴

Draw timelines to illustrate the underlined language items.

1. Don't ring me at 8.00: I'll be having dinner.
2. We used to go to Spain every year for our holidays.
3. I haven't played the guitar for ten years.

---

go to **answer key** *p.153*

Clines are associated more with vocabulary teaching and, like timelines, can be used both to illustrate and test various concepts. Clines are effective for series of items that share a certain feature in their core meaning but differ in terms of degree, for example:

Put the following words in the correct place on the cline below.
gale; breeze; hurricane; wind

weak   *strong*

As a testing device, clines have the added benefits of being simple and easy to use, and versatile, e.g. you can involve learners physically if you prepare written flashcards of the items, draw a cline on the board and ask them to come up and put the words in the appropriate place.

---

think!⁵

Look at these groups of items. Which ones lend themselves to informal testing using clines?

1. love, hate, like, loathe, can't stand, don't mind, quite like, not keen on

2. love, like, worship, idolize, admire, fancy, respect

3. freezing, lukewarm, cold, hot, warm, tepid, boiling

4. shout, mumble, shriek, whisper, scream, mutter

---

go to **answer key** *p.153*

---

defining and paraphrasing

The ability to define and paraphrase concepts in English is beyond the reach of most lower level learners, but it is a very useful testing tool at higher levels because it generates a lot of language use and helps to develop an important language skill.

If you want to use this form of testing, you should make sure first that the target items can be defined or paraphrased clearly and succinctly, and second, that they can be explained without requiring language of comparable complexity.

---

think![6]

How would you define or paraphrase these words and phrases? Which items would upper-intermediate learners find difficult to define or explain (because they require language that the learners may not know)?

uniform (n) dreadful kidnap sb get soaked pride
deserve spoil sth throw sth away

---

go to **answer key** *p.153*

written exercises

There is a wide range of written exercise types for practising and testing language items. Exercises which test understanding include: matching, sorting, true / false, and multiple choice. Exercises which practise and test language productively include: gap-fill, sentence completion, stimuli / response, and transformation.

The advantage of one exercise type over another depends on what you are testing and what you hope to achieve. Sentence completion exercises are usually more open-ended than gap-fill exercises, so have the potential advantage of being more generative, allowing more creativity, and possibly provoking more discussion. On the other hand, gap-fill exercises can usually be constructed in such a way that they only allow one correct answer, so they have the advantage of being more focused and perhaps more appropriate if the items you want to test are very specific. Last but not least, they are usually very quick and easy for either the learner or the teacher to mark.

---

try it out writing grammar sheets

I did this with a First Certificate class who were motivated to study grammar.

After one lesson where we looked at conditional forms, I asked students, for homework, to write a personal grammar sheet on the language we had just studied. They could look at the language reference and any other grammar books they liked. They had to put together a grammar summary as they saw it using their own example sentences.

The next day in class, students compared with each other, and any problems or differences were discussed as a class. They gave them in for correction and comments, and then I returned them. We went on to do other grammar summaries like this. They found that producing their own summaries and examples was more memorable and gave them the motivation to explore the area more thoroughly. Some of their results were excellent.

Ruth, Zurich.

---

4 Testing oral interaction informally

Want to know more? Go to intermediate **teacher's book**, **how to ...** teach listening, *p.150*.

Speaking is difficult to evaluate because you have to assess your learners' performance in real time, and without the opportunity for much reflection. Even in formal testing situations where examination boards have established clear written criteria for evaluation, testing is still quite subjective, depending as it does on how the examiner chooses to interpret the criteria. One person's idea of fluency may be another person's 'occasional hesitation', and teachers' perceptions of accuracy can vary considerably.

For most learners, though, the ability to use English effectively in oral communication is precisely why they come to class, and it is therefore important that we try to give our learners some confirmation of their progress. Here are some guidelines.

a Before you do any speaking activity in class, whether quite controlled or free, be clear in your own mind what you want or expect learners to be able to achieve. For example:
   – using target language appropriately
   – achieving an appropriate amount of interaction with other learners
   – achieving an appropriate level of fluency, e.g. speed and naturalness for their level
   – achieving an appropriate level of accuracy for their level
   – keeping going for a reasonable amount of time
   – speaking intelligibly, e.g. pronouncing clearly without imposing a strain on the listener, and so on.

b Try to limit the focus of your attention in any one activity, even if the learners are trying to do several things at once. Don't try to cover all the criteria above. Pick one or two from the selection above, bearing in mind whether the activity is controlled or freer. If you select one or two criteria each time your learners do a speaking activity, over a period of time you will cover a range of criteria.

c If learners are trying to use language which has only recently been studied, don't expect too much of them, unless the activity is very controlled or limited in its scope.

d At the same time, try to notice whether learners are beginning to use language that they have encountered relatively recently; something perhaps that they couldn't use well a few weeks ago, but they are now using more fluently.

e Remember that the yardstick for measuring their progress is how they perform an activity now compared with similar activities one week, or month, or term ago.

Focusing in this way can help you in several ways. Firstly, you can use the criteria you decided on as the basis for your feedback to your learners on either an individual or a group basis. Secondly, the information you gather will help you to decide how best to proceed with the class: what remedial language work will you need to do? Are there any particular communication skills that learners need to practise more?

repeating activities

One final way of testing learners' progress in oral interaction is by comparing 'like with like'; in other words, after a suitable lapse of time, repeat a freer classroom activity, perhaps adapting it slightly for motivation and interest. Then decide whether your learners can now perform the task more fluently and effectively. Here is an activity from the **student's book** which would be suitable for repetition. On the second occasion, you could use the same task, or you could adapt the topics if you wish. Your focus in feedback the second time should probably be wider, or focus on any areas that were weak the first time.

it's your turn!

1 **Think!** Remember a situation where you did something and then realized you shouldn't have done it. (Or something you didn't do, and should have done.) Use these prompts to help you.

> a holiday
> a journey
> a relationship
> something you spent money on
> *your own topic* _____

example
a beach holiday in spring: 'I should have waited until later in the year.'

2 Move round the class, tell your story and listen to other people's. Has anybody had a similar experience to you?

from upper-intermediate **student's book** unit two *p.24*.

conclusion

In this chapter we have looked at:

- what informal testing is and why and when we do it in the classroom
- ways in which learners can test each other and themselves effectively
- a range of techniques for testing understanding at different stages in a lesson
- guidelines and ideas for 'testing' speaking activities in class.

We have looked at materials which lend themselves to specific testing techniques, such as 'test your partner', and we have discussed techniques which can be used for several different purposes, e.g. timelines, clines, concept questions, and paraphrase are all useful both for explaining and testing language. The next time you use a technique for input, perhaps think about how you could also use it for recycling or informal testing at a later date.

answer key

think![3] *p.151*
1 These questions are effective.
2 These questions don't go far enough. You also need to ask *Were they happy / willing to help?* (No).
3 These questions are effective.
4 This question doesn't go far enough. The teacher also needs to ask *Did his answer have different meanings?*

think![4] *p.151*
Don't ring me at 8.00: I'll be having dinner.

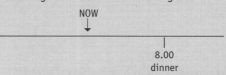

We used to go to Spain every year for our holidays.

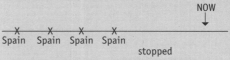

I haven't played the guitar for ten years.

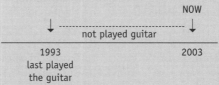

think![5] *p.152*
1 and 3 can be tested on a cline, as they represent degrees of liking and hating or temperature. The items in 2 and 4 differ in meaning as well as degree, so are too complex to include on one cline.

think![6] *p.153*
The first four are suitable for learners to define / paraphrase:
uniform = special clothes people wear at work, e.g. in the police force or at school
dreadful = terrible
kidnap sb = take someone as a prisoner and demand money for returning them
get soaked = get very wet
We think the last four are hard for upper-intermediate learners to define: it is difficult to explain *pride* and *deserve*; to explain *spoil* sth and *throw* sth *away* you need to use words of comparable difficulty, e.g. *ruin* and *get rid of*. *Throw* sth *away* is best demonstrated, and the other three are best illustrated through situations and contexts.

follow up

Ur P 1996 *A Course in Language Teaching* Cambridge University Press (module 2, practice activities, and module 3, tests: Types of test elicitation techniques)

Thornbury S 1999 *How to Teach Grammar* Longman

Parrott M 1993 *Tasks for Language Teachers* Cambridge University Press (chapter 5: Teachers' use of the learners' first language)

Aitken R 1994 *Teaching Tenses* Nelson (very useful on timelines)

how to ... motivate higher level learners

1   Problems of motivating higher level learners

> **think!**[1]
> Motivation can suffer at any time, but can you think of at least two reasons why many learners experience a dip in motivation as they reach upper-intermediate level? Note them down and then read on.

The early stages of learning can be an anxious time in some ways, but most learners have the satisfaction of being able to see their progress from one week to the next. It may be the ability to use the past tense to talk about past experience, or to understand a dialogue in natural spoken English, or to make sense of a restaurant menu that was previously incomprehensible. Such obvious signs of progress are very rewarding and extremely motivating. As learners pass through the intermediate level, their situation changes.

- Progress is not evident in the same way. The giant strides of the early stages are replaced by steps which seem to become ever smaller, until they are hardly visible at all. The learner has now reached a kind of 'plateau'. Progress may still be taking place, but the learners' inability to see it can have a very detrimental effect on their motivation.

- Complacency can also become a problem at this level. Some learners are strongly motivated by their rapid progress and desire to overcome problems in the early stages of learning, but by upper-intermediate level, they are able to express most of their everyday needs, and their urgency and desire begin to evaporate. As motivation flags, progress slows down, with the result that motivation drops even more. They are caught in a downward spiral.

- Some learners at this level suffer from classroom fatigue. They have now worked their way through various levels and coursebooks, and classroom procedures have become routine: the lessons are predictable, the activities are all familiar, the faces are the same. Even the syllabus looks repetitive. In fact, it isn't, but much of the grammar at upper-intermediate level includes headings that are already familiar to any learner who has used an intermediate coursebook: present perfect, past perfect, conditionals, passives, reported speech, and so on. What's new?

- Finally, there is the issue of needs and wants. At lower levels, there is usually a shared belief among learners that they need to cover the basic grammar of the language, learn common high frequency lexis, and devote time to the unfamiliar sounds of a new language so that they are at least intelligible to those around them. Once these basic needs have been met, however, groups may become more disparate. Some will still be driven by a desire to study the grammar, while others may wish to concentrate only on improving their spoken fluency. Some learners want more writing, and often specific kinds of writing, while for others it is irrelevant. Faced with these different needs and wants, most teachers accept there has to be a degree of compromise. Most learners accept it too, but a few find it difficult to sustain motivation if the lesson is not perceived as directly relevant to their needs.

We must stress that dips in motivation do not affect all learners, and neither do they affect all groups. For some learners, their intrinsic motivation carries them through; and for others, motivation can be sustained by external examinations such as Cambridge First Certificate. In any case, for many of those affected, the loss of motivation is both temporary and reversible. It is important, however, that we are prepared for it when it happens, and have measures to combat it. The rest of the chapter looks at a few of these strategies.

2   Helping learners to see their progress

Although many learners reach a kind of 'plateau' where they feel they aren't making progress, this is not necessarily the case. Sometimes, it is simply that progress is less obvious and more subtle; it is best described perhaps as horizontal rather than vertical. Learners continue to expand their vocabulary, they continue to develop different skills such as reading and writing, and they usually make incremental improvements in both accuracy and fluency. But much of this is hard to see and measure, and doesn't replace the thrill of suddenly being able to say something that was previously impossible, or understand something that was previously incomprehensible.

feedback

If progress is not so readily apparent at this level, one of your roles must be to make it apparent; and one way of doing this is through continuous and constructive feedback. At the end of any significant pair or group work activity, tell learners what they have done well, but also what they could improve on next time. This might be their use of language (grammar, vocabulary, and pronunciation), how well they participated, how clearly they expressed their ideas, how well they interacted with and involved each other in the activity, etc. Very often feedback is seen as being identical with correction, i.e. telling people what they got wrong. However, most people are motivated by positive feedback, and if it is important for learners to see their progress, then it is clearly important for them to be aware of what they are doing right. In addition, if you begin with positive feedback, you create a climate in which constructive correction can be more readily accepted.

It is worth remembering that some activities deserve to be repeated, following feedback. It may not be appropriate to do it again immediately – there is the fatigue and familiarity factor to take into account – but many groups appreciate the opportunity to try an activity again, possibly in a slightly different form, and some will become aware they are improving second time around.

tutorials

One potential drawback with class feedback is that much of it may be in response to the contribution of the more vocal minority during activities. To balance this, you could try to organize individual tutorials with everyone in the class, at times in the lesson when the rest of the group are working individually or in pairs. Start with the learners who may get less of your attention in a normal lesson (in other words the less confident or less extrovert learners), and try to plan a timetable in which you can see each member of the group over a specific time period. Less extrovert learners will then have as much of your time as others, and on a one-to-one level may feel more confident in talking to you about their progress. An alternative to individual tutorials is to organize tutorials with pairs or groups of three. However you organize them, you should tell learners in advance, giving them time to think about issues they want to discuss.

Tutorials have other potential advantages:

– they can help you to meet the learners' needs more effectively

– they can give learners a stronger belief that you are interested in them and their progress

– they can give you an opportunity to explain what you are doing and why, and to answer their questions

– they can help to develop rapport

– they can help you to identify problems at an early stage, e.g. class dynamics, student dissatisfaction

– they give you feedback on your teaching.

On the debit side:

– they are very time-consuming

– they can be difficult to organize

– some learners are not used to this kind of one-to-one tutorial and may find it threatening

– you may hear things you don't want to hear

– you may set up expectations which are difficult to meet

– what you learn may give you more work!

---

try it out preparing for tutorials

If you are considering tutorials, it is a good idea to prepare a questionnaire for the learners to complete. This will force them to think about the tutorial in advance, and gives you a starting point for the conversation. The one below is designed as a pair work activity prior to a tutorial, but it could be done individually.

The course so far

With a partner, try to remember:

• the grammar points we've looked at
• the vocabulary areas we've looked at
• some different kinds of speaking activities we've done

Now individually, think of:

• something you enjoyed
• something you learned from another student
• something you didn't enjoy

Tell your partner.

What about you? Have you ...

• done enough English homework?
• used English as much as possible out of class?
• participated enough in class?
• tried to use what you've learned?

Look forward ...

• What would you like to do more of in class?
• What language areas do you need to practise more?
• How can you help yourself more?
• Any questions or worries?

Maggie Baigent, Bologna, Italy

---

try it out learner diaries

Ask learners to buy a little notebook. In it, they write a few thoughts on a regular basis. This could be at the end of each lesson, or each week, depending on how often their classes are. They should write personally to you, and they can write whatever they like:

• about their progress in English
• any queries they have about English
• how they feel in the class
• what they like / don't like doing in class
• what they are doing outside class to improve their English.

They don't need to write at great length, and you should not correct their English unless they specifically ask you to. Collect in these diaries regularly (take a few at a time, so that you don't have to respond to the whole class at once) and write in response to their comments and queries. These diaries can give you a great deal of insight and can enable you to help individuals where possible.

---

self-assessment

Learners can benefit a great deal from class feedback and individual tutorials, but they also need to develop the ability to see progress for themselves. We have tried to nurture this in **natural English** by getting learners to reflect on their own performance at the end of the **extended speaking** activities, e.g.

test yourself!

How well do you think you did the extended speaking? Mark the line.

0	10

Many learners will be unfamiliar with this form of self-assessment, especially on something as subjective as free speaking, but we hope that it will have a positive effect on progress. The exact nature of the scoring system is largely irrelevant; the important point is that it is clear and concrete, so learners have a system by which they can compare one performance with another.

3   Materials, activities, and approaches

interest and variety

Every teacher wants to feel that the materials and activities they use with their learners are going to be appropriate, engaging, and productive, but this is particularly true with higher level learners who through years of study may have become jaded with the same activities. There is certainly a challenge for you as a teacher: firstly, to capture your learners' interest and secondly, to keep their interest. Clearly, it is necessary to have

- variety of activity type
- variety of focus (from pair and group work to individual work, to class discussion, use of video, reading, etc.)
- variety of pace.

At a broader level, learners (and teachers) need variety both within the coursebook and beyond it. For instance, if you are exploiting your **student's book** in different ways, adapting it where necessary to your class's needs, using the suggestions from **ideas plus** in the **teacher's book** and creating your own ways of using the material, you can make your lessons more varied. Just as important, however, is to include lessons or parts of lessons where the coursebook is not used, and where you work from your learners' expressed interests and requests (more of this later, in the section on **topics and tasks** on *p.157*). You can provide variety and tailor the lessons to your class by making use of supplementary materials, topical authentic texts from newspapers, TV and radio, and of course, your own materials. Let us now look at ways of exploiting such texts.

---

think! [2]

1 Read this summary of a text you are going to use with higher level learners. Can you think of three pre-reading and three post-reading activities which would be suitable for use with this text? Note them down, then read on.

Cupid Games

The text is about a TV documentary series in which single people who are looking for a partner are found potential 'blind dates' by family members or groups of friends. In one episode, Danny Kingsley, 39-year-old divorced father of two, agrees to let his father and eldest son choose a potential partner for him, and two of his friends also choose him a date. He goes on dates with each new partner and then gives his verdict on their choices.

2 Now look at these suggested pre-reading and post-reading activities.
Which do you think would best suit the text? Why?
Which would best suit your higher level learners? Why?
Which way(s) would you not normally use, but would be prepared to try?

Possible pre-reading activities

- a song related to the theme, e.g. *All by myself*
- a short video extract, e.g. *Blind Date*, a programme where people find a new partner. If there is a similar programme where you teach, you could use it with the sound turned down, and ask learners to imagine what the participants are saying.
- a vocabulary brainstorm on relationships, e.g. *a blind date*, *have sth in common*
- a short questionnaire about blind dates

Possible post-reading activities

- personalization, e.g. learners work in small groups and discuss the following: Which family members and friends would you nominate to find you a new partner?
What kind of person would your family or friends choose for you?
Who would choose the best partner, do you think?
- discussion, e.g. about arranged marriages or dating agencies
- role play, e.g. meeting someone on a blind date

---

a diagnostic approach

Given that higher level learners have different gaps in their knowledge, and that some learners feel that they have 'seen it all before', one strategy you can use is a diagnostic approach: learners complete an exercise or perform a task, and you observe how well they do it. What are they handling well? What are they making mistakes with? In response, you concentrate only on the language or skills that proved difficult, rather than assuming that everything is unknown. This approach can also help learners to see the difference between what they already know and what they still need to learn. Here are a few examples.

- Learners do a communication activity such as a role play (a job interview, for instance) with no pre-teaching. The teacher monitors and takes notes, or the role plays can be tape-recorded or video-recorded and analysed. The teacher then decides what needs to be learnt: vocabulary, greeting and welcoming interviewees, asking questions, taking turns, etc. He / she then teaches or revises the relevant areas in class, and learners do a parallel role play to see how they have progressed.

- Learners are given a short diagnostic test on a language point they have not fully grasped, e.g. *used to do* versus *be used to doing*. Gap-fills, spot the errors, complete the sentences, or sentence transformations can be used. As in the example above, the teacher goes over the exercise and takes the opportunity to teach or explain only the points which proved difficult for the class, rather than assuming that nothing is known.

- Dictogloss / grammar dictation (see intermediate **teacher's book**, *p.146*). A short text such as the advertisement in upper-intermediate **student's book** unit three *p.37* would be suitable. As learners compare their version of the text with the original and perhaps find new language, or language used in unexpected ways, they are able to notice gaps in their knowledge.

- Learner explanations, e.g. learners are asked to explain the difference between pairs of items which differ in terms of structure, meaning, style, or pronunciation. This informs the teacher of any gaps in their knowledge, which can be filled in by other learners, or by you if necessary. At this level, learners have a wider range of language and are more proficient at defining, explaining, or paraphrasing. This not only sets learners a challenge, but values their contributions to the class. This strategy is particularly useful in this context where learners within each class have different gaps in their knowledge.

topics

Learners who have been studying English for years and have covered many of the basic topics such as holidays, work, health, etc. in their coursebooks may well feel reluctant to revisit these areas. It is therefore important at this level to find new topics or to find new angles on familiar topics. Above all, we recommend that you consult your learners on the topics they would like to explore.

> ### think!³
> You want to find out which topics your class are interested in. How could you do this? How could you use this information?

go to **answer key** *p.159*

Beyond the coursebook, you also have available to you a range of topical issues from the real world, which can be accessed via newspapers, the Internet, TV and radio, e.g. the World Service. Even if you cannot obtain a wide range of English language papers or programmes in monolingual contexts, there is news on the Internet, and cable TV is widespread. Even material in the learners' mother tongue can be used as a springboard.

tasks

- With language tasks, <u>length and complexity</u> can play a part in motivating higher level learners: extended speaking activities, discussions, role plays, and simulations all allow learners the time and opportunity to become absorbed in the activity and have a longer period of practice in English.

- Tasks often work well at this level when they are <u>open-ended</u> and provide the opportunity for learners to take things in their own direction. As a result, different groups will have different outcomes, and they will be more motivated to hear about each others' results. In our data for the **Nasty Neighbours** extended speaking activity, for instance, groups produced widely differing scenarios since they had chosen different characters from the photos, different locations, and different disputes. They were all very interested and often amused to hear each others' stories.

go to upper-intermediate **student's book**, *p.100*

- Finally, there is one way in which you can affect the degree of difficulty in activities: <u>time pressure</u>. If you give learners time to plan and rehearse an activity, it will be easier for them than if they have to do it in a spontaneous and unrehearsed fashion. To increase the level of challenge, give them less time to prepare.

learning through English

Learners at this level are often very motivated in class when they are learning facts and skills through the medium of a second language, for instance, reading or listening texts which give them facts or insights. Equally, peer presentations where learners talk about their jobs, hobbies, or anything else of interest may provide relevant and interesting input, and English simply becomes a channel for this. Our experience is that higher level learners are motivated to develop skills such as *how to give a good presentation* or *how to conduct a successful interview*, which can have benefits beyond the classroom.

This is an issue that you may wish to think about when you choose your own texts for classroom use: will the content tell your learners something new that will be interesting for them?

4   The role of the learner

consulting your learners

The extent to which teachers consult their learners on what they want or need to learn, and how they want to learn it, varies enormously. At higher levels, however, many teachers find that their learners have more divergent needs and they also have the ability to express them. Consequently, consultation tends to be more widespread. Learners may want more say in the choice of topics, but they may also wish to make clear the types of activities they prefer and how they want to spend the classroom time. This information can be gathered through informal discussion, individual or group questionnaires, and individual tutorials, as mentioned above. The information you receive will enable you to make adjustments to your timetable and your use of your coursebook; supplementing, rejecting, or adapting material where appropriate. You may decide to dedicate specific, regular class time to 'requests', either particular language points or skills in which learners express an interest. Indeed, if the language points are not too complicated, you could ask learners to research them, and 'present' them to the class. This may make the language points more memorable and provide a different focus.

project work

Many teachers like to involve upper-intermediate learners in project work; this can be extremely motivating when the focus of the project is well-chosen, and can encourage learners to use a range of skills. Producing a class website, a newsletter, or a video can be an excellent way to involve everyone, and because these activities have a clear outcome or product, they give a sense of achievement, not to mention something to show to their peers or family.

Want to know more? Read **Project Work**, Diana Fried-Booth (OUP).

English outside the classroom

In addition to learner involvement within the class, there is enormous potential at this level for learners to continue using English beyond the classroom. Training in the use of monolingual dictionaries in class time will enable and hopefully encourage learners to use dictionaries when they need them outside. They can also make use of the constantly growing sources of entertainment and information on TV and the Internet as well as in books, newspapers, and magazines.

> ### try it out
> My upper-intermediate class meets three times a week. At the beginning of the year, we had a lesson where we brainstormed the different sources of English outside class: films, TV, satellite TV, Internet websites, music, newspapers and magazines, etc. Learners then agreed that once a month, a lesson or part of a lesson would become a 'recommendations swapshop'. Each learner would briefly talk about something they had done in English that they would recommend to the group – an English-speaking film, a website, or whatever. Sometimes this is done as a mingling activity, and sometimes as a group discussion. Learners make a note of other people's recommendations to follow up themselves.
> *Hedda, Belgium*

5 The language syllabus

At the upper-intermediate level, learners will meet some new grammar, e.g. the future continuous and/or the future perfect, or possibly the past conditional and/or mixed conditionals. To some extent though, 'new' grammar does taper off at this level, and much of the syllabus consists of consolidating and refining learners' knowledge and use of grammar introduced at pre-intermediate and intermediate levels. This often results in a more global approach: past simple, past continuous, and past perfect are brought together under the heading 'narrative' tenses; passives are analysed across a wide range of tense forms; different ways of expressing the future are contrasted, and so on. As language choice increases, so does the level of challenge, but for some learners, the fact that the names remain largely the same gives them a sense that they've seen it all and done it all before.

improving accuracy

You may need to counteract this perception by pointing out exactly why you are bringing together different language forms in this way. Choosing the correct structure where many forms are available is a true test of language accuracy, and this is one of the major challenges at this level. Many can now speak reasonably fluently, but producing accurate English in real time is hard. This was evident throughout our research data, as the two extracts below show. Both are taken from recordings of learners doing the **extended speaking** activity in unit eleven *pp.134* to *135*, and both show that the learners were able to interact quite freely and fluently in English and express quite complex ideas. If there is a weakness, it is that their level of fluency is not yet matched by a comparable degree of accuracy, and indeed, that their accuracy is erratic. They can get a structure right in one utterance, and then get it wrong in the next. There are a lot of errors which the learners could easily correct for themselves if they were monitoring their speech more carefully.

---

think!⁴

Look at the extracts below. Can you find two examples of:

1 incorrect forms of past modals
2 the wrong modal verb being used
3 past participles not being used
4 the wrong lexical item
5 lack of direct object

Learners read and then discuss a case study about two friends, one of whom borrows money from the other for his wedding, and then can't pay him back.

extract 1

A *For me the first problem maybe was that Jeff shouldn't have borrow to Christopher so much money, because maybe he knows that he couldn't return the money, and maybe the situation it's normal, because they are friends but he has to think about if he couldn't returned the money.*

B *Yeah, but I think he shouldn't have promised what he will pay the next month, because both of them known what he's not very well with money.*

C *The problem is not that. I think that the problem is Jeff, no Christopher shouldn't have acted like that, he's his friend, and he knows that anyway he's gonna get the money back.*

A *Sorry? Anyway ...?*

C *He's gonna get the money anyway, so longer time maybe or he might have ...*

B *No, but for the moment ... he promised what I pay you back in a month.*

C *If he has like problems, or economic problems or he has just buy a new house or something, he can pay now.*

A *Yes, but are you sure that this money will be return?*

C *I don't know.*

extract 2

A *What was the first problem and who was responsible?*

B *For me it was Jeff because he want to marry without money, and maybe the wedding reception ...*

A *The problem was he wanted to do a wedding reception very expensive.*

C *He couldn't afford it.*

A *And if you know you can't pay after, you have not to organize.*

D *Personally I think ...*

C *Would you be able to say 'no'?*

A *No, I couldn't.*

C *You know that it's a mistake?*

D *I don't know, I don't think so, not mistake, personally, sometimes people would like to have big ceremony for wedding.*

C *Yes, but if you can't afford it, you just can't do it, because ...*

D *But Christopher at the time think that ...*

C *He could pay, yes.*

D *Yes.*

A *But it wasn't a sure thing, he wasn't sure of it. If he wasn't sure of financial condition, he would have think of it.*

D *But I think that Jeff have no responsible because Jeff believe can repay, pay back to Christopher at the time.*

from **natural English** upper-intermediate research data

go to **answer key** *p.159*

We believe that most learners at this level want feedback on accuracy, and have now reached a level where they are more capable of assimilating rules of use. At lower levels, there is so much to worry about that learners should be happy just to negotiate their way towards achieving a communicative aim, without feeling that it has to be accomplished without making a single mistake. It's not dissimilar to driving. For a learner driver, getting from A to B without mishap is the first priority; worrying about how smooth the gear changes are comes later. So too with language learning. It is only when learners are already reasonably fluent that they are in a position to refine their knowledge and skills to incorporate more subtle aspects of the language with greater accuracy.

expanding lexis

Another major area of challenge at this level is *lexis*¹. Here the scope is endless, so it is an aspect of language development which should be very motivating. Higher level learners should be trying to expand both their receptive and productive vocabulary. Receptive vocabulary needs to be increased in order for learners to cope with the demands of longer, more authentic spoken and written texts. Productively, this is the

*lexis*¹ go to glossary for numbered items *p.159*

level at which learners should aim to become less reliant on a very small range of basic words and phrases, and start expanding their knowledge of more specific items. Rather than relying on *good* to describe a meal, a play, a moment, a companion, an idea, or a cook, they will communicate more effectively by choosing the appropriate adjective: *a delicious meal, a thrilling play, a suitable moment, a delightful companion, a brilliant idea,* or *a skilful cook.* And of course, an important area for development is the number and length of lexical phrases they can use. Here is an example from the **student's book.**

---

natural English
making and responding to requests

2.4

These requests can be used in spoken or informal written English.

requests

I was wondering if you could _____ ?

Do you think you could (possibly) _____ ?

Is there any chance you could _____ ?

responses

Sure, _____ .

I'll see what _____ .

I'm afraid I can't – _____ .

Listen and fill the gaps. Practise the requests and responses with a partner.

from upper-intermediate **student's book**, *p.53*

Want to know more about vocabulary issues? Go to **how to ...** develop lexis at higher levels *p.160.*

---

conclusion

In this chapter, we have looked at:

- some reasons why higher level learners often experience dips in motivation

- some strategies to combat this, e.g. giving constructive feedback, organizing one-to-one or pair tutorials, and encouraging self-assessment, which all help learners to see their own progress

- ways in which you can gain and keep the interest of higher level learners, e.g. choosing materials with a high degree of interest and variety, using a diagnostic approach, involving learners in the choice of topics and tasks, and giving learners the opportunity to learn new facts and skills which may be useful outside the classroom

- aspects of language that learners generally need to improve on at this level, e.g. improving accuracy and expanding lexis.

---

answer key

think![3] *p.157*

How could you find out which topics your group are interested in?
In small groups, learners could brainstorm topics which interest them, perhaps given a framework of hobbies, entertainment, work, social / political issues. Alternatively, you could give learners a list of topics (based on coursebook topics perhaps) and ask them to rank them in order of interest.

How could you use this information?
You may then decide to allocate time on a regular basis to these topics if they are not in your coursebook. Set up discussions based on questions generated by the learners themselves, bring in reading / listening texts for discussion, use the topics as the basis of learner presentations: short five-minute talks leading to group discussion.

think![4] *p.158* possible answers

1 *shouldn't have borrowed; would have **think** it* (should be *thought*, but the meaning is also wrong – see 2).
2 *He has to think about it* should be *He should have thought about it; you have not to organize* should be *you shouldn't organize it; would have think of it* should be *should have thought about it;*
3 *borrow, return, buy, think*
4 *borrow* should be *lend*: Jeff *shouldn't have lent Christopher the money; economic problems* should be *financial problems; financial conditions* should be *financial situation; have no responsible* should be *is irresponsible.*
5 *think about **it**, organize **it**.*

---

glossary

lexis[1] / **vocabulary** We use these terms interchangeably to mean the words or phrases of a language, rather than its grammar. Traditionally, however, vocabulary has been largely viewed as consisting of individual words.

---

follow up

Harmer J 2001 *The Practice of English Language Teaching* Longman (chapter 3 section C on motivation)

Williams M *Motivation in Language Learning* in English Teaching Professional (October 1999)

Littlejohn A *Motivation: Where does it come from? Where does it go?* in English Teaching Professional (April 2001)

Lewis M 2000 *Teaching Collocation* LTP (Lewis emphasizes the importance of lexical phrases or pre-fabricated chunks, and also discusses accuracy and fluency with regard to level, *pp.173–5*)

how to ... develop lexis at higher levels

1 Introduction

Beginners need vocabulary, intermediate learners need vocabulary, advanced learners need vocabulary. In fact, whatever level a learner is at, vocabulary expansion is viewed as a high priority, and is often essential for progress to a higher level. But while the need for lexis remains constant, the type of lexis required may change. In order to survive and communicate basic messages, most low level learners need quite a lot of nouns, a range of common verbs, and a small stock of *fixed*[1] and *semi-fixed expressions*[2] which they can produce automatically, e.g.

How are you?   I think so.   What does that mean?
Never mind.   Let's go.   No, that's all.

Learning common collocations (*a bad cold, black coffee, go to university, get a job*) is also essential right from beginner level.

Want to know more about collocation and lexical phrases? Go to intermediate **teacher's book, how to ...** activate vocabulary *p.136*.

Once learners are able to meet their basic needs with ease and a reasonable degree of accuracy, they can start to concern themselves more with other areas of vocabulary.

2 Aspects of lexis

By upper-intermediate level, learners should aim for more subtle nuances of meaning, they should be linking their thoughts together more clearly and cohesively, using the appropriate style when they speak or write, and, it goes with out saying, building up a more comprehensive bank of collocations and expressions. Let's consider these in more detail.

modifying, extending, and commenting

As learners progress, one important way in which they develop is attaining greater fluency, and this in turn gives them the capacity to express themselves in more complex ways, and at greater length. One way you can assist them is to introduce lexis which builds on what they know and will enable them to (1) modify, (2) extend, and (3) comment on what they are saying.

fixed expressions[1] go to **glossary** for numbered items *p.166*

1 The example below takes expressions that intermediate learners already know and use (*I'm (not) sure, I don't really know*), but slots in **modifiers** common in spoken English (*pretty* and *too*), as well as adding extensions (*to be honest*), and offering alternatives (*I haven't a clue*), so that learners can express the same ideas more precisely, with a wider range of language – and sound more natural.

natural English
saying how sure you are   2.4

I'm (pretty) sure (about that).
I don't really know, to be honest.
I'm not (too) sure (about that).
I haven't a clue. ☺

Listen and write the questions you hear.
Practise the questions and answers with a

from upper-intermediate **student's book**, unit two *p.28*

2 This second example below takes learners beyond the ubiquitous *I agree / I don't agree*, and provides them with varied and natural ways of both agreeing with and challenging other people's opinions; in other words, it extends their range of expression.

natural English
agreeing with and challenging opinions

'I think we should have more men than women on the island.'

agreeing	challenging
Yes, that makes sense.	Why do you say that?
that seems sensible.	I can't see the point of that.
I think you're right.	I don't see why.

Practise saying the phrases to yourself.

from upper-intermediate **student's book**, unit three *p.38*

3 The final example on *p.161* introduces phrases that learners can use to **comment** on and express their attitude to the information they are communicating.

natural English
expectation and surprise

Use these words and phrases for something that was <u>expected to happen</u>:

She passed her test, **as you might expect**.
He kept going and **inevitably** /ɪnˈevɪtəbli/ he ran out of petrol.

Use these phrases for something that was <u>not expected</u>:

He ran across the road and, **to my surprise / amazement**, he threw flowers at me.
It was almost dark but, **for some reason**, he didn't have his lights on.

from upper-intermediate **student's book**, unit five *p.60*.

In our experience, learners find this quite challenging even at upper-intermediate level. This **natural English** box forms part of an activity where learners have to describe a driving incident around a given framework, and have the opportunity to incorporate one or two expressions of expectation or surprise. The previous two **natural English** boxes also have associated practice activities.

think!¹

Think of suitable language for upper-intermediate learners to extend or modify these sentences. The … indicates where you can put the additional language.

1 (angrily) Where … have you been?
2 (interrupting) … Can I speak to you?
3 (accusing sb) That was … stupid … .
4 It was … a … relief to get back home.

In these sentences, replace the underlined phrases with suitable alternatives for upper-intermediate level.

5 Can I <u>speak to you?</u>
6 If I were <u>you</u>, I'd take the job.
7 People came from <u>every country</u>.
8 Can you <u>watch</u> my bags for one minute?

go to **answer key** *p.166*

teaching chunks

Almost all the examples so far in this chapter show vocabulary being taught not through individual words, but as part of fixed expressions, e.g. *to be honest* or semi-fixed expressions, e.g. *to my surprise / amazement*. Presenting phrases will be an important part of vocabulary teaching at any level. At higher levels though, learners can obviously cope with longer chunks of language, and they can explore new meanings and patterns of familiar language. For example, upper-intermediate learners will all know the verb *tell*, but how many know and use it with the meaning *recognize*, in the patterns given in the **natural English** box opposite?

6 Look at the phrases in the **natural English** box and complete the first example with a phrase from the text.

natural English
expressions with *tell (recognize)*

_____ a silk scarf and an acrylic one.
I can't tell one type of beer **from** another.
Can you tell what someone's nationality is, just by looking at them?
Can you tell the difference between one type of mineral water and another?

In A / B pairs, ask / say something about:

A – decaffeinated coffee and ordinary coffee
 – someone lying or telling the truth
 – different brands of fruit juice
 – a crocodile and an alligator

B – different brands of pasta
 – someone's job and their appearance
 – real leather and fake leather
 – good wine and cheap wine

from upper-intermediate **student's book**, unit ten *p.116*.

One potential difficulty with teaching 'chunks', for both teachers and learners, is that many consist of words that, individually, are all familiar to learners at this level, e.g.
the other day
for some reason
I'd find it hard to do that
it's up to you
I didn't mean to
have a go

From a learning point of view, this should make such phrases relatively easy to master (there are no new forms to remember), but the danger is that learners will not recognize them as 'new' vocabulary, or indeed, as vocabulary at all. This is a particular problem with written text: the vocabulary items that learners usually focus on are the individual words they don't recognize, and some of these will probably be low frequency items of little long term value. You may find, therefore, that you will have to take much of the responsibility for highlighting useful phrases and lexical patterns, i.e. pointing them out in a text, checking that learners understand them, writing them on the board, asking learners to repeat them and use them in other contexts. If you are working with a monolingual group, it may be enlightening to show your learners that they would be unlikely to put together many of these phrases accurately by translating from their first language. In other words, these are phrases that need to be learned as lexical items, just as learners recognize they need to learn *collar*, *collapse*, or *conceited*.

think!²

Read the joke. <u>Underline</u> three individual words and three lexical chunks which upper-intermediate learners may not know and may find generally useful.

> Two moose hunters from Texas are flown to a lake in Alaska in the middle of nowhere. They manage to kill a large moose each. When the plane returns to pick them up, the pilot looks at them and says, 'This little plane won't lift all of us, the equipment and both those animals. You'll have to leave one behind. We'll never make it over the trees to take off.'
>
> 'That's baloney,' says one of the hunters.
>
> 'Yeah, you're just a coward. Last year we came out and killed two moose, and the pilot wasn't afraid to take off!'
>
> The pilot gets angry and says, 'Right! If he did it, then I can do it. I can fly as well as anyone!'
>
> They load up and start to take off. The plane almost makes it, but doesn't manage to clear the trees at the end of the lake. It turns upside down, scattering the baggage, moose and passengers all over the place.
>
> Still alive, the pilot looks up and says, 'Where are we?'
>
> One of the hunters puts his head up, looks around and says, 'I'd say ... about 100 metres further than last year!'

go to **answer key** p.166

link words and phrases

At intermediate level and below, learners produce quite short utterances which don't usually require a wide range of linking devices. Even when link words are required, learners rarely have the knowledge or processing capacity to work out how to use them in real time. This becomes an issue at a higher level when learner output is longer and more complex. Effective linking not only adds sophistication, it also helps learners to sound more natural and encourages the production of longer, more coherent chunks of language.

Traditionally, clause combination has often been left until this level, with the result that teachers may spend considerable amounts of time teaching adverbs of concession, e.g. *however*, *in spite of*, or addition, e.g. *moreover*, *furthermore*, and so on.

Want to know more? Go to **Practical English Usage** by Michael Swan *pp.151* to *158*.

If there has been a weakness here, it has been the concentration on *discourse markers*³ which characterize written English, with far less attention paid to those used predominantly in spoken English. Both are likely to be important at this level, and if learners can recognize a wide range of linking devices from spoken and written English, this will help them to anticipate what is going to come up in the next part of the *discourse*⁴. In other words, there is a significant receptive pay-off for learners, in addition to their obvious value to learners as part of their productive vocabulary. Here is one exercise for you to do, which you could also use or adapt for your own learners. .

think!³

How do you think these sentences might continue? What do the link words in bold suggest?

1 We left the door key under the plant **just in case** _____.

2 The lights were all blazing away **even though** _____.

3 I don't like his current girlfriend much. **Mind you,** _____.

4 I'm not going to the wedding – it's too far away. **Besides,** _____.

5 I asked my teenage son to tidy his room last night and **predictably,** _____.

6 I've lent him money twice before – **the trouble is,** _____.

go to **answer key** p.166

There are also sequences of linkers which are used when structuring speech or writing, and these can often be applied quite generatively. A simple example is this sequence:

First of all (I couldn't find the car keys) ...
then to make matters worse (there were road works all the way)
but worst of all, (by the time I got there the party was over).

Such frameworks can be used by learners to connect ideas together and speak at greater length. Here is an example from the natural English box on *p.87*.

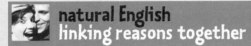

natural English
linking reasons together

There are several reasons why I'd like the job / I'd be good at the job.
First of all, I've had experience in dealing with the public.
Secondly, I'm very patient.
And another thing is that I'm very fond of travelling.

2   Compare your ideas with your partner.

from upper-intermediate **student's book**, unit seven *p.87*.

awareness of style

As learners become more proficient, an awareness of different levels of formality takes on greater significance. Even if most of a learner's language is reasonably fluent and accurate, errors of style can create misunderstandings without the learner being aware of it. Moreover, listeners do not always make allowances for errors of style and assume that someone with a good level of English 'should know better'. We once witnessed a proficient, (and polite) young male tourist receive a very frosty look from an older, female bank cashier after the following exchange took place when the tourist was changing money.

cashier: *How would you like the cash?* (five-pound notes, etc.)
tourist: *I don't mind, love.*

The tourist had probably heard this term of endearment from other shop assistants (it is quite common in British English), and assumed that by using it himself he might sound similarly warm and friendly; sadly not the case.

spoken and written English

One important stylistic contrast in British English is between the various forms of the written and spoken language. If you are using a written text in class, you can point out to learners how similar ideas might be expressed in spoken English. This not only helps to develop their awareness of different styles, but also provides an opportunity to teach useful vocabulary, as in this example, where the learners have already encountered the formal verbs in a written text.

natural English
spoken v. written English

We tend to use phrasal verbs and idioms more in spoken English. In written English, there's often a more formal equivalent.

more formal	more informal
Your telephone has been **disconnected**.	Our phone's been _____ .
They **abolished** the old system.	They _____ the old system.
The boy was **reprimanded** by the teacher.	Joe was _____ by the teacher.

Fill the gaps with these phrasal verbs.

got rid of	told off	cut off

from upper-intermediate **student's book**, unit five *p.63*.

You can also ask learners to 'translate' some of the more formal parts of a text to make it more informal. Notices and warnings are a useful context here. You could ask learners how someone would express the ideas in informal spoken English.

example
smoking prohibited = You can't smoke here.

1 no vacancies (= The hotel is full.)
2 please tender exact fare and state destination (= Please give the exact money (to the driver) and say where you are going.)
3 no exit (= You can't get out here.)
4 cyclists dismount here (= You have to get off your bike here.)
5 do not exceed the stated dose (= You mustn't take more medicine than it says on the packet.)

It is useful to point out to learners the information on style in dictionaries, as this will enable them to check new items for style and note it down as they learn them. You can give your class a set of lexical items covering a range of styles, e.g. formal, informal, neutral. Here is an example:

1 Put the words and phrases under the correct heading, according to style. Use a dictionary to check your answers.

inherit (money)	bequeath sth to sb	be rolling (in money)
be hard up	remuneration	be well-off
purchase	pricey	invest
more formal	**neutral**	**more informal**

go to **answer key** *p.166*

3   Using spoken and written text

For many teachers, the most obvious source of new lexis is text. This is particularly true at higher levels when learners can handle longer authentic texts, and these often provide a rich source of input. This new lexis has the virtue of being contextualized, and there should be a high degree of motivation on the learners' part to understand lexis that forms part of an interesting text (less so perhaps if the text is dull).

learner choice

In addition to any lexis you choose to highlight for your learners, it is a good idea to give them some time to explore the text for themselves. Learners have different needs and interests, and by this level will also have different vocabularies; words and phrases familiar to some learners will be new to others. Restrict learners to checking a limited number of items in class, e.g. two to four, and set a time limit in order to focus their attention. Move round the class giving assistance where necessary.

using tapescripts

Texts are often assumed to be written. However, you should be spending just as much time – in some cases more – on spoken text, otherwise your learners will be getting a very unbalanced lexical diet. Understanding new lexis while you listen is neither practical nor indeed possible in many instances, but after exploiting a spoken text for the development of different listening skills, you can make very good use of the tapescript. We have done this extensively in **natural English**, as some lexical features are more common in spoken English. Here is an example of working from a tapescript, after the learners have listened to the passage several times and completed comprehension tasks.

a Circle all the examples of *so*, *anyway*, and *so anyway*. Why are they used? Check with the **natural English** box on *p.59* of the student's book.

b Find phrases in the tapescript which mean:

1 he spent the night
2 he couldn't get the car to go
3 to his surprise
4 I imagine he was very angry
5 he had no alternative
6 as you can imagine

from upper-intermediate **listening booklet** *p.19*.

text search activities

There are many different kinds of text search activity that you can do with written and spoken texts to help learners with lexis. Here are a few examples:

– Find a word / phrase in the text which means the same as … (*Wait a minute! / What's the matter? / It's easy to find*)

– Circle all the words and phrases in the text which relate to … (*money / friendship / sleep*, etc.)

– Complete these common phrases, then compare with the phrases in the tapescript.
(*I'd had a very late _____; I _____ asleep straightaway; I slept like a _____; I forgot to set the _____*)

– Circle all the examples of *anyway / so anyway*, i.e. a spoken or written connector in the text. What do they mean, and when are they used?

– Transform these sentences. The meaning must stay the same. Then check in the text to find the transformations, e.g.

It will have a big effect on people's lives.
It will make _____ .
(a big difference to people's lives)
We'll give you the information you need.
We'll tell you _____ .
(whatever you need to know)

– Find examples of … e.g. phrases which show that someone is listening with interest; phrases which show that the listener is surprised / doesn't believe the speaker, etc.

4 Anticipating new lexis

Texts are not the only vehicle for a focus on lexis; an alternative approach is to plan speaking activities for the lesson which you think will be of interest to your learners, then anticipate some of the vocabulary that you think will be relevant and useful for the activity, and present it beforehand. If you aren't sure what this language might be, you could do a 'practice run' yourself with another teacher, if possible record it, then make a note of the vocabulary you used.

Want to know more? Go to intermediate **teacher's book, how to …** do free speaking (try it out) *p.164*.

Using this approach, learners will have an immediate opportunity to practise, consolidate, and recycle the new vocabulary. Here is an example of this type of pro-active vocabulary work in **wordbooster** unit five.

1 **Fill the gaps with an appropriate verb. Sometimes more than one is possible.**

cheat	fail	take	get through	do
prepare	sit	come up	turn up	bluff
go on	retake	pass	take place	make a mess of

2 **With a partner, ask and answer the questions.**

the driving test in your country

the practical test

1 Where does the practical test usually _____ ?

2 If you _____ for the test a few minutes' late, are you still allowed to _____ it?

3 If (unfortunately) you _____ the test, how long do you have to wait before you can _____ it? Do you think that's about right?

4 Do people ever _____ in the test?

the written exam

5 Do you have to _____ a written exam as well as a practical one?

6 Is there a specific book you have to use to _____ for the written exam? Do you think that's a good idea?

7 What kinds of questions are likely to _____ in the exam? Do you think the questions are sensible?

8 If you manage to _____ the written, can you _____ to the practical straight afterwards? Or does the practical exam come first?

9 Is it possible to _____ your way through it if you don't know the answers?

from upper-intermediate **student's book**, unit five, *p.61*.

The activity is very controlled, so using the target language should not be difficult. At the same time, new language is personalized and learners have an opportunity for creative output by sharing each other's knowledge and experience.

think![4]

You are planning to do the activity below in which learners will need to express their willingness (or not) to do these things. What phrases might you pre-teach them?

2 **Think!** Which of these would you be prepared to do in your free time? Put a tick ✓, a cross ✗, or 'maybe'.

– Help a child who has problems with reading.
– Take an elderly person's dog for a walk two or three times a week.
– Give up a weekend to clear waste land which will be used for a children's playground.
– Take a small group of teenagers camping for a weekend.
– Babysit three small noisy children regularly for a neighbour.

from upper-intermediate **student's book**, unit seven *p.82*

go to **answer key** *p.166*

5 Self-study

As learners become more proficient, they should find it easier to improve their English and expand their vocabulary outside class. For example, they can

- read books and magazines written in English
- make effective use of ELT monolingual dictionaries
- listen to cassettes and CDs in English
- listen to the lyrics of songs recorded in English
- watch films in English or follow films with English subtitles
- watch one or more of the increasing number of TV channels in English that are available around the world, e.g. CNN
- use the Internet (reading websites and using opportunities to chat on-line
- join English-speaking clubs in many cities around the world.

In theory, these sources are available to everyone, but for lower level learners it is very difficult to benefit from input that is a long way above their own level. Upper-intermediate learners should have the knowledge and confidence to be able to take advantage of these sources, but to do this successfully – in some cases, to do it at all – they will probably need encouragement, and some learners will also need training, which starts in class.

using dictionaries

We have discussed the importance and value of making use of dictionaries in another chapter, and you will also find regular activities in **wordbooster** in the **student's book**, which is designed to teach learners about dictionary features and give them practice in using them. It is also important for learners to keep effective records of the new vocabulary they encounter, otherwise many of these items will be forgotten very quickly.

Want to know more? Go to **how to ...** use dictionaries with learners *p.174*.

keeping vocabulary records

There is no single correct way to keep vocabulary records: ultimately, the best system is the one the learner feels comfortable with and is willing to maintain. If possible though, we think it will help learners to incorporate some of the following suggestions:

- Keep records in a book that is easy to carry around (and have more than one book).
- Divide the book into sections so that the lexis is organized and learners can easily retrieve items they need, e.g. have pages for specific topics, or for verbs followed by a particular preposition, and so on. In some cases, it will be valuable to enter items in more than one place.
- Make a note of the key information about items: the item, the part of speech, the pronunciation, the meaning (in English, or in the mother tongue), and an example showing how the word is typically used. You will need to demonstrate to learners how to do this.

> get away with sth (v) do sth wrong, but not be caught or punished
> People drive above the speed limit and most get away with it.
>
> flood (v/n) /flʌd/ inundar, inundación
> The floods in the south have made thousands homeless.

- Remember that lexis consists of phrases as well as individual words, and in both cases always include the new items in typical examples alongside other words that often combine with them.

  examples
  aware She isn't even <u>aware of the problem</u>.
  get on sb's nerves That noise is really <u>getting on my nerves</u>.

- Try to make the book look interesting, e.g. use pictures or diagrams so that pages are more eye-catching and items stand out.

Without being too dogmatic, you can obviously look at the records your learners are keeping and give advice where you feel it is appropriate. You can also get learners to look at each others' notes for ideas.

learning outside class

To encourage your learners to carry on learning outside class, you can use or adapt this simple activity.

---

try it out learn a word / phrase and teach it

I did this on a regular basis with higher level students I taught during a vocabulary option class.

Between each lesson (they had one every day for a month), I asked each student to find one new word or phrase (from a book, TV, Internet, or wherever). The only conditions were that it had to be, in their view, useful and relevant, and they had to be able to explain it and give clear examples of its use. At the start of the lesson they would then mingle and explain their item and learn others. I set a time limit to focus the learners, but I was also flexible with this if the group was clearly engaged in the activity and useful lexical items were being circulated.

At first, one or two students forgot to do it, and several others chose words or phrases that weren't very useful. However, within a week of persevering with this, students rarely forgot, and the quality of the lexis they introduced improved as time went on. They were motivated to learn other people's items as well as teach their own, and it also provided them with a lot of genuine interaction and practice in explaining and paraphrasing.

I kept a record of all the items brought to class and gave the students short revision tests on the lexis (usually orally) every few days.

Stuart, London.

Again, in theory, you can do this with any level, but it does work more effectively with higher level learners who have the ability to explain and paraphrase quite effectively; with lower levels it can become frustrating if they don't have the language to explain new items satisfactorily.

conclusion

In this chapter we have looked at

- how we can help upper-intermediate learners to express themselves in more complex ways, and at greater length using natural English expressions, chunks, and link words and phrases
- the importance of style at this level, and differences between written and spoken English
- the use of spoken and written text as a major source of new lexis, e.g. exploiting spoken texts by doing text search activities using the tapescript
- a pro-active approach to vocabulary work which involves planning speaking activities and anticipating the vocabulary which will be necessary to accomplish the activity
- ways of training upper-intermediate learners to expand their vocabulary outside the classroom, by for instance, improving dictionary use and record keeping.

answer key

think![1] *p.161*

1 on earth; the hell (informal, and may be offensive)
2 Sorry to bother you.
3 really / very / incredibly; of you
4 such; great / huge
5 have a word with you
6 in your shoes, in your position
7 all over the world
8 keep an eye on

think![2] *p.162*

individual words: *hunter, coward, scatter*
Learners will probably seize on *moose* and *baloney*, although neither is very useful beyond this text.
chunks: *in the middle of nowhere* = somewhere remote; *leave* sth *behind*, (learners would probably say *leave* sth); *make it* = succeed in reaching a place (or one's goal); *(turn) upside down* (there is no other way to express this idea as clearly as this phrase); *all over the place* = everywhere

think![3] *p.162*

1 (**just**) **in case** signals the possibility of an event happening, so it could finish like this: *the children arrived home before us*.
2 **even though** suggests that the rest of the clause will be in contrast or against what one might expect, e.g. *nobody was at home*.
3 **Mind you** indicates you are going to say something which is the opposite of what you have just said, e.g. *she's better than the last one*.
4 **Besides** signals an addition of an extra fact or reason in this case, e.g. *I've got too much work to do at the moment*.
5 **predictably** indicates the speaker's attitude, i.e. *true to character, he hasn't tidied it yet*.
6 **the trouble is** warns the listener that a negative point will follow, e.g. *he never pays it back*, or *I'm a bit short of money myself at the moment*.

1 *p.163*

more formal bequeath, remuneration, purchase
neutral inherit, be well-off, invest
more informal be rolling in money, be hard up, pricey

think![4] *p.164*

This language is from a **natural English** box in upper-intermediate **student's book**, unit seven *p.82*.
I'd be willing / prepared to do that.
I wouldn't mind doing that.
I'd be (a bit) reluctant to do that.
I'd find it (a bit) hard to do that.

glossary

a fixed expression[1] An expression in which the individual words combine with a special meaning and these words cannot be changed, e.g. *never mind* not *never care*; *the tip of the iceberg* not *the top of the iceberg* or *the top of an iceberg*; *a red herring* not *a reddish herring*.

a semi-fixed expression[2] An expression which allows a limited degree of change, e.g. *it's up to you / him / her, have a nice day / swim / meal*.

discourse markers[3] Words and expressions which in different ways show how the discourse develops and is constructed, e.g. *As I was saying*, relates to something that was said before; *however*, signals and emphasizes a contrast; *by the way …*, indicates a change of subject.

discourse[4] Pieces of language which are longer than a sentence.

follow up

Swan M 1995 (second edition) *Practical English Usage* Oxford University Press

Lewis M 1997 *Implementing the Lexical Approach* LTP

Lewis M 2000 *Teaching Collocation* LTP

McCarthy M 1990 *Vocabulary* Oxford University Press

how to ... teach reading

1 How do we read?

Reading can be divided into two categories: reading that takes place <u>inside</u> the classroom, and reading that happens <u>outside</u> the classroom. With the former, texts are usually (but not exclusively) chosen by you, the teacher, and they normally have specific learning goals, which might be one or more of the following:

- to develop specific reading skills
- to teach language contained in the text
- to act as a springboard for other skills activities.

Given the limited amount of classroom time available, texts will necessarily be kept quite short, and the reading will be both concentrated and <u>intensive</u>. In contrast, reading outside class will probably include some longer texts which can be read in a more leisurely way, and often just for pleasure with no accompanying task. This is sometimes referred to as <u>extensive</u> reading.

We will consider how you can influence your learners' extensive reading in the final section (see *p.172*), but much of this chapter will be devoted to the exploitation of texts and the development of reading skills inside the classroom.

2 Key skills in reading

The ability to read efficiently involves the application of various skills, and knowing when it is appropriate to use each one. In this section, we look at

- background knowledge
- prediction
- skimming and scanning
- contextual guesswork
- interpreting a text.

In section 3, **Exploiting a text** (see *p.169*), you will find related practical teaching ideas.

background knowledge

Language learners often suppose the only difficulty in reading a second language is in getting to grips with a new language. In fact, understanding a text often entails more than just understanding the language. Familiarity with the text type, e.g. newspaper articles, advertisements, business letters, novels, e-mails, etc. plus the topic of the text itself, and sometimes the writer's culture and way of life, are all factors that can significantly influence our understanding of what we read.

> **think!**[1]
> Irrespective of language, what might make the following British texts easier or more difficult to understand?
> - a newspaper article about a forthcoming referendum
> - a report on the first day's play of the latest test match
> - a joke in a magazine
> - some examples of teenage text messages
> - a summary of last week's episodes of a soap opera
> - a poem

go to **answer key** *p.173*

activating schemata

The different knowledge that we bring to a text is called *schemata*[1], and it is vital that learners activate the relevant schemata when they approach a text, and don't become so preoccupied with language that they overlook this important element. It is equally true, of course, that if learners don't possess the relevant schemata, they are likely to encounter far greater difficulty with the text. That is something you need to be aware of when selecting or exploiting texts in class. For example, a *referendum* might be a concept that requires careful explanation for learners from some cultures before they can make any sense of a text on the subject. For Swiss learners, however, referenda are a very familiar part of their culture, so the text will be more transparent.

prediction

If learners are able to use their background knowledge to recognize the text type and topic, they may be able to go on and predict much of the content of the text. As they read, their guesses will prove to be either right or wrong. If a person can do this regularly – particularly where their predictions are mostly confirmed – they not only read faster and more efficiently, but also get positive feedback from their reading, which in turn, encourages them to read more. If the reader is not able to predict or doesn't try to do so, reading will be slower and more difficult. As a result the reader may become demotivated and read less. In practical terms, this means:

- encourage prediction with your learners, regardless of nationality
- guide their predictions so that they are more likely to be accurate
- recognize that some cultures will find this particularly difficult, and will therefore need more cultural / background information before they read.

There are practical suggestions for prediction on *p.169*.

If a text contradicts our expectations, that is also significant and will probably influence the way we read the text. For one thing it means the content is surprising and possibly more interesting, but it may also signal key information that the reader needs to process more carefully and attentively.

schemata[1] go to **glossary** for numbered items *p.173*

go to **answer key** p.173

think!²

Read this opening to a text. What would you expect to come next?

> DIETING UNDER STRESS
> By ROS CRUM
> This diet is designed to help you cope with the stress that builds up during the day.
> BREAKFAST
> Half a grapefruit, 1 slice wholemeal toast, 3 oz. skimmed milk.

Your knowledge of food and dieting will obviously influence your predictions here, but most of you will probably have anticipated information about a fairly frugal lunch, possibly containing fish, pulses, vegetables, and /or salad. In fact, the next line is as follows:

> LUNCH
> 4 oz. steamed chicken, 1 portion of spinach, 1 cup of herbal tea, 1 chocolate biscuit.

Did you predict the *chocolate biscuit*? Why not? How has this now changed your perception of what text type this may be, and what might come next? Think about it for a minute or two, then compare your ideas with the rest of the text in the answer key.

skimming and scanning

Sometimes we want or need to read a text very quickly in order to get a general idea of what it is about (the gist of the text), but without worrying too much about the finer details. This is known as skimming, and it is an important skill as it helps us to become faster and more efficient readers. We may decide after skimming the text that it warrants a second reading to get more detailed information; otherwise we can move on without spending unnecessary time on it.

A different skill involves reading through a text in order to find very specific information. In this case, the reader ignores much of the information simply because it isn't relevant to their reason for reading the text in the first place. This is known as scanning, and it would be the normal way we approach reading a bus or rail timetable; searching for information about the specific bus or train we want to catch.

With some texts, we need to use both of these reading strategies. For example, you might read this chapter quickly to get the gist of it, then come back to it later and scan it for a specific piece of information or reader activity that you vaguely remember from your first reading.

contextual guesswork

Even native speakers of a language come across words and phrases in their reading that they don't recognize or understand. In such circumstances, they can:

1 look up the meaning in a dictionary
2 guess the meaning for themselves using the context and possibly the form of the word itself
3 ignore the item and read on in the hope or belief that its meaning isn't crucial to an understanding of the text.

The same options are open to second language learners, the main difference being that it will happen much more frequently for the vast majority of learners, and using the dictionary each time would become extremely time-consuming. It is therefore necessary for learners to make greater use of the second and third options: guess the general meaning from the context, or ignore the item and move on. This latter option is not necessarily a sign of laziness: ignoring a word or phrase may be the sensible decision if the item does not seem to be obviously useful or of great relevance to an understanding of the text.

think!³

In this text, we have changed a few of the words to nonsense words. Can you guess what they might mean, and are they important to an understanding of the text?

> (Peter is in his fourth year of teaching at a boys' grammar school.)
> Teaching had never been Peter's first choice of brindol: he wanted to join the Air Force, then discovered he was darband. But on this hot budder, trying to persuade 4D of the beauty of Shakespeare, the classroom was the last place he wanted to be, and Edwards and Jones at the back were not helping matters. He'd already told them off for pargling in their seats and now one of them was ...

go to **answer key** p.173

interpreting a text

In order to understand certain texts, the reader has to go beyond the literal meaning and interpret what the writer is saying. Read this short text and answer the questions.

> (From an infant *News Book*; the saga starts two weeks before the birthday.)
> 14 days to go: It is my birthday. I hope to get a horse.
> 12 days to go: Mummy says she likes horses too.
> 8 days to go: I can't wait to get a horse for my birthday.
> 3 days to go: Daddy says horses cost a lot of money.
> 2 days to go: I will call it Prince if it is a boy.
> Birthday: I got a hamster for my birthday. It is called Goldy.
> The day after: Mummy is scared of Goldy. Daddy helps me to hold it. I think Mummy would have liked a horse better.
>
> **Questions**
> 1 Does the child think she will get a horse for her birthday?
> 2 Does the mother think the child is going to get a horse?
> 3 Does the father intend to buy the child a horse?
> 4 Is it true the mother would have liked the child to have a horse?

With the probable exception of number 1, one cannot answer these questions with any certainty. Yet, we would be surprised if your answers were not 1 yes, 2 no, 3 no, and 4 no. These are not the answers the child would give, but we interpret the story told from the child's point of view, and we do this by activating our background knowledge of a child's innocence and also the relationship between parents and their young children. The child wants a horse and the mother is happy to go along with this fantasy in the certain knowledge that it won't actually happen. The father has no intention of buying a horse but tries to let the child down gently by mentioning the cost. The child clearly does not want to hear this. It turns out the mother doesn't even like the hamster, so we are inclined to take the view that she was probably against the child being given any kind of animal for a present. In other words we interpret the whole story and fill in all the gaps left by the child's perception of the situation.

In this and many other texts, it is our background knowledge or shared schemata that enables us to interpret the text. Without this knowledge a text may be quite impenetrable, and for learners from a completely different culture, this is one of the biggest hurdles to overcome.

3 Exploiting a text

From a practical point of view, there are a number of things you can ask learners to do

- before reading
- while reading
- and after reading a text.

Let's examine each one in turn.

pre-reading activities

motivating learners to read

You will have certain aims in mind in any activity you use or devise which leads learners into a text, but the emphasis will often vary, depending on the learning context and the learners themselves. Primarily, though, you need to motivate learners to read and arouse interest in the content or the writer. This may seem obvious, but most texts used in class are not selected by the learners themselves and therefore they may not be texts they would normally choose to read; you have to provide them with a reason for reading. This may be particularly relevant where learners want to concentrate on listening and speaking, and are less keen to devote class time to reading.

activating schemata

Activities which stimulate interest in a text will also help learners to activate schemata (see p.167), and enable you to see whether they have sufficient background knowledge to tackle the text successfully. If, for instance, your text assumes learners are familiar with a TV game show such as *Blind date* or *Who wants to be a millionaire?*, then find out what they know at this stage. Ask them in pairs to brainstorm what they know about the games. Elicit their ideas, and then feed in any extra information which may be necessary for them to read the text successfully.

setting appropriate reading tasks

Many learners approach reading texts with a view that all words in it are important, and that they will only have a thorough understanding of the text if they have read it word-for-word. This is clearly something that you want to discourage. If you use tasks which focus learners on the gist of the text, or ask them to find the most interesting information (and set a time limit), this will go some way towards discouraging word-for-word reading. A positive outcome, where learners achieve the task successfully, will be good for their confidence.

Here are some specific ways you can help to motivate learners, familiarize them with the content, and set appropriate reading tasks. (An interesting task can sometimes compensate for a less than exciting text.)

---

think!⁴

As you read the ideas, annotate the list like this:

✓ the ones you use
✓✓ the ones you'd like to use
✗ the ones you don't use / wouldn't use

☐ Use the headlines, titles, captions, headings, and photos or illustrations which accompany a text to encourage prediction before learners read. These can also be used to elicit what learners already know about the topic and can be a useful way to diagnose what background information you need to tell them in advance.

☐ Write a number of key words or phrases from the text on the board, and see if learners can guess what the text is about. For instance, the words below come from the text in the **student's book** on *p.120*. Learners could look at the vocabulary in pairs and try to piece the story together before they read.

Jean Humphries	mid-forties	facelift	glamorous
husband	horrified	daughter's education	
confidence	better mother		

☐ Tell learners the topic of the text, and lift out key sentences from it. Learners have to say how the sentences might end, then read to check their ideas, as in the example below.

1 **Foreign correspondents are given training before they go to trouble spots. Read these extracts. How do you think they finish?**

1 You learn basic and advanced first aid, how to treat gunshot wounds and burns, and how to prepare for extreme _____.

2 There's nothing optional about the training – if you haven't done the course, you _____.

3 I've reported a lot from trouble spots around the world and the one thing I've learnt is that getting out can be more difficult than _____.

4 When reporting somewhere for the first time, it's often worth contacting the aid agencies, religious communities, and any other _____ .

2 **Read the article and check your answers.**

from upper-intermediate **student's book**, unit six p.71

☐ Learners read the first sentence or paragraph of the text, then predict how it might continue, e.g. you could show learners this opening paragraph from the text on *p.83* and ask them what the rest of the text is likely to be about.

It was the end of my first term teaching English at Lanzhou University in China and I was looking forward to a winter break in Shanghai where it was warmer. Three days before departure, however, I spent a bad night alternately **shivering** and **sweating**, and finally I called a doctor. He diagnosed pneumonia, so that put an end to my travel plans, and instead I spent just over a week in a small three-bed **ward** in the university hospital.

from upper-intermediate **student's book**, unit seven p.83

Most learners will probably say that it will describe the period spent in hospital. You can then ask them in pairs to predict what specific aspects she will describe. They are quite likely to make some accurate predictions, but some surprises will occur when they read the text, especially if they know little about Chinese hospitals. (This is in fact what makes the text interesting.)

☐ Learners are given brief notes on the content of each paragraph in a text, and have to put them in a logical order. They then read to see if their order is correct, as in the example below.

---

1 You're going to read about a woman who participated in a month-long scientific experiment. Put these paragraph topics in a logical order. Compare with a partner.

  a the conditions she lived in for a month

  b the purpose of the experiment

  c the after-effects of the experiment

  d how scientists created the conditions for the experiment

  e her feelings during the experiment

2 Read the article and complete the glossary. Was your order of paragraphs the same?

from upper-intermediate **student's book**, unit five *p.62*

☐ Make use of personalization by asking learners to discuss issues to do with the topic before they read. This might include discussion questions or answering questionnaires. In the example below from unit twelve, learners are going to read a text about someone who became a contestant on a quiz show (*Who wants to be a millionaire?*). First, learners answer the questions about themselves, then read the text and answer the same questions about the contestant, Alli.

---

4 Think! Prepare to answer these questions.

  1 Would you like to be a contestant on this show? Why / why not?

  2 How might you prepare for the quiz?

  3 Who would you phone for help on one question?

  4 How would you feel during the show, and at the end?

  5 If you won, how might it change your life?

5 Compare your ideas with a partner.

1 Read the article and complete the glossary.

2 How would Alli answer the questions in **lead-in exercise 4**?

from upper-intermediate **student's book**, unit twelve *p.138*

☐ Give learners the topic and some pre-set questions. In pairs, they have to imagine possible answers before they read. It can be very satisfying to make a clever guess!

☐ Tell learners the topic of the text, e.g. a woman on holiday who loses her passport, and ask them to produce their own questions about it. With a suitable text, this can be more motivating than setting the questions yourself.

This final activity is quite an attractive one, and can work very well, though it has potential drawbacks. Supposing the text does not answer the learners' questions? Won't they find this frustrating and disappointing? If one or two questions remain unanswered, that is largely predictable, and shouldn't be a cause for concern. If the majority of their questions remain unanswered, however, then there is a problem somewhere which you need to identify. Perhaps the text does not lend itself to this type of task, or possibly the learners need the topic to be more clearly defined. It may be that the learners (or certain learners) are not very good at predicting. In this case, you have discovered one reason why texts may be difficult for them. In future, they will need more information before reading, and probably more practice with this kind of task.

In all of the activities above you have a number of issues to consider.

– Firstly, have you <u>set a clear task</u>, and are you certain learners know what to do?

– Secondly, are you going to <u>set a time limit</u> to encourage speed reading, and if so, how long should it be? It pays to be a little flexible if everyone is taking longer than the time you set. If you don't set a time limit, you will need to be prepared for learners finishing at different times. It helps to have a short activity up your sleeve for faster readers which will not interfere with the activities you are planning to do next. They could compare their answers in pairs, for instance.

– Thirdly, are you going to <u>clarify the reading aims</u> for your learners? In other words, are you going to explain why you are asking them to predict content or work to a time limit, for instance?

– Finally, you need to have a clear policy on <u>vocabulary pre-teaching</u>. If you pre-teach all the vocabulary learners are unlikely to know in an authentic text, you may well change the aim of the lesson from developing a sub-skill of reading to vocabulary learning. It is also probable that learners will become too focused on this new vocabulary when they read the text, which could prevent them from reading the text naturally to understand the key information. At the other extreme, if you explain nothing, they may be unable to understand the gist.

So, what should you pre-teach? As a general rule:

– only explain items that are essential to achieving the task set (other items can wait until later).

– try not to make this more than three to four items. (If many more items than this are needed to understand the gist, it may indicate that the task is too detailed, or the text is very difficult.)

activities to do while reading

Learners clearly need to concentrate while they are reading, which is a very active process despite the term 'receptive skill'.

If you have pre-set a task such as true / false questions, transferring information to a grid, reading to confirm predictions, etc. learners have both the task and the reading to juggle at once. Some teachers ask learners to read a text and underline every word they don't know. It would depend on the text and the number of unknown items, of course, but this seems to us a risky approach. Firstly, the focus of reading once again becomes specific vocabulary rather than reading the text for meaning. Secondly, how do you deal with all the items they have underlined, especially as learners will have selected different items? You may find the next half-hour uncomfortably devoted to on-the-spot definitions and explanations.

It is important not to distract learners by writing on the board, for example, or asking questions while they are reading. Use the time instead to <u>observe</u> how they are reading.

– Are learners following the text slowly word-for-word with their finger? If so, you can try some <u>speed reading techniques</u> using the overhead projector or posters, and revealing sentences for a short time only.

– Is anyone using their dictionary to check every word they don't know? You may need to discourage this approach if they are to become more efficient readers.

There are certain purposeful activities learners can do while reading. One of them is to <u>react</u> to the text as they read, putting ticks, crosses, or question marks for points they agree / disagree with or aren't sure about (as you did in the previous section), or putting comments in the margin.

If you can reinforce the idea of pre-reading tasks which help with reading skills, you will be helping learners to read more effectively.

post-reading activities

After learners have completed the pre-set tasks, you may want to exploit the text more fully. Further reading tasks, language exploitation, and extending to other skills are all possibilities, and the way you follow up the text will depend on what your learners need to do most, and what the text is most suitable for. Further reading activities will include those which develop particular sub-skills, e.g. reading for detailed comprehension, interpreting meaning, guessing vocabulary from context, etc. Most coursebooks also take the opportunity to exploit new language in texts, both grammar and vocabulary. This is an example from a reading text in the **student's book** on *p.95*. Learners go on to use the linking phrases in a narrative of their own.

---

natural English
linking events in a sequence

When you want to link a series of bad events in a story to show how a situation got worse and worse, you can use these phrases:

At first …
As time went by (however) …
The situation deteriorated (when) …
Things got much worse (when) …
Eventually, things came to a head (when) …

Find words / phrases in the text with same meaning as the phrases above.

from upper-intermediate **student's book**, unit eight *p.95*

A major pitfall with text work is what might be called 'the vocabulary graveyard': a protracted stage where learners go through all the unknown words in the text after which these items are often ignored or forgotten. Valuable time is spent on

---

them regardless of their likely value to learners. A better strategy would be to encourage learners to select and prioritize a limited number of items per text. Jeremy Harmer has an excellent suggestion for this below.

---

try it out meaning consensus

We can get students to work together to search for and find word meanings.

– Individual students write down three to five words from the text that they want to know.
– They compare with another student and come up with a new joint list of only five words. This means they will probably have to discuss which words to leave out.
– Two pairs join to make new groups of four and once again they pool their lists and end up with only five words.
– Finally, students can look for meanings of their words in dictionaries and / or the teacher can answer questions about the words which groups have decided on.

This process works for two reasons. Firstly, students may be able to explain some words which other students did not know. Secondly, by the time they get to the meanings, the students really do want to know them, because the intervening process has encouraged them to invest some time in the search. 'Understanding every word' has been changed into a co-operative learning task in its own right.

from Jeremy Harmer **The Practice of English Language Teaching** (see **follow up**)

---

contextual guesswork

Contextual guesswork is another common post-reading activity. An important point about developing this skill is that you don't ask learners to guess the meaning of words that are simply not guessable from context. You have two main ways of encouraging learners to focus on contextual guesswork:

– you highlight words or phrases in the text, and ask learners to define or explain them
– you provide definitions or explanations yourself, and ask learners to find words or phrases in the text to match them.

In the **student's book**, we have included contextual guesswork on a regular basis in the text **glossaries**. We have tended to use the second of these approaches and focused on a limited number of items at a time. Here is an example in which learners have to find three vocabulary items in the text, and then add two more new words or phrases of their own choice:

---

stretch your mind make the fullest use of your mind
appeal to sb interest or attract sb
_____ (para 1) ⑥ learn / study for a test / exam
_____ (para 4) take a risk
pay off (your) debts   pay money you owe people
_____ (para 5) money you borrow to buy a house
your own new words
_____ (para __) _____
_____ (para __) _____

from upper-intermediate **student's book**, unit twelve *p.139*

Well-chosen texts will also act as a springboard for other skills such as speaking and writing. If a text is particularly provocative, it would be sensible to let learners discuss it soon after reading, before they become too involved in language study. Texts can lend themselves to discussion or role play (see **Millionaire hopefuls – go for it!** *p.139*, for an example). Writing can be a natural development too: reading an e-mail and writing a response, writing to the letters page about a newspaper article, completing a consumer questionnaire, and so on.

4 Choosing your own texts

If you are lucky enough to have the freedom and the resources to use your own texts in class, how do you choose them?

choosing appropriate texts

Ideally, a text should interest everyone and should be the right level, in other words challenging but comprehensible. It should be of manageable length: anything much over 500 words will be quite time-consuming, so it has to be particularly interesting. The issues of level and length raise the question of whether you should be looking for authentic texts, adapted authentic texts, or simplified texts written specifically for foreign learners. At upper-intermediate level – indeed at most levels – we believe you should be working largely with <u>authentic</u> sources (texts written by native speakers for native speakers), but these have to be carefully chosen so that they are comprehensible and not demotivating.

adapting texts

There may also be valid reasons for adapting texts for classroom use. If the learners are likely to become pre-occupied with trying to understand a lot of difficult items, you could do some judicious paraphrasing to include more useful lexis, and restrict the number of items that will be of very limited value. Texts in the real world will almost always have lexical items that will be unknown to learners, so we would not recommend removing low frequency items completely.

With regard to length, you can often shorten texts by removing whole paragraphs from the body of the text without losing any of its essential information or internal coherence. Newspaper and magazine texts in particular are often full of repetition. The important point is that it should still read like a natural text. You can show it to another teacher and ask them what they think. If they are not immediately aware that it has been doctored in some way, it probably still reads as an authentic text – or a good approximation of one.

jigsaw reading

A different option is to keep the text in its entirety but divide it into sections to reduce the reading time for each individual learner. For example, A reads the first part, B reads the second part, and then they tell each other what they have read. Some texts lend themselves to this, particularly those which offer a series of arguments for and against a proposition, or those in which the chronological order of events is important. (For an example of jigsaw reading, look at the main text in unit one, *p.10*.) You can also consider recording part of the text and using it as a listening passage. This is often suitable for short stories and narratives.

a range of text types

If you are responsible for selecting the majority of texts used in class, you should also consider the text types that are most relevant to your class. Where there is no reason to concentrate on one or two specific text types, it is sensible to try to include a range in order to broaden learners' reading skills and provide variety.

> ## think![5]
>
> How many of these sources do you use regularly ✓✓ or occasionally ✓? Do you think there are any text types you could or should use more often?
>
> - [ ] articles from newspapers
> - [ ] song lyrics
> - [ ] articles from magazines
> - [ ] formal letters; informal letters and e-mails
> - [ ] questionnaires
> - [ ] brochures and leaflets
> - [ ] Internet websites
> - [ ] advertisements
> - [ ] extracts from literature
> - [ ] cartoons and jokes
> - [ ] forms (application forms, etc.)
> - [ ] signs and notices
> - [ ] maps, timetables, etc.
> - [ ] instruction manuals

5 Extensive reading

> ## think![6]
>
> Which of these do you think are true of learners who do a lot of extensive reading, i.e. reading for pleasure in their own time?
>
> - The more they read, the better they become at reading.
> - Learners develop a wider vocabulary and can use more varied sentence constructions.
> - They are better at writing, and more confident at speaking.
> - Candidates for public exams such as TOEFL, FCE, and CPE who read outside class do better in these exams than those who don't.
>
> In fact, all the statements are widely accepted by teachers intuitively, but have also been backed up by research.

Want to know more? Read **The Secret of Reading** by Prowse (see **follow up**).

The issue for the teacher is more to do with motivating learners to read in their own time, and on their own terms. One point worth making to learners is that the quality of what they read is not as important as they may think. Gossip magazines and cartoon books may not seem very 'virtuous' reading material, but learners may well find them more accessible and motivating than a worthy novel. Nor do texts need to be long: browsing magazines, dipping into books and reading in short bursts regularly is a positive approach. The important thing is that they read what they find stimulating, and if they choose a text or a graded reader which they don't enjoy, they should stop reading it and find something they do like.

how you can help

The teacher's role is therefore to encourage reading outside class, and this will mean suggesting sources available to the learners. Help them by suggesting readers, magazines, or papers in English, or where to find websites suited to their interests. If available, a class set of readers appropriate for the learners' level and cultural background can be a useful start. Begin by getting learners to look at the front cover picture and title, predict the content, and have a look at any illustrations. They can then read the summary on the back cover to see if their assumptions were accurate. Read the first few paragraphs aloud to involve them in the story, then ask them to say what might happen next, before they start reading themselves, and carry on in their own time. Another approach is to use a 'library' of readers: see the suggestion below.

---

try it out reader boxes

In our school, we put together for each level a box of suitable and varied graded readers (for a class of 15, we put 20 to 24 books in). We included thrillers, adventure stories, adapted well-known classics, factual books, etc. A few have cassettes which students can borrow from the library and listen to at the same time – in fact, these are incredibly popular.

I take a box into class and display the books, explaining that they can borrow a book to read in their own time. I show them a few of the books in particular, tell them a little about each one, and then say what kinds of books are in the collection. This is to whet their appetite. They then come and pick a book each – occasionally there is an unseemly rush for them! Certain students need a bit of help and advice so I talk to them and make suggestions. If a student doesn't want to do it, I let it go.

We agree a time limit (in my context, a week is long enough, but I'd leave longer overseas). The following week, students bring their books back and tell each other about them in small groups, saying too what they liked / didn't like. They can recommend books to each other and then they all borrow another book, and so on.

If a book is unpopular, we change it. I don't do comprehension tasks – I just want them to enjoy reading.

Rachel, London

If you would like to try this idea, but work in a school without these resources, you can encourage each learner to buy a different reader so that they can swap them within the class.

conclusion

In this chapter, we have looked at

- the different ways we read, i.e. intensive and extensive
- the various skills we need in order to read efficiently, i.e. activating schemata, prediction, skimming and scanning, contextual guesswork, and interpreting a text
- practical activities for exploiting a text, including a wide range of appropriate pre-reading activities, designed to motivate learners to read, activities to do while reading, and post-reading activities to further exploit the text, e.g. contextual guesswork, or using the text as a springboard for speaking or writing activities
- issues to consider when choosing your own texts for a class, e.g. what kind of texts to choose, how to adapt texts, and the importance of using a range of text types
- encouraging learners to read outside the classroom.

think![1] *p.167*

Even speakers of the same language will have different degrees of difficulty with these texts. Texts about a referendum (politics), a test match (cricket), and a TV soap opera will be easier for those with a knowledge of the subject matter. The text messages and the poem will both contain stylistic features which may be easier for those who are familiar with these text types. Understanding the joke may require a familiarity with a sense of humour that is peculiarly British.

think![2] *p.168*

DIETING UNDER STRESS
MID-AFTERNOON SNACK
Rest of the chocolate biscuit packet, 2 pints of chocolate ice cream.
DINNER
2 loaves of garlic bread with cheese, 1 large pizza, 4 large whisky macs, 3 Mars bars or packets of crisps.
LATE EVENING SNACK
Entire Black Forest Gateau.
RULES
1 If you eat something and no one sees you eat it, it has no calories.
2 If you drink a Diet Coke with a Mars bar, the calories of the Mars bar are cancelled out by the Diet Coke.
3 Food used for medicinal purposes such as hot chocolate, brandy, toast, Sara Lee cheesecake, don't count.
4 Movie-related foods do not have additional calories because they are part of the entire entertainment package, and not part of one's personal fuel – such as milk shakes, buttered popcorn, Murray Mints and Mars bars.
5 Broken biscuits contain no calories; breaking causes calorie leakage.
6 Foods of the same colour have the same number of calories e.g. spinach and pistachio ice cream, or mushrooms and white chocolate.
REMEMBER: STRESSED backwards spells DESSERTS

think![3] *p.168*

Brindol and *budder* are both guessable from the context and the co-text (the words around them). *Brindol* must be career / profession and *budder* must be a period during the day, morning or afternoon. *Darband* and *pargling* are not so guessable, although *darband* is obviously something negative that prevented him from joining the Air Force and could well be a physical condition. (In fact, the answer is *colour blind*, but it could be *epileptic / diabetic*, etc.) *Pargling* is obviously an undesirable action, because they got told off, and is probably to do with sitting. (In fact, they were *slouching*, but it could have been *wriggling*.) None of the nonsense words is crucial to a general understanding of the text, but *darband* and *pargling* are important for a detailed understanding.

schema (s) schemata (pl)[1]: our existing knowledge of the world that we bring to a text, e.g. the type of text, the subject matter, the typical language that is used, language patterns, etc.

follow up

Nuttall C 1996 *Teaching Reading Skills in a Foreign Language* Macmillan Heinemann

Harmer J 2001 *The Practice of English Language Teaching* Longman (chapters 14 and 15)

Prowse P October 1999 *The Secret of Reading* in English Teaching Professional (issue 13)

Prowse P January 2000 *Open Your Books* in English Teaching Professional (issue 14)

how to ... use dictionaries with learners

1 Why use dictionaries?

Although a dictionary is usually the first book (often the only book) that people think of buying when they start learning a foreign language, it is possibly the most underused and widely abused of all learning resources. Part of the problem is that dictionaries are a special kind of reference source, and normally require some learner training before they can be used effectively. Learners who don't receive this training may fail to make the best use of their dictionary, or worse still, become so disenchanted with it as their frustration grows, that they stop using it altogether. Some learners also assume that any dictionary will do, and once they have one, they assume there will be no need to buy another. (See section 3 **Which dictionary?**)

In fact, dictionaries have a great deal to offer, and never more so than in the last ten years. The development of computer-based *corpora*[1], begun around 1980 and growing continuously, has enabled dictionary makers to build up vast amounts of information about the way native speakers actually use a language (see the next section on **Corpora**). The current generation of dictionaries now has much more useful and reliable information to offer the user than was the case twenty years ago, ten years ago, or even five years ago. They are getting better all the time.

Dictionaries are also an easy learning tool to tap into.

- Learners invariably respect and trust the information they contain.
- Most learners like having dictionaries around, and this willingness to use them can be nurtured in all sorts of positive ways.
- Good ELT dictionaries are available in every part of the world; and given the amount of information they contain and the years of research that goes into every new edition, they offer tremendous value for money.

Finally, and perhaps most important of all is that learners who are trained to use dictionaries effectively can continue to make progress in their learning beyond the classroom. This is particularly important for learners who only attend formal lessons for perhaps one or two hours a week.

2 Corpora

In the past, successive generations of dictionaries were largely based on the ones that preceded them, and the data they were based on was mostly written text plus a limited amount of largely anecdotal evidence from spoken English. All that changed in the 1980s, due to the ability of computers to handle vast amounts of information, which can be analysed and displayed in all sorts of ways. Now, all major ELT dictionaries are developed from a large *corpus*[2] of spoken and written text, including British and American English. Among these are: The Oxford Corpus Collection, The Longman Corpus Network, The COBUILD Bank of English, The Cambridge Language Survey, and the British National Corpus.

These corpora are growing all the time. For example, when the first edition of the *Collins COBUILD Learner's Dictionary* was published in 1987, it was based on a written corpus of 20 million words (considered very large at the time). Eight years later, a new edition of the dictionary was published, but based on a corpus of written and spoken English exceeding 200 million words. Admittedly spoken English still represents a relatively low percentage of the overall data (five to ten percent is typical), although 10 to 20 million words of spoken English is still a lot of data.

These corpora have provided dictionaries with much more data, and much more reliable data. We now have accurate information about the frequency of words in current usage and the frequency of individual meanings of words; and several dictionaries are passing on some of this information to users. *Collins COBUILD* includes five frequency bands covering the most common 15,000 words. The *Longman Dictionary of Contemporary English* (*LDOCE*) signposts the 3,000 most frequent words used in both spoken and written English, using the symbols S1, S2, and S3 for spoken, and W1, W2, and W3 for written. 1 = 1,000 most frequently used words; 2 = 2,000 most frequently used words; 3 = 3,000 most frequently used words. In the first example below, S1 indicates that the word is among the 1,000 most frequently used words in spoken English.

> **S1 W2 anyway** /ˈeniweɪ/ *adv* [sentence adverb] **1** used to say that someone does something or something happens in spite of a problem: *He said that he didn't know much about computers but that he'd try and help us anyway.*

> **S1 W2 might** /maɪt/ *modal verb negative short form* mightn't
> **1** if something might happen or might be true, there is a possibility that it may happen or be true but you are not certain: *Who knows – England might win the next World Cup!*
>
> *Longman Dictionary of Contemporary English*

> **might** /maɪt/ ◆◆◆◆◆
>
> **Might** is a modal verb. It is used with the base form of a verb.
>
> **1** You use **might** to indicate that something will possibly happen or be true in the future, but you cannot be certain. ❏ *There's a report today that smoking might be banned totally in most buildings. The two countries might go to war. I might well regret it later. He said he might not be back until tonight.* MODAL vagueness = may
>
> *Collins Cobuild English Dictionary for Advanced Learners*
>
> ◆◆◆◆◆ This means that this word is within the 680 most common words.

corpora[1] go to **glossary** for numbered words or phrases *p.180*

Corpora also give us vital information about the contexts in which you are most likely to meet a word, and the way in which they are often used with other words, i.e. collocation. Look at this entry for *restless*.

> **restless** /ˈrestləs/ *adj.* 1 unable to stay still or be happy where you are, because you are bored or need a change: *The audience was becoming restless.* ◊ *After five years in the job, he was beginning to feel restless.* 2 without real rest or sleep: *a restless night* ▶ **restlessly** *adv*: He moved restlessly from one foot to another.
>
> *Oxford Advanced Learner's Dictionary*

This tells us that *audiences, jobs,* and *sleep* are among the most common contexts for *restless*, and that the adjective commonly collocates with the verb *feel*, and the noun *night*.

3   Which dictionary?

bilingual dictionaries

In the early stages of learning, many students rely on pocket-sized bilingual dictionaries: they are quick and easy to use, and learners find it reassuring to have the support of their first language. As these dictionaries operate through one-to-one equivalents, there is obviously simplification and some distortion, but it is still a sensible option for certain basic vocabulary at a time when learners need all the support they can get. In any case, at beginner and elementary levels, monolingual dictionaries are probably far too daunting for all but the most ambitious or determined learners. However, it is important that learners don't stop there. They should consider adding a more substantial bilingual dictionary as their level improves; one that does more than offer single word translations of a lexical item without reference to its different meanings and contexts.

monolingual learner's dictionaries

By the time they reach intermediate level, learners should be able to benefit from one of the monolingual learner's dictionaries, written specifically for that level. (See **follow up** at the end of this chapter for recommended titles.) They not only provide more detailed information than many bilingual dictionaries, they also reduce the reliance on translation and immerse the learner more fully in the target language.

At upper-intermediate level, learners can start making effective use of the larger monolingual learner's dictionaries on offer (see **follow up**). The *defining vocabulary*³ is still simplified as compared with dictionaries written for native speakers, and as each new generation of dictionaries emerge, there are more and more features to help and motivate users: full colour in some places; study pages; usage notes; charts and tables; help with vocabulary development; frequency information, and so on.

specialist dictionaries

Dictionary support doesn't stop there either. A range of specialist dictionaries can help learners with specific topics, e.g. business English, or specific areas of the language, e.g. phrasal verbs and idioms. A different type of dictionary that organizes lexis semantically and topically (under the titles *Activator, Wordfinder,* or *Word Routes*) can help learners in a different way to expand their productive vocabulary and become more accurate (see **follow up**).

4   Dictionary training in the classroom

The **think!** tasks in this section are designed for teachers, but many of them can be adapted and used with learners for dictionary training in the classroom.

There are different skills involved in dictionary use. When looking up a word, dictionary users have to learn how to

1 find the word or phrase they are looking for.

2 select the correct meaning (if there is more than one).

3 understand the explanation and additional information.

4 use dictionaries productively, e.g. noticing and extending their knowledge of common collocations that accompany a particular item.

Let's look at these in turn.

finding words

For the majority of learners used to Roman script, finding a word in a dictionary won't cause any problems, with the possible exception of words beginning with a letter that doesn't exist in the mother tongue, such as *w* in Spanish. For learners who use a different script, however, finding a word may be a challenge, and you will probably need to help them with this skill. Games against the clock in which learners have to organize a list of vocabulary items in alphabetical order can help learners to focus on initial letters, and then they will need to practise the same skill using dictionaries.

finding phrases

A problem common to most learners arises when trying to find a phrase in the dictionary. (Indeed, some learners are not aware that dictionaries include the meaning of phrases.) First of all, can learners recognize that the item they don't know is part of a phrase? This can happen if they encounter a phrasal verb in which the particle is separated from the base verb, e.g.

He couldn't make the sign out in the darkness.
They called the meeting off.

Secondly, learners need to know where to find the entry for a phrase. Which part of the phrase should they look up? With the idiom, *break the ice*, will you find the definition at *break* or *ice*? Dictionaries vary on their policy. The activity below from the **student's book**, unit eleven **wordbooster**, helps learners to find out about this aspect of dictionary use.

use your dictionary

It isn't always easy to find the meaning of a phrase in a dictionary. Start with the first content word (noun, verb, or adjective).

blue *noun* **1** [C,U] the colour that is blue.
2 blues [pl] a sad, slow, style of music that came from the southern US: *a blues singer* – (see also RHYTHM AND BLUES) **3 the blues** [pl] (*informal*) feelings of sadness: *Don't be surprised if you get the blues for a while after your baby is born.* **4 out of the blue** (*informal*) unexpectedly: *A phone call from Jane right out of the blue.* (see also A BOLT FROM THE BLUE / OUT OF THE BLUE ⇨ BOLT³)

Longman Dictionary of Contemporary English

If you wanted to check the meaning of 'out of the blue' in the sentence *He turned up on my doorstep out of the blue*, you would first look at the entry for *blue*.

But if you wanted to check 'a bolt from the blue' in the sentence *It arrived like a bolt from the blue*, you should look under bolt.

1 **Underline the words in each sentence which form a set phrase.**

   examples

   If you fail the test, it'll be <u>your own fault</u>.

   <u>With a bit of luck</u>, he'll pass the exam.

   1 I have no sympathy for those two boys: they're selfish and stupid.
   2 He's 19 years old, but his mother still treats him like a child.
   3 Several children were injured but we don't know who's to blame.
   4 I think he was wrong to buy the flat in the first place.
   5 I don't see the point of trying to help them if they don't want it.
   6 Put yourself in her shoes – what would *you* have done?
   7 Well, to cut a long story short, I asked her to marry me and she said yes.
   8 He's in a bad mood today – don't take any notice of him.

2 **In the phrases in exercise 1, which word would you look up in a dictionary to find the phrase? Circle it. Use a dictionary to check the meaning of any new phrases.**

from upper-intermediate **student's book**, unit eleven *p.131*

You can devise similar activities to use with your learners. You will need to consult the introduction of your particular dictionary to find out how phrases are entered. With most dictionaries, some items will be cross-referenced, e.g. *on the tip of my tongue* may be explained at *tip* but cross-referenced at *tongue*; *kick the bucket* may be explained at *kick* but cross-referenced at *bucket*.

finding the right meaning

When they meet a new word or phrase, many learners look up the item and immediately assume they have found what they are looking for. However, a lexical item often has several different meanings, so learners need to get into the habit of scanning the different meanings to find the one they are looking for in this particular context. It is also not unusual for learners to look up a particular word form, only to discover several lines into the explanation that they are in the wrong *word class*[4], e.g. they are looking under the entry for *book* as a noun, when in fact, they want the entry for *book* as a verb.

Almost all dictionaries number the different meanings of an item, but some help you find them more quickly by using key words next to the target item. These are called *guide words* in *Cambridge International Dictionary of English (CIDE)*, and *shortcuts* in *Oxford Advanced Learner's Dictionary (OALD)*, and they give an approximate indication of each individual meaning. For example:

mug CONTAINER /mʌg/ *n* [C] a container with a handle on one side used esp. for hot drinks such as tea or coffee. It is usually bigger than a cup and used without a SAUCER. • *The shop sells coffee pots and mugs with bright designs.* • *I made myself a large mug* **of** *cocoa* (= enough to fill a mug) *and went to bed.* • *(esp. Am)* A **beer** mug is a heavy glass with a handle and usually with patterns cut into its side, out of which you drink beer.

mug STUPID PERSON /mʌg/ *n* [C] *esp. Br infml* a person who is stupid and easily deceived. • *He's such a mug, he believes everything she tells him.* • If you describe an activity as **a mug's game**, you mean that it will not bring money or satisfaction to the person who does it: *"Working in an office is a mug's game," she said.*

mug FACE /mʌg/ *n* [C] *infml* someone's face • *I don't want to see your* **ugly** *mug around here again.* • *(slang)* A **mug shot** is a photograph taken by the police of a person who has been charged with a crime: *A poster with mug shots of wanted men was on the wall.*

Cambridge International Dictionary of English

bite /baɪt/ *verb, noun*
verb (**bit** /bɪt/, **bit·ten** /'bɪtn/)

<u>USE TEETH</u> **1** ~ **(into/through/off sth)** to use your teeth to cut into or through sth: [VN] *She was bitten by the family dog.* ◊ *Stop biting your nails!* ◊ [V] *She bit into a ripe juicy pear.* ◊ *Does your dog bite?* ◊ *(spoken) Come here! I won't bite!* (= you don't need to be afraid) ◊ *He bit off a large chunk of bread / He bit a large chunk of bread off.*

<u>OF INSECT/SNAKE</u> **2** to wound sb by making a small hole or mark in their skin: [VN] *We were badly bitten by mosquitoes.* ◊ [V] *Most European spiders don't bite.*

<u>OF FISH</u> **3** [V] if a fish **bites**, it takes food from the hook of a FISHING LINE and may get caught

<u>HAVE EFFECT</u> **4** [V] to have an unpleasant effect: *The recession is beginning to bite.*

Oxford Advanced Learner's Dictionary

dictionary organization

It is important to remember that dictionaries vary in the way they organize the different meanings of a word. Some dictionaries order the meanings strictly in terms of **frequency** (the most common meanings coming first); other dictionaries may balance the frequency of a particular meaning with what they consider to be the <u>core meaning</u> of an item, and put that first. For example, if you look up *see* in *LDOCE*, the first meaning given is *understand, realize*, e.g. *I can see that you're not very happy with the situation*. *OALD*, however, gives the *ability to see with one's eyes* as the first meaning of *see*.

---

think!²

Look at these words and definitions. Which definition would you expect to come first in a dictionary if the meanings were listed in order of frequency?

1 bonnet
    a. a hat tied on with ribbons
    b. the metal lid over the front of a car

2 breakdown
    a. the failure of a system or relationship
    b. when a car or piece of machinery stops working

3 settle
    a. to put an end to an argument or disagreement
    b. to make yourself or someone else comfortable in a new position, or put something carefully in a particular position

4 pound (noun)
    a. a unit of money
    b. a unit of weight

Does the dictionary you use list meanings in order of frequency?

---

go to **answer key** *p.180*

---

try it out

I've used this technique as a way of revising vocabulary from previous lessons.

1 I demonstrate this activity first by writing a word on the board, e.g. *interrupt*, and asking students in pairs to write down a dictionary definition for the word. We then hear and discuss each pair's definition, and compare with a dictionary.

2 I give each pair two words (to be revised) on a slip of paper. They have to write a 'dictionary definition' (this can include synonyms, paraphrases, descriptions, etc.) They can't consult a dictionary at this stage.

3 Each pair takes turns to read their definition to the class, without saying the word. The class have to guess what it was.

4 Students then look at dictionaries to compare their definition with the dictionary definitions, and decide which they like best.

This activity is popular with my students, because it requires both accuracy and attention to meaning, and they enjoy the challenge. They also get the opportunity to practise paraphrasing and defining.

Christiane, Paris.

---

understanding the explanation and additional information

pronunciation

You can enable your learners to become more self-sufficient by teaching them phonemic script and relating it to dictionary work.

Want to know more about introducing phonemic script to learners? Go to intermediate **teacher's book, how to ...** teach phonemic script *p.168*.

You can ask learners to look at new words (perhaps from a **wordbooster** section or in a text) and check how they are pronounced with a partner, then in a dictionary if in doubt. If learners do this on a regular basis, they become very familiar with phonemic script and the dictionary becomes an important self-access tool which they are not afraid to use.

Learners also need to understand how stress is marked in the dictionary they are using. In most cases, words are given in phonemic script with a stress mark before the stressed syllable, although *Collins COBUILD* underlines the stressed syllable.

po.ta.to pə'teɪtəʊ‖-toʊ/   (Longman Dictionary of Contemporary English)
po.tato /pə'teɪtəʊ; *AmE* -toʊ/   (Oxford Advanced Learner's Dictionary)
potato /pəte<u>ɪ</u>toʊ/   (Cobuild English Dictionary for Advanced Learners)

Stress on compound nouns is shown like this:

potato chip /.'.. ./   (Longman Dictionary of Contemporary English)
po.tato 'crisp   (Oxford Advanced Learner's Dictionary)
pot<u>a</u>to crisp   (Cobuild English Dictionary for Advanced Learners)

grammar

Dictionaries provide a considerable amount of information about the grammar of lexical items, largely in the form of symbols and abbreviations. There are too many to teach your learners in one go, but certain abbreviations are essential, and as long as learners know where the key to the symbols is, they can check for themselves.

---

think!³

These symbols are from a range of ELT dictionaries. What do they mean? Which ones should your upper-intermediate learners know?

n	adj	adv	poss	pl	U
pp	prep	sth	det	phr v	V-ERG

---

go to **answer key** *p.180*

lexical information

Dictionaries obviously define and explain words, and in recent years, ELT dictionaries have become increasingly responsive to learners' difficulties with overlapping meaning, and provide feature boxes explaining the difference between easily-confused words. This is, of course, an excellent resource for any teacher at the planning stage. A clear understanding of the difference between *attractive, beautiful, handsome,* and *good-looking* will help you to deal with these items confidently in your lesson, and you only need to check in the *Study Notes* in *LDOCE* to get help. The *OALD* has a similar feature, called *Which word?*

---

think!⁴

Think for a minute about the difference in meaning between these pairs of words.

> *ashamed* and *embarrassed*; *destroy* and *spoil*

Compare your ideas with the feature boxes below.

WHICH WORD?
ashamed / embarrassed

You feel **ashamed** when you feel guilty because of something wrong that you have deliberately done: *You should be ashamed of treating your daughter like that.* Do not use **ashamed** when you are talking about something that is not very serious or important: *I am sorry that I forgot to buy the milk.* ◊ *I am ashamed that I forgot to buy the milk.* You feel **embarrassed** when you have made a mistake or done something stupid or feel awkward in front of other people: *I was embarrassed about forgetting his name.*

Oxford Advanced Learner's Dictionary

USAGE NOTE: DESTROY
WORD CHOICE: destroy, ruin, spoil
Destroy means to damage something so badly that it no longer exists or cannot be repaired: *Whole areas of the city were destroyed.* | *a drug to destroy cancer cells* | *Their traditional way of life has been destroyed.* You **ruin** or (less strong) **spoil** something good or useful. It then usually still exists, but no longer has its good qualities or features: *Too much sugar can ruin your teeth.* | *You've completely spoiled my day.*

Longman Dictionary of Contemporary English

In addition to explaining the meaning of a word, dictionaries usually show you the context in which it most often occurs, and the other words which are most likely to appear with it (collocations).

Look at the feature below:

Words frequently used with **'meaning'**	
adjectives	actual, deep, hidden, intended, literal, real, symbolic, true
verbs	catch, decipher, determine, discover, get, grasp, understand

Macmillan English Dictionary for Advanced Learners

Here is an activity you can use with learners, using the *OALD*, to alert them to this feature. You can adapt this exercise to any other relevant items.

collocation in dictionaries

1 **Look at the dictionary entries and answer the questions.**

  1 What nouns are used with *latest*? Think of two more.

  2 What kinds of things could you *flick through*?

lat·est /ˈleɪtɪst/
- *adj.* [only before noun] the most recent or newest: *the latest unemployment figures* ◊ *the latest craze / fashion / trend* ◊ *her latest novel* ◊ *Have you heard the latest news?*

> **PHRV** ˌflick 'through /ˌflɪk 'θruː/ to turn the pages of a book, etc. quickly and look at them without reading everything.

entries from Oxford Advanced Learner's Dictionary

---

2 **Use your own dictionary. What collocates with these in the context of learning or reading?**

  1 to dip into _____   4 to look up _____

  2 _____ by heart   5 _____ the gist

  3 to skip _____

from upper-intermediate **student's book**, unit one *p.12*

language variety and style

Dictionaries will also indicate varieties of English, e.g. British English, American English, Scottish English, etc. as well as styles and registers, e.g. humorous, formal / informal, slang, taboo; medical, literary, poetic, etc.

in·effable /ɪnˈefəbl/ *adj.* (*rare, formal*) too great or beautiful to describe in words: *ineffable joy*

Oxford Advanced Learner's Dictionary

---

think!⁵

Which items in *italics* are:

formal   informal   informal + disapproving?

  1 They *withheld* the financial information.

  2 He's just a *wise guy*.

  3 I was feeling quite *jittery* before the test.

  4 That new receptionist is a real *know-all*.

  5 I had a *presentiment* that something was going to happen.

  6 I gave her £10 and then we were *quits*.

go to **answer key** *p.180*

This might be a good way of recycling vocabulary with your learners; they could discuss the style / register (and meaning, if necessary) of the words you have given them with a partner, then check in their dictionaries.

using dictionaries productively

Dictionaries contain such a wealth of information it is a shame that the majority of learners use them only to look up the meaning of a word; this is just the tip of the iceberg. There are many ways in which they can find out extra information when looking up new words, and also extend their vocabulary.

collocation

As we have shown, learners will find plenty of generative collocations when they look up words.

word families

Some dictionaries highlight these in a special feature, but learners can always check derivatives when they check vocabulary in the dictionary. To familiarize them with this feature, ask learners to look up two or three verbs and find several derivatives for each, e.g. *success*, *successful* (adj); *succeed* (v).

compounds

Give learners a word which forms the first part of many compounds, e.g. *shop* or *traffic*, and ask them to see how many compounds they can find in the dictionary.

illustrations

Dictionaries are now very good at providing illustrated pages of topic vocabulary, e.g. fruit and vegetables, clothes, etc. and learners find these enjoyable to study. You could ask them to brainstorm clothes, for example, and then ask them to build on these using the illustrations in a monolingual dictionary.

synonyms and opposites

These are given in certain dictionaries (*Collins COBUILD* is particularly good at this), and it is useful for learners to record these as they study them, e.g. if they look up *tidy*, they can learn the opposite *untidy*, and if they look up *row* /raʊ/ they will discover the synonym *quarrel*. Cross-referencing enables students to learn more than one word, e.g. at *locker room* learners are asked to compare with *changing room*. You could give learners five sentences with a word underlined, which they have to look up in a dictionary and replace with an opposite, e.g. *polite* (*rude / impolite*), *tactful* (*tactless*), *shallow* (*deep*).

study pages / language portraits

Some dictionaries have whole pages devoted to aspects of vocabulary and grammar. For example, you could ask learners to look at the *Study Page B10–11* (phrasal verbs) from *OALD* for homework to consolidate any analysis you have done in class.

specialist dictionaries

Oxford Wordfinder, *The Longman Activator*, and *Cambridge Word Routes* organize vocabulary by topic and context, and are a useful way to expand vocabulary.

---

try it out dictionary mimes

1 Divide the class into small groups, each with a dictionary. Decide as a class which two pages to concentrate on. Give the group ten minutes to look through the words on the pages and think of suitable ways of miming as many as possible of the headwords.

2 Groups take turns to mime the words they have chosen. The audience shout out the words they spot from the mimes. It doesn't matter if groups choose several of the same words – this simply reinforces learning. The mimes, however, must be different.

Wright J *English Teaching Professional* (see **follow up**)

---

5 Classroom management

Making dictionaries available in the classroom has significant benefits for the teacher and learner.

- If the group is working individually or in pairs on a written text, learners can use their dictionaries as an authoritative source, which frees up the teacher to spend more time with learners needing individual help.

- Using dictionaries to check vocabulary in a text means that each learner can focus on the items they don't know, and to some extent, work at their own pace.

- Dictionaries can be used to encourage interaction and discussion: for instance, learners can look up information in their dictionaries and then compare their understanding with other learners.

- It goes without saying that dictionary use provides some of the most motivating and realistic reading practice.

There are, however, practical considerations that you need to think about.

- If you plan to ask your learners to use dictionaries to check certain items, you'll need to look them up first to ensure that the dictionaries provide the information you expect.

- You don't want learners spending the whole lesson with their heads in a dictionary if it means they are not talking to other learners when they should, or not listening to you when they should. You will need to establish clear guidelines for times when learners can and cannot use their dictionaries. For instance, at the beginning of a speaking activity, make it clear that the activity is just speaking, and not one where dictionaries should be used. Another case might be where you ask learners to read a text without a dictionary first, pointing out that this would slow them down considerably, and reassuring them that they can use their dictionaries at a later stage.

- You may want to discourage higher level learners from using small, bilingual dictionaries. They are capable of using the more informative and appropriate monolingual dictionaries which are widely available. You may be able to encourage some learners to use CD ROM dictionaries which may provide oral models of headwords as well as games and exercises.

- If you are in a situation where learners are using a range of dictionaries in the classroom, you may find that they provide different or even contradictory information, which can be unsettling for learners. On the other hand, these differences can provoke interaction and encourage more processing of the information. You just need to be prepared for this to happen and deal with it positively.

- To make effective use of dictionaries in a class, don't think that each learner has to have their own dictionary. One dictionary between two (or even three) learners is fine, and it also means that learners aren't working in complete isolation and can share their understanding of the information. If your school doesn't have many resources, you can encourage learners to bring their dictionaries to class.

conclusion

In this chapter we have looked at

- why you should encourage your learners to use dictionaries

- advances in dictionary production and what this means for teachers and learners

- appropriate dictionaries for different stages of learning

- how to train learners to use dictionaries effectively, for instance, finding the word or phrase they are looking for; finding the correct meaning; understanding and making productive use of the wide range of information that is available

- the ways in which using dictionaries benefits the class as a whole, together with some practical considerations to think about.

Learner training in the use of dictionaries can make good, short activities providing a change of focus at various stages in a lesson. If you feel your class are not getting the most out of their dictionaries, you could try adapting some of the tasks suggested here and using those in the **student's book** with your learners as a way of raising awareness and encouraging more dictionary use.

answer key

think![1] *p.175*

particularly S1,W1

chat S2

key (n) S2, W3

key (adj) S2 , W1

however S2, W1

thereby W3

think![2] *p.177*

These answers are based on the *Longman Dictionary of Contemporary English (LDOCE)*, which lists items in order of frequency.

1 b is first; 2 a is first; 3 b is first; 4 b is first (which surprises us). For an interesting comparison, here are the results from the *Oxford Advanced Learner's Dictionary (OALD)*, which does not list items in order of frequency.

1 a is first; 2 b is first; 3 a is first; 4 a is first.

think![3] *p.177*

n: noun; adj: adjective; adv: adverb; poss: possessive; pl: plural; U: uncountable; pp: past participle; prep: preposition; sth: something; det: determiner; phr v: phrasal verb; V-ERG: ergative verb.

We think most of these are necessary for intermediate and above, with the exception of *poss, det,* and V-ERG.

think![5] *p.178*

These answers are based on *OALD*.

1 formal

2 informal + disapproving

3 informal

4 informal + disapproving

5 formal

6 informal

glossary

corpus (s)[2], **corpora (pl)**[1] a body of linguistic data (either written text or a transcription of recorded speech) which is stored on a computer and is available for different kinds of analysis, e.g. how often a word occurs, what other words it collocates with

defining vocabulary[3] the items used in dictionary definitions

word class[4] part of speech, e.g. noun, verb, adjective, etc.

....

follow up

Wright J 1998 *Dictionaries* (Resource Books for Teachers) OUP. Highly recommended.

Wright J 1997 *Using Dictionaries in Class: Resource or Reference?* ETP (issue 3 p.22)

Ilson R (ed.) 1985 *ELT Documents 120: Dictionaries, Lexicography and Language Learning* OUP

....

recommended dictionaries

These dictionaries have been produced specifically for intermediate level learners. Some have been available for many years and we would recommend that learners always look for the latest edition.

Oxford Wordpower Dictionary (OUP)

Longman Active Study Dictionary (Longman)

Cambridge Learner's Dictionary (CUP)

Collins COBUILD Learner's Dictionary Intermediate

These dictionaries have been produced for upper-intermediate and advanced level learners. Again, we would recommend learners look for the most recent edition.

Oxford Advanced Learner's Dictionary (OALD)

Longman Dictionary of Contemporary English (LDOCE)

Cambridge International Dictionary of English (CIDE)

Collins COBUILD English Dictionary for Advanced Learners

Macmillan English Dictionary for Advanced Learners

These are specialist dictionaries which organize words into groups with similar meaning and use.

The Longman Essential Activator (intermediate to upper-intermediate)

The Longman Language Activator (upper-intermediate to proficiency)

Oxford Learner's Wordfinder Dictionary

Cambridge Word Routes (these are translation dictionaries organized by topic or concept; there are versions in French, Spanish, Catalan, Italian, and Greek.)

language reference key

unit one

1.1
1 locking
2 waiting
3 hiking, cycling, etc
4 driving
5 forgetting

1.2
1 worth
2 to
3 pointless
4 of
5 good / use

1.3
1 Could you stop talking please? I'm trying to work.
2 ✓
3 I think he regrets buying that car.
4 ✓
5 Did you mean to break the window, or was it an accident?

1.4 1a, 2a, 3a

1.5
1 I wish I could read without glasses.
2 I wish I was / were on holiday.
3 I wish I'd brought my sunglasses.
4 I wish I hadn't spent all my money on that camera.
5 I wish they hadn't given us that horrible vase.

unit two

2.1
1 You should borrow the extra money.
2 Carole should have left earlier.
3 The teacher should have told them off.
4 'Carefully' should have two 'l's.
5 I should have warned the neighbours about the party.

2.2 *sample answers*
1 we still got there late.
2 the weather wasn't very nice.
3 I didn't really believe him.
4 I still think I failed.
5 (it's) a bit cold

2.3
1 D
2 S
3 D
4 S
5 S

2.4
1 He's unlikely to come.
2 My bag is bound to be the last one off the plane.
3 I don't suppose they'll win.
4 It's likely to start raining before lunchtime.
5 I dare say there will be a lot of people on that train.

unit three

3.1
1 me
2 yourself
3 –
4 themselves
5 –

3.2
1 He had a shave and left.
2 I don't feel very well today.
3 The children hurt themselves in the playground.
4 ✓
5 Jenny never went to school; in fact she taught herself to read.

3.3 1a, 2a, 3b, 4b, 5a

3.4
1 will / 'll have to
2 don't have to
3 have to
4 mustn't
5 must

3.5
1 mustn't
2 will have to
3 mustn't
4 I've got to
5 must

3.6
1 He can't come – he's **got** to go to the dentist.
2 Don't you think we ought **to** leave soon?
3 When I was young, we weren't **allowed** to stay up late.
4 You should**n't** leave your bag here – someone might steal it.
5 I don't think you**'re** allowed to park in front of this entrance.

3.7
1 David climbed the mountain soon after breakfast.
2 Helena prepared her presentation prior to meeting her new boss.
3 It started raining shortly before the accident happened.
4 While she was living in Saudi Arabia, Christine studied Arabic.
5 Cherie has lost weight since having her / the baby.

unit four

4.1
1 cat's paws
2 doctors' clinic
3 the girls' mother
4 committee's report
5 my parents'

4.2
1 The end of the film was very sad.
2 I gave the money to Jake's uncle.
3 He has just been made the sales manager.
4 Can we sit at the front of the train?
5 We'll see you at the bus station at 10.00.

4.3
1 be arriving
2 know
3 live / be living
4 be spending
5 be having

4.4
1 in
2 by
3 anyway
4 still
5 This

unit five

5.1
1 rang; spoke / had spoken
2 had already tidied up; got
3 was; had spent
4 remembered; had forgotten
5 was; had stayed

5.2 *sample answers*
1 they'd been playing football.
2 he'd been to a wedding.
3 she'd missed the bus.
4 he'd been running.
5 she'd fallen over.

5.3
1 It was such hard work that I gave up the job.
2 His sister was so bright that she got the top job.
3 We went back the following year because it was such a beautiful resort.
4 He was so bad-tempered that I left him.
5 They were such lovely gardens that we stayed all afternoon.

5.4
1 U an absolutely wonderful garden
2 G an extremely expensive city
3 G; U extremely dirty; absolutely freezing house
4 G; G extremely noisy but absolutely charming children
5 U an absolutely dreadful film

5.5
1 a bit
2 quite
3 a bit
4 quite
5 rather

unit six

6.1
1 My bicycle was stolen last night.
2 I've been told that it's a great restaurant.
3 The final decision will be made tomorrow by Sir John Mackintosh.
4 Fireworks were invented by the Chinese.
5 Children under 16 aren't served in this bar.

6.2
1 have been
2 was; has been
3 was
4 has just been; have been
5 was

6.3
1 He is believed to be a millionaire.
2 It is thought (that) Pedro Gonzales will win the election.
3 The new manager is known to be very efficient.
4 He is said to have lost a fortune.
5 It is believed (that) the man's identity will never be established.

6.4 *sample answers*
1 Could you tell me what time it starts?
2 Do you know why this door doesn't open?
3 Could I ask you what you think about it?
4 I was wondering if you are / were busy tonight.
5 I'd like to know if he found the hotel.

unit seven

7.1 1 are expected to
2 wasn't supposed to
3 wasn't expected to
4 aren't supposed to
5 you'll be / are expected to

7.2 1 Have you always liked
2 posted
3 spent
4 Has she ever had
5 has run

7.3 1 just
2 yet; since
3 before
4 always
5 ever

7.4 1 haven't seen
2 haven't got
3 worked; has lived
4 've cut
5 has lived

7.5 1a, 2b, 3b

7.6 1 U
2 C
3 U
4 U
5 C
6 U
7 C
8 U
9 U
10 U

7.7 1 a bit / piece of advice
2 a piece / bit of information
3 an item of news
4 a slice of bread
5 a blade of grass

7.8 1 P, plural verb
2 P, plural verb
3 U, singular verb
4 U, singular verb
5 P, plural verb

7.9 1 do, will
2 would
3 will / does (emphatic)
4 will / does
5 would

unit eight

8.1 1 He promised to help me.
2 She suggested we go out / going out.
3 He denied doing it.
4 She admitted that she stole the money / stealing the money.
5 He threatened to tell my parents.

8.2 1c, 2d, 3a, 4e, 5b

8.3 1 from
2 for
3 of
4 from
5 of

8.4 1 although
2 despite
3 in spite of
4 however
5 although

8.5 1 in spite of / despite
2 , although / in spite of the fact that / despite the fact that
3 However, / Nevertheless,
4 despite / in spite of
5 Mind you, / Still, / However,

unit nine

9.1 1 no
2 yes
3 yes

9.2 *sample answers*
1 more
2 better
3 fatter
4 more
5 more expensive / valuable

9.3 1 in the shop / you've ever seen
2 of my life / I've ever known
3 you've ever seen
4 in the street / I've ever met
5 in the world

9.4 1 Take some sandwiches in case you get hungry.
2 I went into town in order to buy some books.
3 I had to stay in bed as I had a migraine.
4 Take that overcoat, otherwise you'll be cold.
5 I went to the library so that I could work in peace.

9.5 1 otherwise
2 so that
3 in case
4 As
5 in order to

unit ten

10.1 1 ✓
2 Is love the most important thing?
3 ✓
4 People say that exercising is the best way to lose weight.
5 ✓

10.2 1 unemployed
2 elderly
3 rich
4 homeless
5 injured

10.3 1 a; the; the
2 the
3 a; The; the
4 a
5 the

10.4 in 1, *the piece of paper* has been mentioned before (a); *the bin* is the only one (c)
in 2, *the chair* is defined in the context (b)
in 3, *the one* has been mentioned before, i.e. the restaurant (a); *the cinema* is the only one (c)
in 5, *the sun* is the only one (c)

10.5 1 She lives opposite the man who committed the crimes. D
2 My brother Joe, who has never been involved in any accidents, must be the world's safest driver. ND
3 The photos I showed you were all taken by a professional photographer. D
4 Henry, who is becoming more and more eccentric, often comes to dinner with us. ND
5 That was the book I was telling you about. D

10.6 1 The dustman who empties our rubbish has won the lottery.
2 A car which was stolen last night contained secret government documents.
3 A private detective who works for the princess has been accused of robbery.
4 I found a credit card (which / that) I lost several days ago.
5 A woman whose cat was rescued from a tree has paid the rescuer £1,000.

10.7 1 The volcano, **which** local people had been worrying about for years, suddenly erupted on Saturday.
2 Twenty Olympic athletes, **who** were accused of taking drugs, have received a formal apology.
3 The gallery, **which** had only been open for six months, had to close owing to lack of support.
4 Alison Mansell, **whose** parents were at the performance, sang the solo with great skill.
5 The money was stolen from my bank account, **which** was very upsetting.

unit eleven

11.1 1a, 2b, 3b

11.2 1 I wouldn't **have** phoned your mother if I'd known where you were.
2 If he**'d** told me earlier, I would have changed the arrangements.
3 We would have got here on time if we had**n't** missed the train.
4 What would have happened **if** she'd lost the documents?
5 Dina would **have** cut herself if her mother hadn't taken the scissors away.

11.3 1a, 1b; 2a; 3b; 4a, 4b; 5b

11.4 1 She said she would finish it later.
2 He said it was no good.
3 She said she wouldn't come.
4 He said they'd broken the front window.
5 They said he'd been sent to prison.

11.5 1 Anita explained (that) the road was / had been blocked the day before / the previous day because of the snow.
2 Dave promised (that) he wouldn't forget to bring the money.
3 Sue mentioned (that) she would be late that night.
4 Liam suggested (that) we invite / invited Patsy to the party.
5 The policeman warned me that the journey would be quite dangerous.

12.1 1 He wanted to know **whether** / **if** his job was safe or not.

2 Sue **was** wondering why the delivery had been delayed.

3 The receptionist asked me whether I **had** stayed there before.

12.2 1 He asked her what her name was.

2 He wanted to know why Pam had left so early.

3 He asked me if I could park in such a tiny space.

4 She was wondering where Colin had taken the kids.

5 He wanted to know if I knew them.

12.3 1 as / like

2 as

3 like / such as

4 like

5 as

Great Clarendon Street, Oxford OX2 6DP

Oxford University Press is a department of the University of Oxford. It furthers the University's objective of excellence in research, scholarship, and education by publishing worldwide in

Oxford New York

Auckland Bangkok Buenos Aires Cape Town Chennai Dar es Salaam Delhi Hong Kong Istanbul Karachi Kolkata Kuala Lumpur Madrid Melbourne Mexico City Mumbai Nairobi São Paulo Shanghai Taipei Tokyo Toronto

Oxford and Oxford English are registered trade marks of Oxford University Press in the UK and in certain other countries

ISBN 0 19 4373355

Edited by Theresa Clementson

Printed in China

Acknowledgements

The Publisher and Authors would like to thank the following for permission to reproduce photographs:
Getty images: cover and throughout (Uwe Krejci/2 people); pp.159, 160, 161, 162, 163, 171 (Rutz Manfred/ear).
Commissioned photograph by Steve Betts, p.149.